Resource Generation and Economic Growth
on the Code of Conduct of an Effective Government

资源生成与经济增长
兼论有为政府行为准则

陈云贤 著

内容简介

本书共有八部分内容,具体包括:区域政府是中观经济市场主体,资源生成与供给侧三驾马车推动经济增长,斯密的第三本书与政府双重属性理论,区域政府竞争与政府超前引领,区域资源配置效率与经济增长新引擎,市场经济双重主体与中观经济三大定律,成熟市场经济是强式有为政府与强式有效市场相融合的经济,微观、中观、宏观经济行为分析与政府经济行为的几点共识。

本书为力图探索与破解世界各国经济学理论与经济实践中"政府与市场"关系的难题而作。愿其能在经济学说的历史沿革进程中做出贡献。

图书在版编目(CIP)数据

资源生成与经济增长:兼论有为政府行为准则 / 陈云贤著. —北京:北京大学出版社,2023.11
ISBN 978-7-301-34652-5

Ⅰ.①资… Ⅱ.①陈… Ⅲ.①中国经济—经济增长—研究 Ⅳ.①F124.1

中国国家版本馆 CIP 数据核字(2023)第 229083 号

书　　　名	资源生成与经济增长:兼论有为政府行为准则 ZIYUAN SHENGCHENG YU JINGJI ZENGZHANG: JIANLUN YOUWEI ZHENGFU XINGWEI ZHUNZE
著作责任者	陈云贤　著
策 划 编 辑	王显超
责 任 编 辑	赵天思　李娉婷
标 准 书 号	ISBN 978-7-301-34652-5
出 版 发 行	北京大学出版社
地　　　址	北京市海淀区成府路 205 号　100871
网　　　址	http://www.pup.cn　新浪微博:@北京大学出版社
电 子 邮 箱	编辑部 pup6@pup.cn　总编室 zpup@pup.cn
电　　　话	邮购部 010-62752015　发行部 010-62750672　编辑部 010-62750667
印 刷 者	涿州市星河印刷有限公司
经 销 者	新华书店
	787 毫米 ×1092 毫米　16 开本　16 印张　458 千字 2023 年 11 月第 1 版　2023 年 11 月第 1 次印刷
定　　　价	98.00 元

未经许可,不得以任何方式复制或抄袭本书之部分或全部内容。
版权所有,侵权必究
举报电话:010-62752024　电子邮箱:fd@pup.cn
图书如有印装质量问题,请与出版部联系,电话:010-62756370

This book aims to discuss and solve the difficulty of addressing the relationship between government and market in global economic theories and practices. The author hopes that this book will contribute to the evolution of economics.

本书为探索与破解世界各国经济学理论与经济实践中"政府与市场"关系的难题而作。愿其能在经济学说的历史沿革进程中做出贡献。

Preface

This book is a concise edition of the author's study on mezzoeconomics over the years. The following viewpoints are put forward in this book in a concise and clear manner:

(1) regional governments are the market entity of mezzoeconomy;

(2) a regional government utilizes the supply-side troika to boost economic growth in the field of resource generation;

(3) the economic behavior of a government stems from its inherent "quasi-macro" and "quasi-micro" attributes;

(4) the government of a region or a country compete and cooperate around market factor, market environment and market space in economic projects, industrial chain support, and import and export trade;

(5) a government must achieve foresighted leading in different stages of economic development in order to keep ahead and achieve sustainable growth;

(6) regional governments and enterprises jointly form a double-wheel drive for market economy development;

(7) macroeconomy, mezzoeconomy and microeconomy are correlated;

(8) a mature market economy is the fruit of an effective government fusing with an efficient market;

(9) a region or a country should create new engines of investment, innovation and regulations.

This book aims to discuss and solve the difficulty of addressing the relationship between government and market in global economic theories and practices. The author hopes that this book will contribute to the evolution of economics.

January 3, 2023
Guangzhou, China

序

  本书可以说是笔者多年来研究中观经济学的一部精简本。它非常精炼且旗帜鲜明地提出：

(1) 区域政府是中观经济的市场主体；

(2) 区域政府在资源生成领域运用供给侧三驾马车助推经济增长；

(3) 政府的经济行为冲动源自政府自身内在的"准宏观"与"准微观"双重属性；

(4) 一个区域或一个国家的政府在经济项目、产业链配套与进出口贸易中，围绕着市场要素、市场环境、市场空间等方面展开竞争与合作；

(5) 在不同的经济发展阶段，要取得领先优势，实现可持续增长，政府需要超前引领；

(6) 区域政府与企业共同形成市场经济发展的双轮驱动力；

(7) 宏观、中观、微观经济三者的互动存在关联效应；

(8) 成熟市场经济是强式有为政府与强式有效市场相融合的经济；

(9) 一个区域或一个国家应形成推动经济增长的投资新引擎、创新新引擎和规则新引擎。

  本书为探索与破解世界各国经济学理论与经济实践中"政府与市场"关系的难题而作。愿其能在经济学说的历史沿革进程中做出贡献。

2023 年 1 月 3 日

中国·广州

Contents

Introduction   Regional Government Is a Market Entity of Mezzoeconomy / 002
      I. "9-in-3" Competition Among Regional Governments / 004
      II. A Regional Government Utilizes the Supply-side Troika to Boost Market Economy / 008
      III. Country, Region and Enterprise Are Correlated / 010
      IV. There Are Dual Drives for the Development of Market Economy / 014

Chapter I   Resource Generation and Supply-side Troika Boosts Economic Growth / 020
      I. Resource Generation and Economic Growth / 020
      II. Government Is the First Investor in the Field of Resource Generation / 036
      III. Supply-side Troika Boosts Economic Growth / 040
      IV. The Boundary for An Effective Government to Adjust the Three Types of Resources / 046

Chapter II   Smith's Third Book and Dual Attributes Theory of Governments / 052
      I. Adam Smith's Third Book and the Dual Attributes of Government / 052
      II. Government's "Political Achievements" and Official's "Outlook on Political Achievements" / 058
      III. Objective Function of Government's Economic Activities: the Fiscal Revenue Determination Mechanism / 068
      IV. Indicator Function of Government's Economic Activities: the Regional Competitiveness Determination Mechanism / 072

目录

导　言　区域政府是中观经济市场主体 / 003
　　一、区域政府之间存在"三类九要素"竞争 / 005
　　二、区域政府在供给侧运用三驾马车推动市场经济发展 / 009
　　三、国家·区域·企业之间存在关联效应 / 011
　　四、市场经济发展存在双重驱动力 / 015

第一章　资源生成与供给侧三驾马车推动经济增长 / 021
　　一、资源生成与经济增长 / 021
　　二、政府是资源生成领域的第一投资人 / 037
　　三、供给侧三驾马车助推经济增长 / 041
　　四、有为政府调节三类资源的边界 / 047

第二章　斯密的第三本书与政府双重属性理论 / 053
　　一、斯密的第三本书与政府双重属性 / 053
　　二、政府"政绩"与官员"政绩观" / 059
　　三、政府经济活动的目标函数——财政收入决定机制 / 069
　　四、政府经济活动的指标函数——区域竞争力决定机制 / 073

Chapter III　**Regional Government Competition and Government's Foresighted Leading** / 082

    I. The Characteristics of Regional Government Competition / 082

    II. The Manifestation of Regional Government Competition / 086

    III. The Spillover Effect of Competition Policy and "Voting with Feet" to Select a Regional Government / 112

    IV. Government's Foresighted Leading / 116

    V. Disruptive Innovations in the Theory of Government's Foresighted Leading / 121

Chapter IV　**Regional Resource Allocation Efficiency and New Engine for Economic Growth** / 128

    I. Comparison of Regional Resource Allocation Efficiency and Enterprise Resource Allocation Efficiency / 128

    II. The Growth Stage Dominated by Industrial Economy / 132

    III. The Growth Stage Dominated by Urban Economy / 136

    IV. The Growth Stage Dominated by Innovative Economy / 140

    V. The Growth Stage Dominated by Shared Economy / 144

    VI. Gradient Transference of Regional Economic Competition / 148

    VII. New Engine for Economic Growth / 154

Chapter V　**Dual Entities of Market Economy and Three Mezzoeconomic Laws** / 160

    I. Carbon Emissions and Carbon Market (Case) / 160

    II. Modern Market Economy / 176

    III. Mature Effective Government / 178

    IV. Dual Entities of Market Competition / 180

    V. Three Mezzoeconomic Laws / 182

    VI. On Competitive Neutrality / 186

第三章　区域政府竞争与政府超前引领 / 083
　　一、区域政府竞争特点 / 083
　　二、区域政府竞争表现 / 087
　　三、竞争政策溢出效应与"用脚投票"选择区域政府 / 113
　　四、政府超前引领 / 117
　　五、政府超前引领理论的颠覆性创新 / 121

第四章　区域资源配置效率与经济增长新引擎 / 129
　　一、区域资源配置效率与企业资源配置效率比较 / 129
　　二、产业经济驱动主导的增长阶段 / 133
　　三、城市经济驱动主导的增长阶段 / 137
　　四、创新经济驱动主导的增长阶段 / 141
　　五、共享经济驱动主导的增长阶段 / 145
　　六、区域经济竞争梯度推移 / 149
　　七、经济增长新引擎 / 155

第五章　市场经济双重主体与中观经济三大定律 / 161
　　一、碳排放与碳市场(案例) / 161
　　二、现代市场经济 / 177
　　三、成熟有为政府 / 179
　　四、市场竞争双重主体 / 181
　　五、中观经济三大定律 / 183
　　六、关于竞争中性 / 187

Chapter VI A Mature Market Economy Is the Combination of Strong Effective Government and Strong Efficient Market / 192

    I. Classification of Efficient Market and Types of Effective Government / 192

    II. Potential Economic Growth Rate and Real Economic Growth Rate / 198

    III. Washington Consensus and the Middle Income Trap / 200

    IV. The Mode of Integrating Effective Government With Efficient Market and the Evaluation of It / 204

    V. A Strong Effective Government and a Strong Efficient Market Contribute to a Mature Market Economy / 208

Conclusions Consensus on Micro, Mezzo, and Macroeconomic Analysis and Government's Economic Behaviors / 218

    I. Analysis of Micro, Mezzo, and Macroeconomic Behaviors / 218

    II. Code of Conduct of an Effective Government / 230

    III. Mezzoeconomics and China / 236

    IV. Mezzoeconomics and the World / 239

第六章 成熟市场经济是强式有为政府与强式有效市场相融合的经济 / 193
　　一、有效市场划分与有为政府类型 / 193
　　二、潜在经济增长率与现实经济增长率 / 199
　　三、华盛顿共识与中等收入陷阱 / 201
　　四、有为政府与有效市场相融合的模式组合及评价 / 205
　　五、强式有为政府 + 强式有效市场 = 成熟市场经济 / 209

结　语　微观、中观、宏观经济行为分析与政府经济行为的几点共识 / 219
　　一、微观、中观、宏观经济行为分析 / 219
　　二、有为政府行为准则 / 231
　　三、中观经济学与中国 / 237
　　四、中观经济学与世界 / 239

The reasonable core of mezzoeconomics will effectively address the relationship between government and market in economic theories, and refine the successful practices and experience of China's reform and opening-up over the past 40 years. It will become a new engine for discovering the current and future market drives for the economic development of various countries around the world, effectively solve relevant problems in the economic development of various countries around the world, essentially boost their sustainable economic development, and seek to build new systems and paths for building global economic governance!

中观经济学的合理内核,将有效破解经济学理论中的"政府与市场"关系的难题,并将提炼中国改革开放四十多年来的成功实践与经验,发掘世界各国现在与未来的市场驱动力与经济新引擎,从而有效破解世界各国经济增长中的相关难题,实质推动世界各国经济的可持续发展,并探索构建全球经济治理的新体系、新路径!

Introduction

Regional Government Is a Market Entity of Mezzoeconomy

In view of China's successful experience in reform and opening-up and the reform and innovation in the world market economy theory, the author draws the conclusion that enterprises and regional governments are market entities in microeconomy and mezzoeconomy respectively after analyzing the third book of Smith: *On Government and Law*. Smith is the founder of economics.

In 1759, *The Theory of Moral Sentiments* by Smith, representing his first book, was published. In this book, he analyzed the orientation of individual behavior and proposed that an individual's "selfinterest" and "sympathy" for others were combined as an invisible hand that promoted his survival and development in society. In 1776, his second book, *The Wealth of Nations*, was published, in which he analyzed the orientation of corporate behavior and proposed that the "selfishness" of a corporation and the "altruism" of commodity production were combined as an invisible hand that promoted the survival and development of the corporation in the market economy. From 1777 to 1790, Smith attempted to complete his third book, *On Government and Law*, in which he analyzed the orientation of state government behavior and tried to reveal the intrinsic drivers of economic development in a country and the intrinsic balance between states by discussing the basic economic functions and administrative characteristics of the government. Smith attempted to identify the economic fields where states would be likely to compete with each other and the rules that they would rely on for coordination and maintain together. Pitifully, the relationship between the state government and the market

导 言

区域政府是中观经济市场主体

基于对中国改革开放成功经验的思考和对世界市场经济理论改革创新的探索,笔者从经济学鼻祖斯密的第三本书《政府与法律论》入手分析,得出"企业是微观经济市场主体,区域政府是中观经济市场主体"的结论。

1759年,斯密的第一本书《道德情操论》问世,该书从分析个人行为取向的角度提出,一个人的"自我心"与对他人的"同理心"的融合,形成了一只看不见的手推动个人在社会中的生存与发展。1776年,斯密的第二本书《国富论》问世,该书从分析企业行为取向的角度提出,一个企业的"利己性"与商品生产的"利他性"的融合,形成了一只看不见的手推动企业在市场经济中的生存与发展。1777—1790年,斯密力图研撰第三本书《政府与法律论》[①],该书从分析国家政府行为取向的角度,探讨一国政府的经济基本职能与政府管理行为特征,从而试图揭示国家经济发展的内在动力、国家与国家之间的内在牵制力。斯密试图分析国家与国家之间将可能在哪些经济领域展开竞争,又将靠什么规则来相互协调。

---

① 陈云贤:《经济新引擎:兼论有为政府与有效市场》,外语教学与研究出版社,2019,第13—19页。

that he would ultimately conclude if he continued his research would completely undermine and overturn his claim that the government serves as a night watchman in *The Wealth of Nations*. Smith was caught in an inextricable paradox, and his third book eventually fell through.

Then, the history of world economics has continued to this day thanks to the several basic conclusions drawn in *The Wealth of Nations* in 1776. First, the market economy focuses on the industrial economy and industrial resources; second, the government serves as a night watchman in the industrial economy; third, enterprises are entities in the market economy. However, the author argues that enterprises are entities in the market economy, but only in the microeconomic dimension.

I. "9–in–3" Competition Among Regional Governments

Microeconomics researchers basically study the economic behavior of an individual economic production unit (enterprise) and its consequences by analyzing resource allocation in the context of resource scarcity. During their research, they focus on the price determination mechanism among main economic variables. Finally, the research results and its development constitute a series of theories. By studying microeconomics, students are expected to understand and grasp the laws of microeconomic operation, so as to effectively implement management, reform and innovation in enterprises.

Differently, macroeconomics researchers basically study the economic behavior of the active unit (state) in the total socioeconomic process and its consequences by analyzing resource utilization in the context of resource allocation optimization in a country. During their research, they keep their eyes on the determination and operation mechanisms of national income among economic growth variables. On this basis, the relevant core indicators, theoretical models, growth and volatility trends, regulation and management approaches, international market theories, etc. can be drawn. By studying macroeconomics, students are expected to understand and grasp the laws of macroeconomic operation, so as to effectively practice macro management, reform and innovation.

Different from the foregoing two, mezzoeconomics researchers basically study the economic behavior of regional economic development units (regional governments) and its consequences by analyzing resource allocation on the basis of resource generation. During their research, they focus on the determination mechanism of regional fiscal revenue and the structural mechanism of fiscal expenditure. Finally, the research results and its development

然而，沿着这一研究思路得出的国家政府与市场的关系，将完全颠覆与推翻他在《国富论》中对政府作为守夜人的角色的定位。因此，斯密陷入了难以自拔的矛盾之中。最终，他的第三本书夭折[①]。

于是，世界经济学说史，沿革1776年《国富论》的几个基本结论延续至今。第一，市场经济聚焦在产业经济与产业资源上；第二，在产业经济中，政府是守夜人的角色；第三，企业是市场经济主体。然而，笔者的研究认为，企业是市场经济主体，但它只是微观经济市场主体。

一、区域政府之间存在"三类九要素"竞争

微观经济学的研究主体主要是单个经济生产单位（企业）的经济行为及其后果；研究对象是资源稀缺条件下的资源配置问题；研究焦点是其主要经济变量中的价格决定机制。微观经济学的研究内容及其展开形成了系列理论。学习微观经济学有利于了解和把握微观经济运行规律，有效实施企业管理、改革和创新。

宏观经济学的研究主体主要是社会经济总过程的活动单位（国家）的经济行为及其后果；研究对象是一国资源配置优化中的资源利用问题；研究焦点是其经济增长变量中的国民收入决定及其运行机制。宏观经济学的研究内容及其展开形成了相关核心指标、增长与波动模型、调节与管理理论、国际市场理论等。学习宏观经济学有利于了解和把握宏观经济运行规律，有效实施宏观管理、改革和创新。

中观经济学的研究主体主要是区域经济发展单位（区域政府）的经济行为及其后果；研究对象是资源生成基础上的资源配置问题；研究焦点是影响区域政府

---

① 详见本书第二章内容。

constitute the Resource Generation Theory, the Dual Government Attribute Theory, the Regional Government Competition Theory, the Four-stage Resource Allocation Theory, the Government Foresighted Leading Theory, the New Economic Engine Theory, the Dual-Entity of Market Competition Theory, the "Double Strong Forms" Theory in a mature market economy, etc. By studying mezzoeconomics, students are expected to understand and grasp the laws of mezzoeconomic operation, to build a scientific governance concept, to develop a scientific governing code of conduct and make a scientific choice of policy instruments, and to promote sustainable economic development.

The author argues that regional governments compete for "Nine Factors in Three Categories" (the "9-in-3" Competition) in the mezzoeconomic dimension.

The first category is the regional economic development level, including ①project competition; ②supporting industrial chain competition; ③import and export competition.

The second category is regional economic policies, including ④infrastructure competition; ⑤talent and sci-tech competition; ⑥fiscal and financial competition.

The third category is the regional economic management efficiency, including ⑦policy system competition; ⑧environmental system competition; ⑨management system competition.

In this framework, the objective function and the indicator function of regional government competition are the fiscal revenue determination mechanism and the regional competitiveness determination mechanism, respectively. The core influencing factors and key supporting conditions for these two functions are basically derived from the "9-in-3" Competition.

In the mezzoeconomy, regional government competition can be defined in narrow and broad senses. Regional government competition in the narrow sense is mainly manifested in the competition of regional governments for "quasi-operative resources", namely, urban infrastructure construction and the establishment and implementation of related policy support. Specifically, competition in this sense mainly occurs in urban infrastructure, and is essentially the competition in the determination of regional fiscal investment expenditure. Differently, regional government competition in the broad sense includes competition for operative resources (industrial economy), non-operative resources (livelihood economy) and quasi-operative resources (urban economy); it is essentially the competition among regional governments for the objective functions and indicator functions of industrial development, urban construction and social livelihood, namely, the competition of regional fiscal revenue determination and regional competitiveness determination.

竞争的主要经济变量，即区域财政收入决定机制与财政支出结构。中观经济学的研究内容及其展开形成了资源生成理论、政府双重属性理论、区域政府竞争理论、四阶段资源配置理论、政府超前引领理论、经济新引擎理论、市场竞争双重主体理论和成熟市场经济"双强机制"理论等。学习中观经济学有利于了解和把握中观经济运行规律，确立科学的执政理念，制定科学的执政行为准则，优化政策工具选择，推动经济可持续发展。

笔者认为，区域政府之间在中观经济领域存在"三类九要素"竞争[1]。

第一类是区域经济发展水平，它包括①项目竞争；②产业链配套竞争；③进出口竞争。

第二类是区域经济政策措施，它包括④基础设施竞争；⑤人才、科技竞争；⑥财政、金融竞争。

第三类是区域经济管理效率，它包括⑦政策体系效率竞争；⑧环境体系效率竞争；⑨管理体系效率竞争。

其中，区域政府竞争的目标函数是财政收入决定机制，区域政府竞争的指标函数是区域竞争力决定机制。区域政府竞争的目标函数和指标函数的核心影响因素和关键支持条件主要来自"三类九要素"竞争。

在中观经济领域，区域政府之间存在狭义的竞争和广义的竞争。狭义的区域政府竞争主要体现在区域政府对"准经营性资源"，即对城市基础设施建设及其政策配套与落实的竞争，其实质是在区域公共投资性支出决定方面的竞争。广义的区域政府竞争，包括对可经营性资源（产业经济）、非经营性资源（民生经济）和准经营性资源（城市经济）的竞争，其实质是区域政府在产业发展、城市建设、社会民生中目标函数和指标函数方面的竞争，即区域财政收入决定机制和区域竞争力决定机制方面的竞争。

---

[1] 详见本书第三章内容。

II. A Regional Government Utilizes the Supply-side Troika to Boost Market Economy

Keynes proposed in *The General Theory of Employment, Interest, and Money* published in 1936 that a country must adopt expansionary fiscal policies to stimulate investment and consumption in order to achieve full employment and boost economic growth. Since then, from the perspective of stimulating economy and expanding employment, scholars have put forward that it is wise use the troika (investment, consumption and export) to boost economic growth.

The author believes that Keynes' economics is flawed in resource scarcity and resource generation.

Resource generation and resource scarcity are both inseparable aspects of resource allocation.

Resource generation, also known as generative resource, is not a planned product, but a product that already exists or must exist with the development of the times. It goes from being static to being dynamic and from being non-productive to being productive, and forms economic effects therewithin.

In the development and utilization of generative resource, the government forms the following troika on the supply side to promote the development of market economy.

(1) Supply of factor, including tangible factors (such as space resource, deep-sea resource, and polar region resource) and intangible factors (such as technology resource and data resource). It unveils the connotation and transformation process of micro enterprise's factor of production in various countries around the world.

(2) Supply of environment, including hard environment (such as urban infrastructure and ecological protection) and soft environment (such as policies and management efficiency). It unveils the connotation and transformation process of business environment in various countries around the world.

(3) Supply of market, including the transverse market system (such as developing industrial economy, urban economy, and international economy) and the longitudinal market

system (such as building and improving market factors, market organizations, market legal system, market supervision, market environment, and market infrastructure). It unveils the market development, market system improvement, and the transformation process of the connotation of market economy in various countries around the world.

二、区域政府在供给侧运用三驾马车推动市场经济发展

凯恩斯在1936年出版的《就业、利息和货币通论》中提出一个国家要实现充分就业，促进经济增长，需要采取扩张性的财政政策，刺激投资和消费。在此之后，有学者从拉动经济、扩大就业的视角出发，提出用投资、消费、出口三方面发力的三驾马车拉动经济增长。

笔者的研究认为，凯恩斯的经济学理论在资源稀缺与资源生成方面存在一些问题。

笔者认为，资源生成与资源稀缺是资源配置中的一对孪生儿，是资源配置中不可分割的两个方面。

资源生成即生成性资源，它不是计划设定的产物，而是原已存在或随着时代进程客观需要存在，由静态进入动态、由非生产性进入生产性，并在其中形成经济效应的产物。

在对资源生成领域的开发和利用中，政府在供给侧形成以下三驾马车来推动市场经济发展。

(1) 要素供给，包括有形要素(例如开发太空资源、深海资源、极地资源等)和无形要素(例如开发技术、数据资源等)；它涉及世界各国微观企业生产要素的内涵及其变革。

(2) 环境供给，包括硬环境(例如投资城市基础设施、生态环保等)和软环境(例如制定政策措施、提高管理效率等)；它涉及世界各国营商环境的内涵及其变革。

(3) 市场供给，包括市场横向体系(例如开拓产业经济、城市经济、国际经济等)和市场纵向体系(例如建设与完善市场要素、市场组织、市场法治、市场监管、市场环境、市场基础设施等)；它涉及世界各国市场领域的开拓与市场体系的完善，以及市场经济内涵的变革。

III. Country, Region and Enterprise Are Correlated

The author believes that macroeconomy, mezzoeconomy and microeconomy are correlated in the national income of a country, the tax sharing in a region, and the total taxes paid by enterprises (tax type and tax rate). This correlation effect is shown in Figure 0-1.

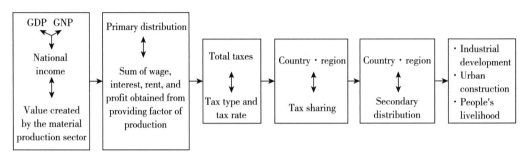

Figure 0-1　Correlation Effect of Macroeconomy, Mezzoeconomy and Microeconomy

The national income determination mechanism in macroeconomy, the fiscal revenue determination mechanism in mezzoeconomy, and the commodity price determination mechanism in microeconomy all focus on the amount of total taxes. The amount of total taxes depends on a country's economic development level, economic policies, and economic management efficiency (the effects of regional government in "9-in-3" Competition).

Fiscal revenue is one of the supporting factors for the sustainable and high-quality development of a country's economy. Regional governments consider the fiscal revenue determination mechanism as the objective function of competition because: ①they need to be supported by increased fiscal revenue scale as their functions extend and their role in economic coordination intensifies; ②they need to be backed by increased fiscal revenue scale as the population in the region grows and the total demand for regional public services by the public increases; ③they need to be supported by increased fiscal revenue scale as regional urban scale increases and social public investment grows; ④they need to be backed by increased fiscal revenue scale as regional technological level rises, promoting them to keep exploring new fields of technology and production; ⑤they need to be supported by increased fiscal revenue scale as regional social welfare undertakings get expanded. The *People's Daily* published an article on May 21, 2021, which put forward that "we should let finance play a greater role in the new journey", and further elaborated that work should be done to ①promote and build a modern industrial system; ②safeguard and promote the layout of major regional projects; ③advance and coordinate the development of urban-rural integration.

三、国家·区域·企业之间存在关联效应

笔者研究认为，宏观、中观、微观经济关联效应的扭结点是：国家的国民收入、区域的税收分成和企业的税收总额(税种、税率)。这一关联效应可用图0-1来表示。

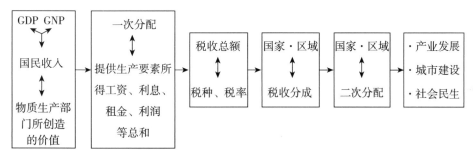

图0-1 宏观、中观、微观经济关联效应

宏观经济的国民收入决定机制、中观经济的财政收入决定机制和微观经济的商品价格决定机制，它们三者的聚焦点都在税收总额的大小上；而税收总额取决于一国的经济发展水平、经济政策措施与经济管理效率(区域政府的"三类九要素"作用力)。

财政收入是一国经济可持续高质量发展的支持要素之一，区域政府把财政收入决定机制作为竞争目标函数的主要动因包括：①区域政府职能不断扩张，其经济调控功能增强，需要扩大财政收入规模做支撑；②区域人口增长，民众对区域公共服务需求总量增加，需要扩大财政收入规模做支撑；③区域城市规模不断扩大，社会公共投资不断增长，需要扩大财政收入规模做支撑；④区域科技水平不断进步，推动区域政府不断开拓新的科技领域和生产领域，需要扩大财政收入规模做支撑；⑤区域社会福利事业不断扩大，需要扩大财政收入规模做支撑。《人民日报》2021年5月21日发表文章，提出"让财政在新征程中发挥更大作用"，对此还进行了进一步阐述：①促进和构建现代产业体系；②保障和推动区域重大项目布局；③推动和协调城乡一体化发展。

From the perspective of a state, fiscal and tax policies safeguard the national economy and the people's livelihood. They mainly include ①reform of the fiscal system by further streamlining the relationship between central finance and local finance, and fully leveraging the enthusiasm of both central and local governments; ②improvement of the budget management system by further deepening the reform of budget management system, better implementing national strategies and reflecting policy guidance; ③improvement of the tax system by bettering the modern tax system and letting tax play its role; ④reforms in relevant fields by further improving the government's debt management system, and creating a regulated, safe, and efficient borrowing and financing mechanism for the government.

From the perspective of a region, both the quality and efficiency of fiscal and tax policies should be raised to boost sustainable economic development in the region. Fiscal and tax policies function to ①raise the efficiency of regional regulation and make the regional economy operate within a reasonable range; ②strengthen the overall planning of financial and tax resources, and strengthen the financial support for deploying major projects in the region; ③facilitate supply-side structural reform in the region and speed up the transformation of the driving force for regional economic growth.

Resources are allocated by enterprises and regional governments. Market economy is an epitome of fundamental economic activities in which the market plays a decisive role in resource allocation. In market economy, there are dual entities: micro enterprises and mezzo regional governments. As shown in Figure 0-2, both of them are indispensable, but should function where they should function.

In addition, country, region and enterprise should run in harmony.

(1) We should grasp the full picture of the modern market system;

(2) We should fully grasp the dual entities of the modern market economy;

(3) We should fully realize that a mature market economy is the fruit of effective government fusing with efficient market;

(4) We should strengthen the coordination of micro, mezzo, and macroeconomic activities.

从国家的角度看，财税政策护航国计民生。它包含四大方面内容：①改革财政体制——进一步理顺中央和地方财政关系，充分发挥中央和地方两个积极性；②完善预算管理制度——进一步深化预算管理制度改革，更好地贯彻国家战略和体现政策导向；③完善税收制度——进一步完善现代税收制度，切实发挥税收功能作用；④积极推进相关领域改革——进一步健全政府债务管理制度，完善规范、安全、高效的政府举债融资机制。

从区域的角度看，财税政策提质增效，可持续推动区域经济发展。它包含三项功能：①提高区域调控效能，促进区域经济运行保持在合理区间；②加强财税资源统筹，增强区域重大项目布局的财力保障；③支持区域供给侧结构性改革，加速区域经济增长动能转换。

资源调配有两个系统：企业和区域政府。市场经济是市场在资源配置中起决定性作用的基础性经济组织活动的表现形式。市场经济有双重主体：微观企业和中观区域政府。二者都不能"缺位"，亦不能"越位"，如图 0-2 所示。

此外，应强化国家、区域、企业三者的协调性。

(1) 应完整把握现代市场体系；

(2) 应完整把握现代市场经济的双重主体；

(3) 应完整把握成熟市场经济是"有为政府"与"有效市场"相融合的经济；

(4) 应强化微观、中观、宏观经济活动的协调性。

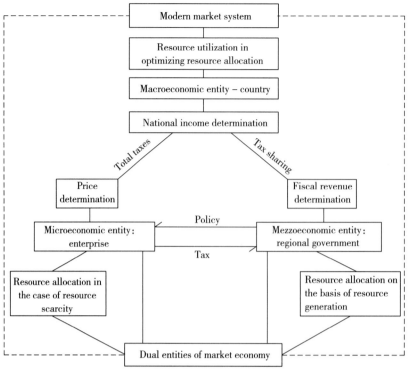

Figure 0-2   Dual Entities of Market Economy

IV. There Are Dual Drives for the Development of Market Economy

The author believes that a complete market system must include two fundamental aspects: the supply side and the demand side.

The former is mainly involved in increment and structure issues, and price seeking and pricing issues, while the latter is mainly involved in inventory and scale issues, and fairness and competition issues.

Regional government is the main actor on the supply side of a region, while enterprises and individuals are the main actors on the demand side of a region.

Fiscal policy mainly functions on the supply side, while monetary policy mainly on the demand side.

Let's first analyze objective function, indicator function, and enterprise resource allocation

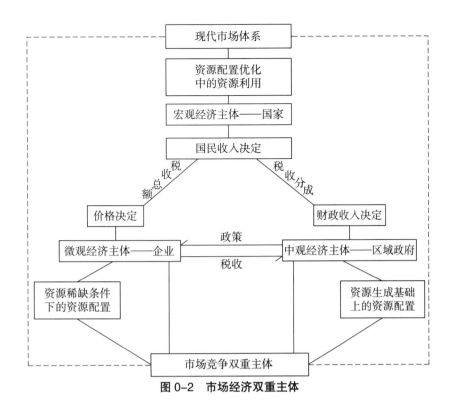

图 0-2　市场经济双重主体

四、市场经济发展存在双重驱动力

笔者认为，一个完整的市场体系，一定包括供给端和需求端两个对立统一的基本方面。

供给端主要解决增量与结构性问题、寻价与定价问题；需求端主要解决存量与规模问题、公平与竞争问题。

区域供给端的主要行为主体是区域政府；区域需求端的主要行为主体是企业和个人。

财政政策的功能作用主要体现在供给端；货币政策的功能作用主要体现在需求端。

我们可以先来分析一下企业竞争的目标函数、指标函数与企业资源配置效

efficiency in terms of enterprise competition. The objective function and the indicator function of enterprise competition is the price determination mechanism and the enterprise competitiveness determination mechanism separately. The key indicators for measuring enterprise resource allocation efficiency in the four stages of economic development include labor productivity in the factor-driven stage, capital productivity in the investment-driven stage, technological progress rate in the innovation-driven stage, and total factor productivity in the wealth-driven stage. The enterprise competitiveness determination mechanism can be demonstrated by the enterprise resource planning (ERP) model.

Let's move on to objective function, indicator function, and regional resource allocation efficiency in terms of regional government competition. The objective function and the indicator function of regional government competition is the fiscal revenue determination mechanism and the regional competitiveness determination mechanism respectively. The key indicators for measuring regional resource allocation efficiency in the four stages of economic development include industrial competitiveness in the stage of developing industrial economy, investment growth rate in the stage of developing urban economy, contribution rate of technological progress in the stage of developing innovative economy, and the effects of regional government in "9-in-3" Competition in the stage of developing shared economy. The regional competitiveness determination mechanism can be demonstrated by the district resource planning (DRP) model.

The entire process of the regional competitiveness determination mechanism is shown in Figure 0-3.

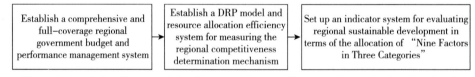

Figure 0-3 Entire Process of the Regional Competitiveness Determination Mechanism

On this basis, we can study the driving effect of per capita GDP and per capita fiscal revenue growth on regional economic growth and their relationship from the perspective of the objective function, or the influence of variables in regional institutional (policy) innovation on the growth of per capita GDP and per capita fiscal revenue at different stages of economic development from the perspective of the indicator function.

We can complete the DRP model in the following four steps.

(1) The determination mechanism for fiscal surplus and "Nine Factors in Three Categories".

(2) Comprehensive measure and objective function.

(3) In the case of limited budget, a regional government may maximize the comprehensive measure by adjusting the proportions of three types of fiscal expenditures.

率。企业竞争的目标函数是价格决定机制；企业竞争的指标函数是企业竞争力决定机制。企业资源配置效率在经济发展的四个阶段的主要衡量指标是：要素驱动阶段表现为劳动生产率；投资驱动阶段表现为资本生产率；创新驱动阶段表现为技术进步率；财富驱动阶段表现为全要素生产率。企业竞争力决定机制可以通过企业资源规划(enterprise resource planning，ERP)模型显现出来。

我们再来分析区域政府竞争的目标函数、指标函数与区域资源配置效率。区域政府竞争的目标函数是财政收入决定机制；区域政府竞争的指标函数是区域竞争力决定机制。区域资源配置效率在经济发展的四个阶段的主要衡量指标是：产业经济导向阶段表现为产业竞争力；城市经济导向阶段表现为投资增长率；创新经济导向阶段表现为科技进步贡献率；共享经济导向阶段表现为"三类九要素"作用力。区域竞争力决定机制可以通过区域资源配置(district resource planning，DRP)模型显现出来。

区域竞争力决定机制的全流程可用图0-3来表述。

图0-3 区域竞争力决定机制全流程

我们由此可以引申研究区域人均国内生产总值和人均财政收入增长对区域经济增长的拉动作用和关系(目标函数角度)；也可以引申研究区域制度(政策)创新的变量在经济发展不同阶段中对人均国内生产总值和人均财政收入增速的影响(指标函数角度)。

我们可以从以下四个步骤来完成DRP模型：

(1) 财政支出盈余与"三类九要素"的决定机制；

(2) 综合测度和目标函数；

(3) 在满足预算约束的条件下，区域政府通过调整三种财政支出的比例，使此综合测度最大化；

(4) Establish a performance evaluation system for regional government.

After thorough studies, the author's core viewpoint is that there are dual drives for the market economy to develop. In the four stages of economic development, there are four "combinations" of regional resource allocation efficiency and enterprise resource allocation efficiency. In other words, in the development process of a country's macroeconomy and market economy, there will be four combinations of mezzoeconomic regional government behavior and microeconomic enterprise behavior. Combination 1: positive regional resource allocation efficiency plus positive enterprise resource allocation efficiency; combination 2: positive regional resource allocation efficiency plus negative enterprise resource allocation efficiency; combination 3: negative regional resource allocation efficiency plus positive enterprise resource allocation efficiency; combination 4: negative regional resource allocation efficiency plus negative enterprise resource allocation efficiency. See Figure 0-4 for details.

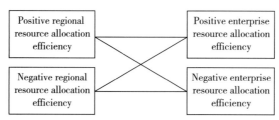

Figure 0-4　Four Combinations of Resource Allocation

To achieve the goal of sustainable and high-quality economic development, a country should have positive regional resource allocation efficiency plus positive enterprise resource allocation efficiency. That is to say, the country should allow the market to determine resource allocation and better leverage the dual drives of regional government and enterprise.

Based on the foregoing, the following conclusions can be drawn:

(1) regional government is the market entity of mezzoeconomy;

(2) there are dual entities of market economy;

(3) regional government competition and enterprise competition are correlated on one hand and different in essence on the other hand;

(4) an effective government should achieve scientific foresighted leading;

(5) coordinated macro, mezzo and microeconomic activities are required by a country's economic growth;

(6) the economic growth of countries around the world requires a new engine.

(4) 设定区域政府绩效评估体系。[1][2]

笔者经过认真研究，认为核心观点是，市场经济发展存在双重驱动力。在经济发展的四个阶段进程中，区域资源配置效率与企业资源配置效率存在四种"叠加"方式。即在一国宏观经济、市场经济的发展进程中，中观经济的区域政府行为与微观经济的企业行为将产生四种组合：组合一，区域资源配置效率与企业资源配置效率的正正叠加；组合二，区域资源配置效率与企业资源配置效率的正负叠加；组合三，区域资源配置效率与企业资源配置效率的负正叠加；组合四，区域资源配置效率与企业资源配置效率的负负叠加，如图0-4所示。

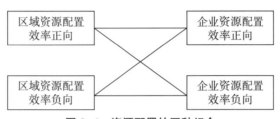

图0-4 资源配置的四种组合

一国经济可持续高质量发展的目标应该是区域资源配置效率与企业资源配置效率的正正叠加。也就是说，应该由市场决定资源配置，更好地发挥区域政府与企业双轮驱动的作用。

至此，笔者得出如下结论。

(1) 区域政府是中观经济市场主体。

(2) 市场经济存在双重主体发生作用。

(3) 区域政府竞争与企业竞争具有联系，更有本质区别。

(4) 有为政府需要进行科学的超前引领。

(5) 一国经济增长需要宏观、中观、微观经济活动保持协调性。

(6) 世界各国经济增长需要新引擎。

---

[1] 覃征鹏、郭东霓、朱朝贵等：《对标最优 顺德发布高质量发展指标体系》，《佛山日报》2019年9月24日。

[2] 江琳：《用好考核指挥棒 树立正确政绩观——解读〈关于改进推动高质量发展的政绩考核的通知〉》，《人民日报》2021年1月19日。

Chapter I

Resource Generation and Supply-side Troika Boosts Economic Growth

As we see in global economic theories, Smith's *The Wealth of Nations* is correlated with industrial economy and scarce resources; Keynes's *The General Theory of Employment, Interest, and Money* is correlated with aggregate demand, aggregate supply, and increasing the supply of scarce resources; and Samuelson believed that: "Economics is the study of how a society chooses to use scarce resources to produce goods and to distribute them to people for consumption." Later generations of economists around the world studied how to regard and expand the theory of resource scarcity in microeconomics and macroeconomics.

Upon studies, the author believes that resource generation and resource scarcity are two inseparable aspects in economic resource allocation.

I. Resource Generation and Economic Growth

The author believes there are reasons behind Smith's failure to propose the law of resource generation. First, Smith published *The Wealth of Nations* in 1776 when the Industrial Revolution in the UK had just begun. Second, around 1776, the urban infrastructure in the UK only included simple roads, bridges, canals, and ports. Third, resource generation includes primary resources, secondary resources, and retrograde resources, and generation conditions of each of them were all absent around 1776.

第一章

资源生成与供给侧
三驾马车推动经济增长

纵观世界经济学说史，斯密的《国富论》与产业经济、稀缺资源相关联。凯恩斯的《就业、利息和货币通论》与总需求、总供给、增加稀缺资源供给相联系。萨缪尔森认为："经济学研究的是一个社会如何利用稀缺的资源生产有价值的商品，并将它们在个体之间进行分配。"① 世界各国经济学后人，则在微观经济学与宏观经济学中，展开如何看待和拓展资源稀缺论的研究。

笔者经过研究认为，资源生成与资源稀缺是经济学资源配置中不可分割的两个方面。

一、资源生成与经济增长

为什么斯密当年没能提出资源生成法则呢？笔者分析有以下几个原因。第一，斯密 1776 年发表《国富论》，当时英国工业革命才刚刚开始；第二，1776 年前后英国的城市基础设施还相当落后，仍仅仅停留在简单的道路、桥梁、运河和港口等设施上；第三，资源生成包括原生性资源、次生性资源和逆生性资源三大类，在当时的历史阶段缺乏生成条件。

---

① 保罗·萨缪尔森、威廉·诺德豪斯：《经济学：第19版：教材版》，萧琛主译，商务印书馆，2013，第4页。

(I) Regional economic resources are divided into three types

From an economic perspective, there are three types of resources in a region. The first type is resources corresponding for industrial development, which are referred to as the operative resources (or private products) in a market economy. The second type is resources corresponding for social and people's livelihoods, which are referred to as non-operative resources (or public goods) in a market economy. The third type is resources corresponding for urban construction (including the entire resource generation), which are referred to as quasi-operative resources (or quasi-public goods) in a market economy and can be converted from non-operative resources (or public goods) into operative resources (or private products).

1. Operative resources (or private products)

$$x_j = \sum_{i=1}^{n} x_j^i \qquad 1\text{-}1$$

In the formula, x_j represents the total amount of the j-th operative resource (or private product), and n represents the number of enterprises (or total number of people) in the economy; x_j^i represents the amount of the operative resource (or private product) owned by the i-th enterprise (or individual). The formula suggests that the total amount of operative resources (or private products) is equal to the sum of the quantity of such operative resources (or private products) owned by all enterprises (or individuals), and that operative resources (or private products) can be allocated among enterprises (or individuals). Therefore, operative resources (or private products) are competitory and exclusive.

2. Non-operative resources (or public goods)

$$X_m^i = \sum_{k=1}^{m} X_k = X_m \qquad 1\text{-}2$$

In the formula, X_m represents the total amount of non-operative resources (or public goods); X_m^i represents the quantity of such non-operative resources (or public goods) owned by the i-th consumer (individual or enterprise); k is a dummy variable, and $\sum_{k=1}^{m} X_k$ indicates that there are m types of resources available for use (i.e. from the 1st to the m-th, from X_1, X_2 to X_m). The formula suggests that any consumer (individual or enterprise) can control non-operative resources (or public goods), and that non-operative resources (or public goods) are non-allocatable among consumers (individuals or enterprises). Hence, non-operative resources (or public goods) are non-competitory and non-exclusive.

3. Quasi–operative resources (or quasi–public goods)

The author believes that the proportion of quasi-operative resources (or quasi-public

（一）区域经济资源分为三类

一个区域，从经济学的角度来看，存在三类资源：第一类，与产业发展相对应的资源——在市场经济中称为可经营性资源（或纯私人产品）；第二类，与社会民生相对应的资源——在市场经济中称为非经营性资源（或公共物品）；第三类，与城市建设（包括整个资源生成）相对应的资源——在市场经济中称为准经营性资源（或准公共物品），即它可由非经营性资源（或公共物品）转化为可经营性资源（或纯私人产品）来使用。

1. 可经营性资源（或纯私人产品）

$$x_j = \sum_{i=1}^{n} x_j^i \qquad 1-1$$

式中，x_j为第j种可经营性资源（或纯私人产品）的总量，n为经济中的企业数（或总人数）；x_j^i为第i个企业（或个人）对这种可经营性资源（或纯私人产品）的拥有量。它表明：第一，可经营性资源（或纯私人产品）的总量等于每一个企业（或个人）对这种可经营性资源（或纯私人产品）的拥有数量之和；第二，可经营性资源（或纯私人产品）在企业（或个人）之间是可分的。可经营性资源（或纯私人产品）具有竞争性和排他性。

2. 非经营性资源（或公共物品）

$$X_m^i = \sum_{k=1}^{m} X_k = X_m \qquad 1-2$$

式中，X_m为非经营性资源（或公共物品）的总量，X_m^i为第i个消费者（个人或企业）对这种非经营性资源（或公共物品）的占有量，k为哑变量，$\sum_{k=1}^{m} X_k$表明总共有m种资源可以用（即从第1种加到第m种，从X_1、X_2加到X_m）。它表明：第一，任何一个消费者（个人或企业）都可以支配非经营性资源（或公共物品）；第二，非经营性资源（或公共物品）在消费者（个人或企业）之间是不可分的。非经营性资源（或公共物品）具有非竞争性和非排他性。

3. 准经营性资源（或准公共物品）

笔者认为，准经营性资源（或准公共物品）在公共部门当中的配置比例（λ）

goods) in the public sector (λ) is under the common influence of the development level of market economy (Y), the fiscal revenue and expenditure including fiscal budget (B) and fiscal expenditure (FE), and the cognitive degree of residents or society (γ). There is a function as follows:

$$\lambda = F(Y, B, \text{FE}, \gamma) \qquad 1\text{-}3$$

To further study the possible functional forms of Equation 1-3, we will first discuss the marginal effect of the foregoing variables on λ.

Firstly, the development level of market economy (Y) is a variable between 0 and 1, and represents the state of economic development between highly underdeveloped economy and highly developed economy. It affects disposable income, which in turn affects the amount of funds flowing into the field of quasi-operative resources (or quasi-public goods). The higher the level of economic development is, the higher the disposable income of residents will be. In this case, the private sector will have increased capability and intention to invest in quasi-operative resources (or quasi-public goods). This indicates that when λ will go smaller, the proportion of operative resources (or private products) converted into operative resources (or private product) will increase. A higher value of λ indicates a lower supply of private funds in the market for quasi-operative resources (or quasi-public goods). If the aggregate demand remains constant, the market will offer higher returns to new funds, thereby accelerating the flow of funds into the private sector. Therefore, according to traditional economic theories, the growth rate of λ is negatively correlated with Y, and a is *a* positive constant.

$$\frac{\partial \lambda / \lambda}{\partial Y} = -a \qquad 1\text{-}4$$

Secondly, the government's investment in quasi-operative resources (or quasi-public goods) is influenced by its fiscal revenue and expenditure. When the fiscal budget (B) is lower than the fiscal expenditure (FE), the government will be short of funds and will promote the conversion of quasi-operative resources (or quasi-public goods) into operative resources (or private products) to reduce its expenditure. The government will also provide higher returns to the private sector due to the insufficient supply of fiscal capital. In this case, the proportion of quasi-operative resources (or quasi-public goods) flowing into the private sector will increase, and λ will go smaller. Therefore, λ is negatively correlated with the ratio of fiscal expenditure to fiscal budget (FE/B). In addition, the government's fiscal expenditure is subject to the original value of λ. A higher λ indicates a higher proportion of quasi-operative resources (or quasi-public goods) provided by the public sector, namely a higher fiscal expenditure. Therefore, the correlation between λ and fiscal revenue and expenditure can be expressed by Equation 1-5, with b being a positive constant.

受到市场经济发展程度 (Y)、财政收支状况——包括财政预算 (B) 和财政支出 (FE)、居民或社会认知程度 (γ) 的共同影响，即存在一个如下函数：

$$\lambda = F(Y, B, FE, \gamma) \qquad 1\text{-}3$$

为了进一步探讨式 1-3 的可能函数形式，我们先来讨论上述变量对 λ 的边际影响。

首先，市场经济发展程度 (Y) 是一个介乎 0 到 1 之间的变量，代表着经济发展水平在高度不发达和高度发达之间的状态。市场经济发展程度会影响可支配收入水平，而可支配收入水平又会影响流入准经营性资源 (或准公共物品) 领域的资金量。如果经济发展程度较高，则居民可支配收入较高，此时私人部门将有能力和意愿投资准经营性资源 (或准公共物品)，即 λ 变小，准经营性资源 (或准公共物品) 转换为可经营性资源 (或纯私人产品) 的比例变高。如果原有的 λ 水平值较高，则意味着准经营性资源 (或准公共物品) 市场上原本的私人资金供给较少，在总需求不变的情况下，市场会给予新入资金更高的收益率，从而加速私人部门资金流入。因此，参考传统经济学理论，λ 的增长率与 Y 负相关，a 为正的常数，即

$$\frac{\partial \lambda / \lambda}{\partial Y} = -a \qquad 1\text{-}4$$

其次，政府对于准经营性资源 (或准公共物品) 的投入会受到政府财政收支状况的影响。如果财政预算 (B) 低于财政支出 (FE)，则政府此时资金不足，将推动准经营性资源 (或准公共物品) 向可经营性资源转换 (或纯私人产品)，以减少政府开支；且政府由于财政资金供给不足，愿意使私人部门获得更高的收益率。在这种情况下，准经营性资源 (或准公共物品) 转向私人部门的比例升高，λ 变小。因此，λ 与财政收支状况，即财政支出与财政预算的比值 (FE/B) 负相关。此外，政府财政支出会受原有 λ 值的影响，如果原有的 λ 值较高，即准经营性资源 (或准公共物品) 由公共部门出资的比例较高，则意味着政府具有更高的财政支出。因此，λ 与财政收支状况的关系可用式 1-5 表示，b 为正的常数。

$$\frac{\partial \lambda / \lambda}{\partial \left(\dfrac{FE}{B}\right)} = -b \qquad 1\text{-}5$$

Lastly, the private sector's investment in quasi-operative resources (or quasi-public goods) is influenced by both the supply and demand of funds and the cognitive degree of residents or society. It should be noted that the cognitive degree of residents or society has different effects on their willingness to invest in different economic stages. In details, when an economy is underdeveloped, namely $Y < Y^*$ (Y^* represents the critical value for economic maturity, which should be country-specific), the higher the cognitive degree of residents or society is, the more aware they are of the driving role of infrastructure investment in economic development, and thus the more willing they are to invest in quasi-operative resources (or quasi-public goods). In this case, λ is negatively correlated with γ. Differently, when an economy is developed, namely $Y > Y^*$, the higher the cognitive degree of residents or society is, the more aware they are of the negative impact of excessive infrastructure investment on sustainable development, and thus the more willing they are to invest in other resources rather than quasi-operative resources (or quasi-public goods) at the same level of return. In this case, λ is positively correlated with γ. Therefore, $\ln\left(\dfrac{Y}{Y^*}\right)$ is added as a correction factor for the above discussion. Another consideration is that the original value of λ has a significant impact on the cognitive degree of residents or society. When a market is underdeveloped, the higher the value of λ is, the stronger residents' preference for investing in public resources will be. On the contrary, when a market is developed, the higher the value of λ is, the stronger the desire of residents to control the scale of infrastructure will be, rather than investing in public resources.

Therefore, the correlation between λ and the cognitive degree of residents or society can be represented by Equation 1-6, with c being a positive constant.

$$\frac{\partial \lambda / \lambda}{\partial \left[\gamma \ln\left(\dfrac{Y}{Y^*}\right)\right]} = -c \qquad 1\text{-}6$$

Based on the above-mentioned analysis, there is a simple formula to express the correlation between the allocation proportion of quasi-operative resources in the public sector (λ) and the development level of market economy (Y), the fiscal revenue and expenditure including fiscal budget (B) and fiscal expenditure (FE), as well as the cognitive degree of residents or society (γ).

$$\frac{d\lambda}{\lambda} = -a\,dY - b\,d\frac{FE}{B} - c\ln\left(\frac{Y}{Y^*}\right)d\gamma \qquad 1\text{-}7$$

Equation 1-7 indicates the dependence of quasi-operative resources (or quasi-public goods) on different variables when they are converted into operative resources (or private products) and non-operative resources (or public goods). Noticeably, in an extreme case of $\lambda=0$, when quasi-operative resources (or quasi-public goods) are completely converted

$$\frac{\partial \lambda / \lambda}{\partial \left(\dfrac{\mathrm{FE}}{B}\right)} = -b \qquad 1\text{-}5$$

最后，私人部门对准经营性资源（或准公共物品）的投入，不仅受到资金供求的影响，还受到居民或社会认知程度的影响。值得注意的是，居民或社会认知程度对于其投入资金意愿的影响在不同经济阶段是不同的：如果经济发展处于落后阶段，即 $Y<Y^*$（Y^* 为经济成熟的临界值，根据各国标准而定），则居民或社会认知程度越高，越能意识到基础设施投资对于经济发展的带动价值，从而越愿意投资准经营性资源（或准公共物品），这时 λ 与 γ 负相关；如果经济发展处于成熟阶段，即 $Y>Y^*$，则居民或社会认知程度越高，越能意识到过度的基础设施投资对于环境可持续发展具有负面影响，从而在同样的收益率水平下，更愿意投资其他资源而非准经营性资源（或准公共物品），这时 λ 与 γ 正相关。因此，我们加入 $\ln\left(\dfrac{Y}{Y^*}\right)$ 作为上述讨论的校正系数。另外需要考虑的是，原有的 λ 水平对居民或社会认知程度有较大影响。如果市场发展落后，则 λ 越高，越会增强居民投资公共资源的偏好；反之，如果市场发展成熟，则 λ 越高，越会加强居民控制基建规模的愿望，而不愿投资于公共资源。

因此，λ 与居民或社会认知程度的关系可用式 1-6 表示，c 为正的常数。

$$\frac{\partial \lambda / \lambda}{\partial \left[\gamma \ln\left(\dfrac{Y}{Y^*}\right)\right]} = -c \qquad 1\text{-}6$$

基于上述分析，我们可以建立一个简单的公式来表达准经营性资源在公共部门当中的配置比例（λ）与市场经济发展程度（Y）、财政收支状况——包括财政预算（B）和财政支出（FE）、居民或社会认知程度（γ）的关系。

$$\frac{\mathrm{d}\lambda}{\lambda} = -a\mathrm{d}Y - b\mathrm{d}\frac{\mathrm{FE}}{B} - c\ln\left(\frac{Y}{Y^*}\right)\mathrm{d}\gamma \qquad 1\text{-}7$$

式 1-7 表达了准经营性资源（或准公共物品）向可经营性资源（或纯私人产品）和非经营性资源（或公共物品）转换时对于不同变量的依赖性。值得注意的

into operative resources (or private products), the operation of quasi-operative resources (or quasi-public goods) will be completely uncorrelated with the fiscal revenue and expenditure, the cognitive degree of residents or society, and other variables. This indicates that there will be no way to use such variables to affect the nature of operative resources.

Equation 1-7 is a differential equation about λ, which can be solved to obtain an explicit solution as shown in Equation 1-8 to visually understand their correlation.

$$\lambda = e^{-\left(aY+b\frac{FE}{B}\right)} \left(\frac{Y}{Y^*}\right)^{-c\gamma} \quad\quad 1-8$$

Equation 1-8 provides an expression for the allocation proportion of quasi-operative resources (or quasi-public goods) in the public sector, which is subject to economic conditions in different periods.

It indicates that the conversion of quasi-operative resources (or quasi-public goods) is going from being non-competitory to being competitory, and from being non-exclusive to being exclusive. The conversion of quasi-operative resources (or quasi-public goods) or generative resources, is influenced by the development level of regional market economy, the fiscal revenue and expenditure, and the cognitive degree of residents or society.

(II) Quasi-operative resources (or quasi-public goods) and three fields of resource generation

Quasi-operative resources (or quasi-public goods) are divided into three layers as shown in Figure 1-1.

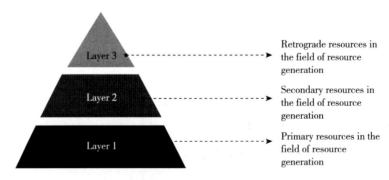

Figure 1-1　Three Layers of Quasi-operative Resources (Or Quasi-public Goods)

1. Primary resources in the field of resource generation

Primary resources of resource generation are divided into tangible factors and intangible factors.

(1) Tangible factors include space resources, deep-sea resources, polar resources, deep-exploration resources, and other resources.

是，极端情况下，即 λ 为 0，也就是准经营性资源 (或准公共物品) 完全转换为可经营性资源 (或纯私人产品) 时，该资源的运作将与财政收支状况、居民或社会认知程度等变量完全无关，即我们不可能借助财政收支状况等变量影响可经营性资源的性质。

式 1–7 是关于 λ 的微分方程，求解可得到一个显式解，如式 1–8 所示，可以方便我们更加直观地理解它们的相互作用。

$$\lambda = e^{-\left(aY + b\frac{FE}{B}\right)} \left(\frac{Y}{Y^*}\right)^{-c\gamma} \quad 1\text{--}8$$

式 1–8 给出了准经营性资源 (或准公共物品) 在公共部门当中的配置比例的表达式，它会根据不同时期的经济状况变化。

它表明，第一，准经营性资源 (或准公共物品) 的转换是一个从非竞争性到竞争性、从非排他性到排他性的过程；第二，准经营性资源 (或准公共物品)，即生成性资源的转换过程受三个因素影响：区域市场经济发展程度、财政收支状况和居民或社会认知程度。

(二) 准经营性资源 (或准公共物品) 与资源生成三大领域

准经营性资源 (或准公共物品) 包括以下三个层面，如图 1–1 所示。

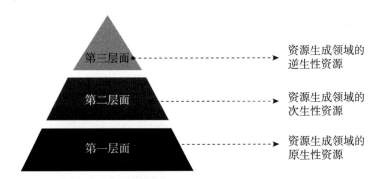

图 1–1　准经营性资源 (或准公共物品) 的三个层面

1. 资源生成领域的原生性资源

资源生成领域的原生性资源包括有形要素和无形要素两个方面。

(1) 有形要素包括太空资源、深海资源、极地资源、地球深探资源和其他资源。

For example, in terms of space resources, exploring the vast universe, developing the aerospace economy, and building an aerospace power represent the unremitting pursuit of countries around the globe. Amongst others, China has created an "affordable" space "villa". Manned spaceflight, lunar exploration, planetary exploration, and application satellites are all gaining comprehensive development around the world.

(2) Intangible factors include technology, data, etc.

Amongst others, data factor means that we use data as a resource or capital.

Data are not a natural factor of production. They are essentially an electronic or non-electronic record of information related to goods, services, or economic entities. It takes a gradual process for data to become a factor of production. In the long term, data factor will eventually penetrate into industrial economy, urban economy and other fields on a large scale, thereby comprehensively improving total factor productivity and promoting a new round of global economic growth. Data factor plays a role in the construction of communication network infrastructure, computing power infrastructure, and digital technology infrastructure with the new-generation information technology to develop the digital industry and promote the digital development of industrial economy and urban economy.

The generation role of data factor is reflected or integrated in the relevant infrastructure projects of intelligent city, including ①intelligent energy project; ②intelligent transportation project; ③intelligent urban management project; ④intelligent logistics project; ⑤intelligent medical project; ⑥intelligent education project; ⑦intelligent agricultural project; ⑧intelligent water conservancy project; ⑨intelligent environmental protection project; ⑩intelligent emergency project; etc. In these regards, in addition to planning and providing infrastructure, the government should also ①determine data property rights; ②supervise data operation; ③develop unified data collection standards; etc.

Therefore, it can be concluded that data play an important role in industrial development, urban construction, and social livelihood.

2. Secondary resources in the field of resource generation

In traditional economic theories, urban infrastructure (hardware and software) is defined as public goods provided by the government for free. However, in the process of urban development, governments around the world contract it to the market and investors. Urban infrastructure (hardware and software) in this book is referred to as secondary resources in the field of resource generation. As a secondary resource, urban infrastructure (hardware and software) refers to public facilities that provide public services for social production and residents' lives, and quasi-public product system used to ensure the normal functioning of national and regional socioeconomic activities and people's daily lives.

以太空资源为例，探索浩瀚宇宙，发展航天经济，建设航天强国，是世界各国不懈追求的航天梦。中国打造出"经济适用型"太空"别墅"。世界各国载人航天、月球探测、行星探测、应用卫星等各领域都在全面发展。

(2) 无形要素包括技术、数据等要素。

例如数据要素，即将数据资源化、资产化。

数据并非天然就是生产要素。数据本质上是对物品、服务或经济主体等相关信息的电子或非电子形式的记录。从资源化到资产化，数据成为生产要素是一个渐进的过程。从长期趋势看，数据要素终将大规模渗透到产业经济、城市经济等领域，全面提升全要素生产率，推动全球经济新一轮增长。数据要素涉及新一代信息技术演化生成的通信网络基础设施建设、算力基础设施建设和数字技术基础设施建设等，可以推进数字产业化和产业经济、城市经济数字化。

数据要素的生成作用体现或融合在智能城市开发的相关基础设施工程上，包括①智慧能源工程；②智慧交通工程；③智慧城管工程；④智慧物流工程；⑤智慧医疗工程；⑥智慧教育工程；⑦智慧农业工程；⑧智慧水利工程；⑨智慧环保工程；⑩智慧应急工程；等等。政府在其中的作用，除了规划与提供基础设施外，还应该包括①确定数据产权；②监管数据运行；③统一制定数据归集标准；等等。

数据要素在产业发展、城市建设和社会民生中具有重要作用。

2. 资源生成领域的次生性资源

城市基础设施(硬件与软件)在原有的经济理论中被定义为公共产品，由政府无偿提供。但在现实的城市发展进程中，世界各国又把它推向市场，由投资者去完成。笔者把城市基础设施(硬件与软件)称为资源生成领域中的次生性资源。作为次生性资源的城市基础设施(硬件与软件)，指为社会生产和居民生活提供公共服务的公共工程设施，用于保证国家和地区社会经济活动和人们日常生活正常进行的准公共产品系统。

Urban infrastructure (hardware and software) is divided into three layers.

The first layer includes urban hardware infrastructure and urban software infrastructure.

(1) Urban hardware infrastructure mostly refers to six types of system infrastructure, including ①energy supply system; ②water supply and drainage system; ③transportation system; ④post and telecommunication system; ⑤environmental protection and sanitation system; ⑥defense and disaster prevention system.

(2) Urban software infrastructure refers to administration, culture and education, healthcare, commercial service, finance and insurance, social welfare, and other social infrastructure.

The second layer indicates the result of the process of urban-rural integration. Productive infrastructure, living infrastructure, environmental infrastructure and social development infrastructure in rural areas are also included in urban infrastructure.

The third layer indicates the result of the process of urban and rural management going modernized. Intelligent city and other series of projects, namely the popular "new infrastructure" and facilities it utilizes, are also included in urban infrastructure.

3. Retrograde resources in the field of resource generation

Carbon dioxide and other five GHGs will immediately form unpopular social public goods in our production and social life once they are discharged into the air. Therefore, these resources are referred to as retrograde resources in the field of resource generation in this book.

The GHGs specified in the CDM Rules of the *Kyoto Protocol to the United Nations Framework Convention on Climate Change and the Paris Agreement* and their conversion are shown in Figure 1-2.

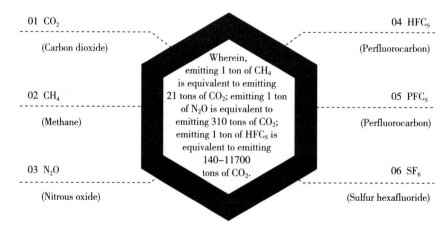

Figure 1-2   GHGs and Their Conversion

城市基础设施(硬件与软件)包括三个层次。

第一层次包括城市的硬件公共设施和软件公共设施。

(1) 城市的硬件公共设施,多指六大系统工程性基础设施,包括①能源供应系统;②供水排水系统;③交通运输系统;④邮电通信系统;⑤环保环卫系统;⑥防卫防灾系统。

(2) 城市的软件公共设施,主要是指行政管理、文化教育、医疗卫生、商业服务、金融保险、社会福利等社会性基础设施。

第二层次是指随着城乡一体化的进程,城市基础设施还包括乡村的生产性基础设施、生活性基础设施、生态环境基础设施和社会发展基础设施。

第三层次是指随着城乡管理现代化的进程,城市基础设施还包括逐步开发和建设的智能城市等系列工程,也就是当今风行的"新基建"及其运用的项目设施。

3. 资源生成领域的逆生性资源

以二氧化碳等六种温室气体的排放为例,其一旦排入大气中,就会立刻形成在人类生产和社会生活中并不被欢迎的社会公共产品。因此,笔者把这类资源称为资源生成领域的逆生性资源。

《联合国气候变化框架公约》京都议定书确定的包含的温室气体与其换算方法如图1-2所示。

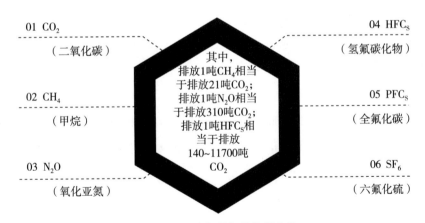

图1-2 温室气体与其换算方法

In response to climate change, the *Kyoto Protocol to the United Nations Framework Convention on Climate Change* and the *Paris Agreement* point out the overall direction of global green and low-carbon transformation.

General Secretary Xi Jinping delivered an important speech at the general debate of the 75th United Nations General Assembly, announcing that China will increase its independent national contribution, adopt more vigorous policies and measures, strive to achieve the peak value of carbon dioxide emissions by 2030 and achieve carbon neutrality by 2060.

Therefore, in terms of carbon emissions, carbon reduction, issuance and trading of carbon emission permits, carbon finance, and carbon market, we are exposed to the development, utilization, containment, and disposal of retrograde resources in the field of resource generation (as shown in Figure 1-3).

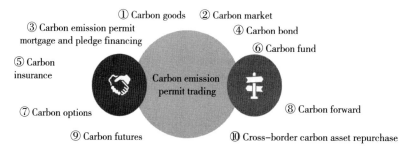

Figure 1-3　Carbon Emission Permit Trading

The result of the development, utilization, containment, and disposal of primary resources, secondary resources and retrograde resources in the field of resource generation represents the result of transformation from quasi-operative resources to operative resources, which can be summarized as follows.

First, it provides factors of production (supply of factor) for the development of industrial economy.

Second, it creates and optimizes the environment and conditions (supply of environment) for the development of industrial economy.

Third, it promotes the development of urban economy and international economy and expands the field and space of market economy (supply of market).

Fourth, the exploration and development of resource generation has become a new engine for a country's economic growth (driving its sustainable economic growth).

Therefore, by exploiting primary resources, secondary resources and retrograde resources in the field of resource generation, the government offers a troika (supply of factor, supply of environment and supply of market) on the supply side to boost the sustainable economic growth of a country or a region.

在应对气候变化的进程中,《联合国气候变化框架公约》京都议定书和《巴黎协定》代表了全球绿色低碳转型的大方向。

习近平在第七十五届联合国大会一般性辩论上发表重要讲话,郑重承诺,中国将提高国家自主贡献力度,采取更加有力的政策和措施,二氧化碳排放力争于2030年前达到峰值,努力争取2060年前实现碳中和。

于是,从碳排放到碳减排、碳排放权凭证发放与交易,再到碳金融、碳市场,就有了一个资源生成领域中对逆生性资源的开发、利用、遏制与处置问题(如图1-3所示)。

图1-3　碳排放权交易

对资源生成领域三类资源的开发、利用、遏制与处置的结果,即准经营性资源向可经营性资源转换的结果,可以概括为以下几点。

第一,它为产业经济发展提供了生产要素(要素供给);

第二,它为产业经济发展创造、优化了环境和条件(环境供给);

第三,它推动了城市经济、国际经济的发展,拓展了市场经济的领域和空间(市场供给);

第四,对资源生成领域的开拓与发展,成为一国经济增长的新引擎(推动着一国经济可持续增长)。

这表明,政府通过开发资源生成领域的三类资源,在供给侧提供了三驾马车(要素供给、环境供给、市场供给),助推着一个区域或一个国家经济的可持续增长。

II. Government Is the First Investor in the Field of Resource Generation

Resource generation is featured with ①changeability; ②economy; ③productivity; ④high risk.

High risk to which resource generation is exposed are embodied in big initial investment, long construction period, high cost and small market, failure of investment recovery, emergency incident, etc. Therefore, unique investment risk, operational risk, and management risk are seen in the field of resource generation. For this sake, the government has to be the first investor in the field of resource generation (private enterprises usually lack the courage, motivation, and strength to invest in such resources).

In the field of resource generation, before turning a non-competitory and non-exclusive generative resource to a competitory and exclusive one, it is required to address the following issues.

(1) Source of funds. The conversion of quasi-operative resources (quasi-public goods) into operative resources (private products) needs to be supported by funds. These funds used by governments around the world for investment are mainly sourced from investment expenditure in the fiscal year budget, bank loan, issuance of government bonds, investment partners, and other methods.

(2) Organization management. Governments around the world use the following means of organization management. First, they make independent investment by establishing state-owned companies to directly charge fees from these projects in installments annually. Second, they make leasing investment by BOT (build-operate-transfer), TOT (transfer-operate-transfer) and other methods. Third, they make joint investment by PPP (public private partnership), PPC (port-park-city), and other forms of joint venture. Fourth, they make joint venture investment by establishing and listing joint venture companies to obtain returns.

(3) Capital operation. Governments around the world carry out capital operation for their investment by the following means. First, they implement the capital operation of franchise right by DBO (design-build-operate), BOT, BOO (build-own-operate), BOOT (build-own-operate-transfer) or other means, using the right of charge, the right of pricing. Second, they also adopt different capital operation methods or cross-apply different capital

二、政府是资源生成领域的第一投资人

资源生成领域具有四大特性：①动态性；②经济性；③生产性；④高风险性。

资源生成领域的高风险性表现及其揭示的问题是：第一，前期投资支出额大；第二，建设周期长；第三，成本高，市场窄小；第四，投资回收可能失败；第五，可能存在突发事件；等等。因此形成了资源生成领域中特有的投资风险、运营风险、管理风险，也使得政府在客观上成为该类资源开发的第一投资人（私人企业通常没有魄力、动力和实力去投资此类资源）。

同时，在资源生成领域，将生成性资源从非竞争性转为竞争性，从非排他性转为排他性，需要解决以下几个问题。

(1) 资金来源问题。从准经营性资源（准公共物品）到可经营性资源（纯私人产品）的转换需要解决资金来源问题。世界各国政府投资的资金来源包括：第一，通过财政年度预算的公共投资性支出；第二，银行贷款；第三，发行政府债券；第四，寻求政府的投资合作伙伴；第五，其他方式。

(2) 组织管理问题。世界各国政府投资的组织管理方式有以下几种：第一，独立投资，世界各国政府组建国有公司直接对项目分年段收费；第二，租赁式投资，政府运用建设—运营—转让(build-operate-transfer，BOT)、转让—运营—转让(transfer-operate-transfer，TOT)等方式收费；第三，合伙投资，政府采取公共私营合作制(public private partnership，PPP)、港口—工业园区—城市(port-park-city，PPC)等合营方式收费；第四，股份式投资，政府组建股份制企业，并通过上市方式获取收益；等等。

(3) 资本运营问题。世界各国政府投资的资本运营方式有以下几种：第一，世界各国政府也通过收费权、定价权等手段，运用设计—建设—运营(design-build-operate，DBO)、BOT、建设—拥有—运营(build-own-operate，BOO)、建设—拥有—运营—转让(build-own-operate-transfer，BOOT)等方式实施特许经营权的资本运营；第二，世界各国政府还会根据各准经营性资源，即基础设施项目不同的特点和条件，采取不同的资本运营方式，或交叉运用不同资本

operation methods in view of various quasi-operative resources (or the characteristics and conditions of infrastructure projects), such as taking PPP as an equity carrier or PPC as a development mode. Third, they adopt other means like REITs (real estate investment trusts) to provide new direct financing support for infrastructure construction, thereby promoting the market-oriented development of infrastructure investment and financing.

Exploitation of resources in the field of resource generation can:

(1) urge governments around the world to transform their functions;

(2) attract a variety of investors;

(3) disperse investment risks;

(4) lure social funds to participate in the construction of urban infrastructure and other projects;

(5) employ market mechanisms to maximize government revenue with the optimal fiscal expenditure structure;

(6) promote economic growth and create a new engine for a country's economic growth.

Exploitation of resources in the field of resource generation suggests that:

(1) high risk involved in the investment and development of quasi-operative resources prompt the government to become the first investor;

(2) the operation of investment in quasi-operative resources makes the government participate in market competition;

(3) the government must follow market rules in investing and constructing quasi-operative resources;

(4) the local government or superior government should be responsible for coordinating, supervising, and managing the conversion of quasi-operative resources.

It is of utmost significance when the government participates in economic activities, especially in urban economic development, and plays a promising role. The government plays an effective role, deepens its effective role, or has its effective role merge with market economy in this aspect. It can be concluded that the exploitation of resource generation is an important entry point for government competition.

The trajectory of government and enterprises participation in economic activities is shown in Figure 1-4.

运营方式，例如采用PPP方式作为股权载体，或运用PPC方式作为开发模式；第三，其他方式，例如房地产投资信托基金(real estate investment trusts，REITs)为基础设施建设提供了一种新的直接融资支持，推动了基础设施投融资的市场化发展。

对资源生成领域开发的意义包括以下几个：

(1) 促进世界各国政府职能转变；

(2) 推动投资主体多元化；

(3) 分散投资项目风险；

(4) 吸引社会资金参与城市基础设施等项目的建设；

(5) 运用市场机制，以最佳的财政支出结构带来最大的政府财政收益；

(6) 促进经济增长，成为一国经济增长的新引擎。

对资源生成领域的开发过程揭示出以下几点：

(1) 在对准经营性资源的投资开发中，其高风险性促使政府成为第一投资人；

(2) 在对准经营性资源的投资运营中，其组织方式促使政府参与市场竞争；

(3) 在对准经营性资源的投资建设中，政府也必须遵循市场规则；

(4) 在转换准经营性资源的过程中，各级政府同时兼有协调、监督、管理的职责(本级政府或上级政府)。

这就是政府参与经济活动尤其是参与城市经济发展、发挥有为作用最主要的方面。政府的有为作用，或政府有为作用与市场经济的相互融合，正是从此领域切入并深入的。可以这么定论，对资源生成领域的开发是政府竞争的重要切入点。

政府与企业参与经济活动的连接轨道如图1-4所示。

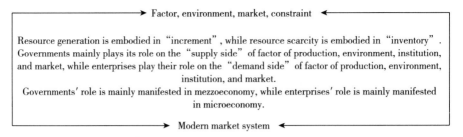

Figure 1-4　Trajectory of the Government and Enterprises Participation in Economic Activities

III. Supply-side Troika Boosts Economic Growth

By exploring the field of resource generation, the government may form a "troika" on the supply side to promote a country's or region's economic development. The supply-side troika refers to the supply of factor, the supply of environment, and the supply of market.

(1) The supply of factor involves tangible factors and intangible factors. It unveils the connotation and transformation process of micro-enterprise's factor of production in various countries around the world.

① Tangible factors include space resource, deep-sea resource, polar resource, etc.

② Intangible factors include technology, data, etc.

(2) The supply of environment includes hard environment and soft environment. It unveils the connotation and transformation process of business environment in various countries around the world.

① The hard environment includes infrastructure, environmental protection, etc.

② The soft environment includes policy, management efficiency, etc.

(3) The supply of market includes transverse market system and longitudinal market system. It unveils the market development, market system improvement, and the transformation process of the connotation of market economy in various countries around the world.

① The transverse market system includes industrial economy, urban economy, international economy, etc.

② The longitudinal market system includes market factor, market organization, market legal system, market supervision, market environment, market infrastructure, etc.

```
        ┌──────→ 要素、环境、市场、约束 ←──────┐
        │  资源生成表现在"增量" │ 资源稀缺表现在"存量"  │
        │  政府行为侧重在生产要素、环境、│ 企业行为侧重在生产要素、环境、│
        │  制度和市场的"供给侧"    │ 制度和市场的"需求侧"        │
        │  政府作用主要表现在中观经济 │ 企业作用主要表现在微观经济   │
        └──────→     现代市场体系    ←──────┘
```

图 1-4　政府与企业参与经济活动的连接轨道示意图

三、供给侧三驾马车助推经济增长

政府通过开拓资源生成领域，可以形成政府在供给侧的三驾马车，推动一国或区域经济的发展。政府在供给侧的三驾马车包括要素供给、环境供给和市场供给。

(1) 要素供给，包括有形要素和无形要素。它揭示出世界各国微观企业生产要素的内涵及其变革进程。

① 有形要素：太空资源、深海资源、极地资源等；

② 无形要素：技术、数据等。

(2) 环境供给，包括硬环境和软环境。它揭示出世界各国营商环境的内涵及其变革进程。

① 硬环境：基础设施、生态环保等；

② 软环境：政策措施、管理效率等。

(3) 市场供给，包括市场横向体系和市场纵向体系。它揭示出世界各国市场领域的开拓、市场体系的完善，以及市场经济内涵的变革进程。

① 市场横向体系：产业经济、城市经济、国际经济等；

② 市场纵向体系：市场要素、市场组织、市场法治、市场监管、市场环境、市场基础设施等。

Keynes mentioned government behavior and intervention in his *The General Theory of Employment, Interest, and Money*. In the book, Keynes reinterpreted the concept of full employment, put forward the principle of effective demand, the theory of determination of national income, the operating rules of three psychological variables, the multiplier theory, the theory of business cycle, and studied the price theory, the wage theory, and the international trade theory.

Therefore, economists believe that Keynes made the following contributions to economics: ①he found new areas for promoting a country's economic growth; ②he believed that the government should intervene in the development of the national economy by means of infrastructure investment; ③he believed that the government should mostly adopt fiscal policies. As a result, Keynes's economic thoughts function as an independent theoretical system in economics.

A successful case was the Roosevelt's New Deal, which put Keynes's economic thoughts into use. The core of Roosevelt's New Deal can be summarized as 3Rs, namely recovery, relief, and reform. Work relief was the most important measure in Roosevelt's New Deal. Roosevelt rectified the banking and financial industry, revitalized the industry, adjusted agricultural policies, established a social security system, set up the Federal Emergency Relief Administration, and vigorously promoted the construction of public works to create jobs and stimulate production and consumption, all of which achieved fruitful results.

However, the author believes Keynes did not essential distinguish public goods and commodity; did not rigorously distinguish and define urban infrastructure construction and industrial economy; did not rigorously distinguish participants in the urban infrastructure construction and those in the industrial economy; did not specify whether the government, one of the participants, should follow market rules when investing in public goods; did not clearly clarify whether the government competes with private investors and investors' alliance when participating in infrastructure investment.

Therefore, the following shortcomings are clearly visible in his economic theory. Firstly, Keynes abandoned Smith's theoretical support, but intentionally or unintentionally relied on Smith's industrial economy market theory. Secondly, he found a new area for promoting a country's economic growth: the development and utilization of urban infrastructure, but failed to find a reasonable theoretical core when discussing government functions. Thirdly, he ignored resource generation in a country's economic growth. Fourthly, he borrowed Smith's theory of industrial resource allocation, but did not discuss the generation and allocation of urban resources. Fifthly, his resource generation was not supported by "institutional construction".

凯恩斯的《就业、利息和货币通论》也涉及了政府行为和政府干预的问题。在该书中，凯恩斯重新解释了充分就业的概念，提出了有效需求原理、简单的国民收入决定理论、三大心理变量的运行规律、乘数理论、经济周期理论，研究了物价理论、工资理论、国际贸易理论。

因此，经济学界认为凯恩斯对经济学做出了贡献：①找到了一国促进经济增长的新领域；②认为政府要干预国家经济的发展，手段、措施和切入点就在于基础设施投资；③认为政府应运用财政政策作为政策主体。于是，凯恩斯特色经济思想作为一个独立的经济学理论体系逐渐形成。

比较典型的成功案例是包含有凯恩斯特色思想的罗斯福新政。罗斯福新政的核心可以概括为3Rs，即复兴、救济、改革(recovery、relief、reform)。以工代赈是罗斯福新政最重要的一条措施，除了整顿银行和金融业、复兴工业、调整农业政策、建立社会保障体系、建立急救救济署等措施，还有大力兴建公共工程、增加就业、刺激生产和消费，这些措施取得了成效。

但笔者认为，凯恩斯经济学理论也存在着问题。第一，凯恩斯经济学理论没有在本质上严格区分公共物品与商品；第二，没有严格区分和界定城市基础设施建设与产业经济；第三，没有严格区分城市基础设施建设参与主体与产业经济参与主体；第四，没有明确参与主体之一的政府在公共物品的投资中是否也应遵循市场规则；第五，没有明确阐明政府在参与基础设施投资时，与私人投资者和投资者联盟，是否也有竞争关系。

因此，凯恩斯经济学理论的缺陷明显地表现出来：第一，凯恩斯经济学理论抛弃了斯密的理论支撑，但又有意无意地依赖着斯密的产业经济市场理论；第二，凯恩斯找到了一国促进经济增长的新领域——城市基础设施的开发和利用，但在论述政府职能时，却又缺乏其理论上的合理内核；第三，凯恩斯在理论上忽略了一个国家经济增长中的资源生成问题；第四，凯恩斯借用了斯密产业资源配置的理论，却又不去讨论城市资源的生成与配置问题；第五，他的资源

Sixthly, he failed to analyze and develop modern market theory and the system of modern economics based on the core principles of economics: resource scarcity and resource generation in resource allocation.

The theory that "Supply-side Troika Boosts Economic Growth" proposed in this chapter is fundamentally different from Keynes's economic theory.

(1) Different behavioral nodes. The theory that "Supply-side Troika Boosts Economic Growth" focuses on pre-event behaviors, while the government intervention specified in Keynes's economic theory focuses on mid-event and post-event behaviors.

(2) Different priorities of adjustment. The theory that "Supply-side Troika Boosts Economic Growth" involves the role of government in three types of generative resources in an all-round way, while the government intervention specified in Keynes's economic theory focuses on the demand side.

(3) Different government roles. Effective government plays as a major market entity in the field of resource generation, while Keynes's economic theory ignores government's role in the market.

(4) Different operational modes. The theory that "Supply-side Troika Boosts Economic Growth" requires the government to lead and carry out supply-side structural reforms to help the market to determine resource allocation and help the government itself to better play its role, while Keynes's economic theory emphasizes government intervention and its role on the demand side.

The theory that "Supply-side Troika Boosts Economic Growth" is similar to the Supply-side Economics to some extent. They are identical in starting with the supply side and emphasizing the analysis of the economic effects of government policies. As for their essential differences, the theory that "Supply-side Troika Boosts Economic Growth" refers to developing and utilizing three types of generative resources and taking fiscal, financial, environmental, efficiency, and legal policies and means to expand the supply of factor, environment and market, boost demand, and promote sustainable economic growth in a region or country. Say's Law denies demand management and government intervention. Therefore, the theory "Supply-side Troika Boosts Economic Growth" and the Supply-side Economics are different in basic theories, government roles, policy tools, and policy objectives.

The author believes that the theory that "Supply-side Troika Boosts Economic Growth" implies a change in the production mode of a region or even a country for the following reasons. First, it expands the connotation of micro-enterprise's factor of production and promotes the transformation of industrial factor of production. Regional governments should develop, utilize,

生成缺少"制度建设"配套；第六，凯恩斯没能以经济学的核心原则——资源配置中的资源稀缺和资源生成为切入点，分析和演化出现代市场理论与现代经济学体系。

本章提出的"供给侧三驾马车助推经济增长"与凯恩斯经济学理论有着本质区别。

(1) 行为节点不同。"供给侧三驾马车助推经济增长"侧重在过程的事前；凯恩斯经济学理论的政府干预表现在事中、事后。

(2) 调节侧重点不同。"供给侧三驾马车助推经济增长"涉及政府作用于三类生成性资源的全方位、全过程；而凯恩斯经济学理论的政府干预着重在需求侧。

(3) 政府作用不同。有为政府在资源生成领域作为市场主体发挥着作用；凯恩斯经济学理论仍然把政府置于市场之外。

(4) 运行模式不同。"供给侧三驾马车推动经济增长"是通过政府引领和供给侧结构性改革，使得市场决定资源配置，同时更好地发挥政府作用；而凯恩斯经济学理论强调政府干预和需求侧作用。

政府使用供给侧三驾马车助推经济增长与西方经济学中的供给学派也不完全相同。两者的相同点是：都将供给侧作为理论的主要出发点；都重视对政府政策的经济效应分析。两者的本质区别是：政府使用供给侧三驾马车助推经济增长，是借助于对三类生成性资源的开发和利用，运用财政、金融、环境、效率、法律等政策手段，扩大要素供给、环境供给和市场供给，带动需求，促进一个区域或一个国家的经济可持续增长；而供给学派中的萨伊定律与需求管理决裂，否认政府干预。因此二者的理论基础、政府作用、政策手段和政策目标不同。

笔者认为，政府使用供给侧三驾马车助推经济增长是一个区域乃至一个国家生产方式的一场变革。第一，它扩大了微观企业生产要素的内涵，推动了产业生产要素的变革。区域政府在遵循市场规律的基础上开发、利用和管理资源生成领域的三类资源，从而把微观企业的要素内涵扩展到现阶段有形要素与无形要素相

and manage three types of resources in the field of resource generation subject to market rules, thereby integrating the connotation of micro-enterprise's factor of production with the current six tangible and intangible factors. Second, it expands the connotation of mezzo business environment and promotes the transformation of a country's business environment. In order to promote sustainable economic growth, regional governments should keep investment and construction and improve the hard and soft environments, thereby promoting the transformation and enhancement of a country's business environment. Third, it expands the scope and space for the role of a country's market, and builds a new multi-level market system. In a transverse market system, both enterprise and government play a role in industrial economy, urban economy, international economy, and other fields. The longitudinal market system involves market factor system, market organization system, market law system, market supervision system, market environment system, and market infrastructure, all of which promote the transformation and expansion of the connotation of market economy in countries around the world. Fourth, it clarifies the positioning and role of a government in the market economy. The effective role of a government is reflected in the allocation of three types of resources on the supply side, policy support, and goal achievement. Fifth, it unveils important new engines for a country's economic growth, namely investment, innovation, and rules.

IV. The Boundary for An Effective Government to Adjust the Three Types of Resources

The government can play a major role in the field of resource generation. By exploiting and using primary resources, secondary resources and retrograde resources in the field of resource generation, the government will form a troika on the supply side to boost the sustainable economic growth of a country. Here are some cases.

◎ **Case 1-1**

On April 26, 2022, the 11th meeting of the Central Commission of Finance and Economics pointed out that work should be done to strengthen the construction of infrastructure in an all-round way. The meeting stressed that the government ought to optimize the layout, structure, functions, and development mode of infrastructure, build a modern infrastructure system, so as to lay a solid foundation for the comprehensive construction of a socialist modernized country. The modern infrastructure system involves ①industry upgrading infrastructure (information, technology, logistics, etc.); ②network infrastructure for transportation, energy, and

融合的六要素中。第二，它扩大了中观区域营商环境的内涵，推动了一国营商环境的变革。区域政府为推动经济的可持续增长，不断进行投资建设，改善硬环境、完善软环境，推动了一国营商环境的变革与提升。第三，它扩大了一国市场作用的领域和空间，构建了全新的多层次市场体系。市场横向体系中，企业和政府作为双重主体，在产业经济、城市经济、国际经济等领域发挥着作用；市场纵向体系包含市场要素体系、市场组织体系、市场法治体系、市场监管体系、市场环境体系、市场基础设施，其六大功能推动着世界各国市场经济内涵的变革与扩大。第四，它阐明了政府在市场经济中的定位及作用。政府的有为作用体现在供给侧对三类资源的调配、政策配套和目标实现上。第五，它发掘和开拓了一国经济增长重要的新引擎，即投资新引擎、创新新引擎和规则新引擎。

四、有为政府调节三类资源的边界

政府在资源生成领域大有作为。政府通过对原生性资源、次生性资源和逆生性资源的开发、利用，形成供给侧三驾马车，推动一国经济的可持续增长。以下是一些具体案例。

◎ 案例1-1

2022年4月26日，中央财经委员会第十一次会议指出：要全面加强基础设施建设。会议强调要优化基础设施布局、结构、功能和发展模式，构建现代化基础设施体系，为全面建设社会主义现代化国家打下坚实基础。现代化基础设施体系包括：①产业升级基础设施(信息、科技、物流等)；②交通、能源、水利等

water conservancy; ③urban infrastructure; ④agricultural and rural infrastructure; ⑤national security infrastructure. The modern infrastructure system will provide significant support for the economic and social development of China.

◎ **Case 1-2**

China's project of "channeling more computing resources from the eastern areas to the less developed western areas" was launched in all aspects on June 15, 2022. National computing hubs will be built in the Beijing-Tianjin-Hebei region, the Yangtze River Delta, the Guangdong-Hong Kong-Macao Greater Bay Area, the Chengdu-Chongqing economic circle, north China's Inner Mongolia Autonomous Region, southwest China's Guizhou Province, northwest China's Gansu Province and Ningxia Hui Autonomous Region. 10 national data center clusters are planned. The overall layout design of China's integrated big data center system has been completed. The project of "channeling more computing resources from the eastern areas to the less developed western areas" has been officially launched in all aspects.

On this occasion, the author proposes that the prerequisite for building an effective government is to rely on market rules and mechanisms. An effective government must keep up with the times, embrace competition and cooperation, and make transparent government affairs. The principle is that the market should determine resource allocation, while the government should play its guiding, coordinating, and pre-alarming roles in the industrial economy, its allocating, participating, and marshoulding roles in the urban economy, and its guarantee, supporting, and improving roles in the livelihood economy. The government may take planning, investment, consumption, price, tax, interest rate, exchange rate, law, and other policies and carry out innovation in terms of concept, institution, organization, and technology. The purpose of a government being effective is to use the supply-side troika to form a leading advantage in economic growth and achieve scientific and sustainable development.

In fact, the connotation of an effective government is reflected in its policy formulation and policy tools, as shown in Table 1-1.

Table 1-1　Policy Formulation and Policy Tools of An Effective Government

Type of resources	Policy formulation	Policy tools
Operative resources	Policy on industrial economy	Planning and guiding, supporting and coordinating, supervising and managing
Non-operative resources	Policy on livelihood economy	Providing general underpinning, maintaining fairness, and making practical improvement
Quasi-operative resources (generative resource)	Policy on urban economy	Planning, participating in construction, and realizing orderly management

网络型基础设施；③城市基础设施；④农业农村基础设施；⑤国家安全基础设施。它将为国家经济社会的发展提供重要的支撑。

◎ 案例1-2

2022年2月，中国的"东数西算"工程全面启动。在京津冀、长三角、粤港澳大湾区、成渝、内蒙古、贵州、甘肃、宁夏等地启动建设国家算力枢纽节点，并规划10个国家数据中心集群。中国一体化大数据中心体系完成总体布局设计，"东数西算"工程正式全面启动。[①]

值此，笔者提出，政府有为的前提是依靠市场规则和市场机制。政府有为的条件是与时俱进、竞争与合作、政务公开。政府有为的原则是市场决定资源配置；政府对产业经济发挥导向、调节、预警作用，对城市经济发挥调配、参与、维序作用，对民生经济发挥保障、托底、提升作用。政府有为的手段是运用规划、投资、消费、价格、税收、利率、汇率、法律等政策，开展理念、制度、组织、技术创新。政府有为的目的是推动供给侧三驾马车，形成经济增长领先优势，实现科学可持续发展。

回到现实，有为政府的内涵表现在有为政府的政策制定及其政策工具的选择上，如表1-1所示。

表1-1　有为政府的政策制定及政策工具选择

资源类型	政策制定	政策工具
可经营性资源	产业经济政策	规划、引导，扶持、调节，监督、管理
非经营性资源	民生经济政策	基本托底、公平公正、有效提升
准经营性资源（生成性资源）	城市经济政策	规划布局、参与建设、有序管理

---

① 王政：《"东数西算"工程全面启动》，《人民日报》2022年6月15日。

The author defines the boundary for an effective government to adjust three types of resources (three types of economies), as shown in Table 1-2.

Table 1–2 The Boundary for an Effective Government to Adjust the Three Types of Resources (Three Types of Economies)

Type of resources	Type of economy	Boundary
Operative resources	Industrial economy	The government should stay out of competition and use industrial policies to guide and restrict the direction, scale, and structure of non-governmental investment
Non-operative resources	Livelihood economy	The government should clarify the basic scope of social demands, and define a reasonable proportion of fiscal revenue and expenditure, thereby improving the direction, scale, and structure of social charitable undertakings and public goods
Quasi-operative resources (generative resource)	Urban economy	The government should optimize the fiscal expenditure structure and create new allocation modes of fiscal resources to better the investment direction, scale, and structure of quasi-operative resources (such as urban infrastructure)

Only in this way can we truly enable the market to determine resource allocation, make the government play its roles better, and distinguish scientific and reasonable economic behaviors from administrative interventions. This indicates the essence of the author's mezzoeconomics!

Hence, it can be concluded as follows:

(1) Resource generation is an important new engine in a country's economic growth;

(2) The government is the first investor in the field of resource generation;

(3) The government should use the supply-side troika to promote economic growth;

(4) The government is a market entity on the supply side, while enterprises are the counterpart on the demand side;

(5) An effective government should follow market rules, define the scope of economic behaviors, and develop norms for economic behaviors.

因此，笔者对有为政府对三类资源(三类经济)的调节边界进行界定，如表1-2所示。

表1-2 有为政府对三类资源(三类经济)的调节边界

资源类型	经济类型	调节的边界
可经营性资源	产业经济	应坚持退出竞争性领域，通过产业政策的引导作用，来制约非政府投资的方向、规模与结构
非经营性资源	民生经济	应明确社会公共需要的基本范围，通过确定财政收支的合理比例，来完善社会公益事业和公共产品的方向、规模与结构
准经营性资源(生成性资源)	城市经济	应优化财政支出结构，通过创新财政资源的配置方式，来提升准经营性资源(城市基础设施等)的投资方向、规模与结构

只有这样，才能真正使市场决定资源配置，同时更好地发挥政府的作用，并把政府科学、合理的经济行为与行政干预区别开来。这是笔者研究的中观经济学的精髓所在！

至此，本章得出如下结论。

(1) 资源生成是一国经济增长中的重要新引擎。

(2) 政府是对资源生成领域开发的第一投资人。

(3) 政府在供给侧运用三驾马车促进经济增长。

(4) 政府是供给侧领域的市场主体，企业是需求侧领域的市场主体。

(5) 有为政府应遵循市场规则，界定经济行为领域，规范经济行为准则。

Chapter II

Smith's Third Book and Dual Attributes Theory of Governments

Chapter I introduces the theory and characteristics of resource generation, analyzes the role of the government in boosting economic growth with the troika on the supply side, and clarifies that the government is the first investor in the field of resource generation. This chapter will explain why the government still has investment behavior choices in high-risk resource generation areas. Behind these are the dual attributes of government.

I. Adam Smith's Third Book and the Dual Attributes of Government

Smith, born in 1723, attended two universities from his 14 to 21 years old, and was awarded the title of university professor at the age of 27. He finished his first work *The Theory of Moral Sentiments* at the age of 36 in 1759, and his second work *The Wealth of Nations* at the age of 53 in 1776. He passed away in 1790 at the age of 67, and left his third work *On Government and Law* unfinished. According to the customs and habits in the UK then, the relevant materials were destroyed.

Smith's tutor proposed that "people can understand theoretically what is good by discovering behaviors that are beneficial to humans". This idea had influenced Smith all the way in his exploration of the (beneficial) behaviors of individuals, enterprises, and even governments.

第二章

斯密的第三本书与政府双重属性理论

第一章着重阐述了资源生成理论及其特征，分析了政府在供给侧运用三驾马车促进经济增长的作用，明确了政府是资源生成领域的第一投资人。这一章将着重阐述为什么在具有高风险性的资源生成领域，政府仍有投资行为选择？原因要从政府存在双重属性说起。

一、斯密的第三本书与政府双重属性

斯密于 1723 年出生，14～21 岁上了两所大学，27 岁被授予大学教授头衔；1759 年，时年 36 岁，完成了第一部著作《道德情操论》；1776 年，时年 53 岁，完成了第二部著作《国富论》；1790 年逝世，时年 67 岁，此前已开始撰写第三部著作《政府与法律论》，但未完成，按当时英国的风俗习惯，相关材料被销毁。

斯密的导师提出"人们可以通过发现对人类有益的行为来认识从理论上来说什么是好的"。这一哲理深深影响着斯密对社会个人、市场企业，甚至国家政府（有益的）行为的探研。

The Theory of Moral Sentiments includes seven parts respectively of the propriety of action; of merit and demerit, or of the objects of reward and punishment; of the foundations of our judgments concerning our own sentiments and conduct, and of the sense of duty; of the effect of utility upon the sentiments of approbation; of the influence of custom and fashion upon the sentiments of moral approbation and disapprobation; of the character of virtue; of systems of moral philosophy.

The Wealth of Nations includes five parts respectively of the causes of improvement in the productive powers of labor, and of the order according to which its produce is naturally distributed among the different ranks of the people; of the nature, accumulation, and employment of stock; of the different progress of opulence in different nations; of systems of political economy; of the revenue of the sovereign or commonwealth.

It was estimated that his third book should had been *On Government and Law*. By analyzing the characteristics of government's economic behaviors, he attempted to figure out what holds the behavioral attribute, intrinsic essence, and essence of a government; what drives the inherent constraint between countries; and what economic means should a government use to safeguard or strive for national interests. For this purpose, he had to study and answer the following five questions. ①What is the relationship between government and law? ②What are the basic functions of national economy and the characteristics of government management behavior? ③What is the inherent driving force behind national development? ④What is the inherent constraint between countries? What common rules are followed if it is "collaboration"? What fields are involved if it is "competition"? ⑤What is the role a government plays in the market economy?

The Theory of Moral Sentiments analyzes individual behavior in society, and believes that individual egotism and empathy are mutually opposed and unified, forming an invisible hand that promotes individuals to survive and develop in social groups. *The Wealth of Nations* analyzes the behavior of enterprises in the market, and believes that its selfishness and altruism are mutually opposed and unified, forming an invisible hand that promotes enterprises to survive and develop in the market economy. Does *On Government and Law* also touch on and analyze the behavior of governments, and believe that their pursuit of interests and coordination are mutually opposed and unified, forming an invisible hand to promote the survival and development of countries? If the answer is no, the third book would be a failure.

If yes, the third book would contradict with the law in *The Wealth of Nations* that government is a night watcher. Pitifully, Smith's third book, which he had studied for nearly 14 years, was

斯密的第一本书《道德情操论》共分为七部分：论行为的合宜性；论功劳与过失，即论奖赏与惩罚的对象；论我们品评自己情感与行为的基础，并论义务感；论效用对赞许感的影响；论社会习惯与时尚对道德赞许与谴责等情感的影响；论好品格；论道德哲学体系。

第二本书《国富论》共分为五部分：论劳动生产力进步的原因，兼论劳动产品在不同阶级人们之间自然分配的顺序；论资本的性质、积累和用途；论不同国家财富的不同发展；论政治经济学体系；论君主或国家的收入。

据分析，斯密的第三本书应当是《政府与法律论》[①]。他从一国政府的经济行为特征入手，试图分析一国政府的行为属性、内在本质、精髓内核靠什么来牵引；国家与国家之间的内在牵制力靠什么来推动；一国政府为了维护或争取国家利益，如何利用经济手段去谋取其利益。为此，他必须至少研究并回答以下五个方面的问题。①政府与法律的关系是什么？②国家经济的基本职能与政府管理行为特征是什么？③国家发展的内在动力是什么？④国家与国家之间的内在牵制力是什么？如果是共同"协作"——靠什么共同规则？如果是相互"竞争"——在哪些领域开展？⑤政府在市场经济中的角色是什么？

在斯密的前两本书中，《道德情操论》分析了社会中的个人行为，认为个人的自我心与同理心相互对立统一，形成了一只看不见的手，推动个人在社会群体中的生存与发展；《国富论》分析了市场中的企业行为，认为企业的利己性与利他性相互对立统一，形成了一只看不见的手，推动企业在市场经济中的生存与发展。那么，《政府与法律论》是否也会触及并分析国家政府的行为，并认为国家政府的逐利性与协调性是相互对立统一的，从而也会形成一只看不见的手推动国家与国家之间的生存与发展呢？答案如果是否定的，第三本书将无法研究下去；答案如果是肯定的，又会与《国富论》中视政府为守夜人的定律相矛盾。最终，斯密研究了接近14年的第三本书未能面世，留给世人一大遗憾。于是，经济学

---

① 陈云贤：《经济新引擎：兼论有为政府与有效市场》，外语教学与研究出版社，2019，第7-19页。

unfinished. Therefore, the explanation of the relationship between government and market in economics is also based on *the Wealth of Nations*: ①market economy refers to the development of industrial economy and industrial resources; ②the relationship between government and market represents the roles they play in industrial economy; ③enterprise is the market entity of market economy.

The author believes that enterprise is only the market entity of microeconomy. Governments utilize the supply-side troika to boost economic growth in the field of resource generation. So, the government is the market entity of mezzoeconomy.

Regional government boasts "dual attributes". First, regional government has a "quasi-macro" or "quasi-state" attribute. This sort of "quasi-state" attribute is reflected in the political, economic, urban, and social functions of the region. The revenue of a "quasi-state" regional government is reflected in the regional fiscal revenue. The expenditure of a "quasi-state" regional government is reflected in its purchasing expenditure (including consumption expenditure and investment expenditure) and transfer expenditure. Second, regional government has a "quasi-micro" or "quasi-enterprise" attribute. ①The "quasi-enterprise" attribute is reflected in that the regional government serves as the agent for economic stakeholders in the region. ②The "quasi-enterprise" attribute is reflected in that the regional government seeks to maximize economic benefits for the region. ③The "quasi-enterprise" attribute is reflected in that the regional government strives to attract investment, capture projects and industrial chain support, expand total import and export trade, and implement relevant policies.

Let's review the issues that Smith's three books attempted to unveil. In *The Theory of Moral Sentiments*, he revealed the behavioral attribute of individuals in social groups, which is manifested as the unity of opposites between self-interest and sympathy (the invisible hand). The underlying motivation is the survival and development of individuals in society. In *the Wealth of Nations*, he tried to reveal the behavioral attribute of enterprises in the market, which is manifested as the unity of opposites between selfishness and altruism (the invisible hand). The underlying motivation is the restraining element of enterprises' property rights (interests). In his third book, he could have unveiled the behavioral attribute of governments, which is manifested as the unity of opposites between quasi-micro and quasi-macro, as well as between profit seeking and coordination (the invisible hand). The underlying motivation could be the constraint of the government's "political achievements". A government's "political achievements" are determined by the dual goals and dual attributes of developing economy and maintaining stability. Therefore, the dual attributes of government are dialectical and unified.

  理论对政府与市场关系的阐述也就自然而然地落脚在1776年《国富论》的定调上，即①市场经济就是产业经济、产业资源开发；②政府与市场的关系就是产业经济中政府与市场的角色关系；③企业是市场经济主体。

  对此，笔者的研究认为，企业是市场经济主体，但它只是微观经济市场主体。政府在资源生成领域运用供给侧三驾马车推动市场经济发展，所以，政府是中观经济市场主体。

  区域政府存在"双重属性"[①]。第一，区域政府具有"准宏观""准国家"的属性。区域政府"准国家"的属性是通过履行本区域政治、经济、城市和社会等职能显现的；区域政府"准国家"属性的收入，是通过区域财政收入显现的；区域政府"准国家"属性的支出，是通过购买性支出（包括社会消费性支出和公共投资性支出）与转移性支出显现的。第二，区域政府具有"准微观""准企业"的属性。①区域政府的"准企业"属性，体现在区域政府是本区域经济利益主体的集中代理上；②区域政府的"准企业"属性，体现在区域政府追求本区域经济利益最大化上；③区域政府的"准企业"属性，体现在区域政府招商引资、抢抓项目和产业链配套、扩大进出口贸易总额及其相关的政策措施配套上。

  此时，我们回顾一下斯密三本书所试图揭示的问题。在《道德情操论》中，斯密试图揭示个人在社会群体中的行为属性，它表现为自我心与同理心的对立统一（看不见的手），其背后动因是个人在社会中的生存与发展问题。在《国富论》中，斯密试图揭示企业在市场中的行为属性，它表现为利己性与利他性的对立统一（看不见的手），其背后动因是企业财产权（利益）的制约因素。在第三本书中，斯密可能试图揭示政府在国家中的行为属性。它表现为准微观与准宏观、逐利性与协调性的对立统一（也是一只看不见的手），其背后的动因应该是政府"政绩"的制约。而政府"政绩"又是由经济发展和维护稳定的双重目标、双重属性所决定的。因此，政府的双重属性是辩证统一的。

---

  ① 区域是个相对的概念，既可以在全球范围内指一个国家，又可在一国范围内指国内所辖各区域。本书中所指区域，为研究方便，大多数属一国范围内的各区域。

II. Government's "Political Achievements" and Official's "Outlook on Political Achievements"

The dual attributes of a government are the inherent driving force behind its pursuit of "political achievements", while its "political achievements" embody its dual attributes.

Governments around the world exist to maintain stability, achieve development, and handle emergency. A regional government has three economic functions: development of industries, urban construction, and safeguarding people's livelihood. The actual situation of a region embodies the regional government's "political achievements" and dual attributes.

1. Industrial development

In 2005, the author served as the chief official in Shunde District, Foshan City, Guangdong Province, China. At that time, the total output value of Shunde District was RMB 601 billion, with the secondary industry accounting for 61% of the total output value, and the home appliance and home electronics industries accounting for 70% of the total industrial output value. The home appliance industry was monopolized by the three giants Midea, Kelon, and Galanz. In order to prevent the regional economic crisis caused by the failure of a single industry or individual enterprises there, in consideration of the actual situation, the author put forward the "three, three, and three" industry development strategy to guide and support the harmonized development of the primary, secondary, and tertiary industries. In particular, we guided and supported three or more pillar trades in each industry, and three or more leading enterprises in each trade, thereby bettering the industrial chain, forming industrial clusters, and achieving sustainable development. In addition, in view of the issues such as weak foundation and shortage of funds in the growth process of a lot of micro, small and medium-sized enterprises (MSMEs), the government of Shunde District set up a credit guarantee fund for them: the regional government allocated a fixed amount of special financial funds and worked together with professional guarantee institutions and commercial banks to provide guarantees and loans for growing MSMEs that had difficulties in obtaining loans from commercial banks due to a lack of sufficient collateral.

The practice has proven that the guiding, coordinating, and early warning measures taken by the government in the economic field then boosted the fine development of the primary industry, the improvement and development of the secondary industry, and the accelerated development of the tertiary industry. As a result, conventional industries were transformed and upgraded, emerging industries cultivated and strengthened, and high-tech industries helped grow rapidly. What's more, a gradient of large, small and medium-sized enterprises and the

二、政府"政绩"与官员"政绩观"

政府的双重属性,是政府追求"政绩"的内在驱动力;政府的"政绩",是政府双重属性的外在表现。

纵观世界各国,国家政府具有三大任务——稳定、发展、对突发事件的处置。仔细分析区域政府,其具有三大经济职能——产业发展、城市建设、社会民生。一个区域的现实状况,既是其政府"政绩"的体现,又是其政府双重属性的外在表现。

1. 关于产业发展

2005年,笔者在中国广东省佛山市顺德区当主官,当时顺德区生产总值601亿元,第二产业产值占比为61%,而其中家用电器和家用电子行业产值又占工业总产值的70%,并且家电行业主要由美的、科龙、格兰仕三家巨头相对垄断。为防范顺德区因单一产业、个别企业可能经营不善而引发的区域经济危机,笔者结合实际,提出"三三三"产业发展战略——引导和扶持第一、第二、第三产业协调发展;在每个产业中,引导和扶持三个以上的支柱行业;在每一个行业中,引导和扶持三个以上的龙头企业;完善产业链,形成产业集群,促进可持续发展[①]。与此同时,面对大量中小微企业成长过程中基础不强、资金短缺等问题,顺德区政府又创新思维,设立中小微企业信用担保基金——区域政府安排定额财政专项资金,与专业担保机构和商业银行联手合作,为那些因缺乏足够抵押物而难以从银行获得贷款的成长型中小微企业提供担保和贷款[②]。实践证

---

① 陈云贤:《超前引领:对中国区域经济发展的实践与思考》,北京大学出版社,2011,第15-32页。
② 陈云贤、邱建伟:《论政府超前引领:对世界区域经济发展的理论与探索》,北京大学出版社,2013,第114-116页。

complementary advantages of industrial clusters have maintained Shunde District's leading position in GDP among 2800 counties in China. In China's reform and opening up, there are numerous successful cases of regional governments' planning, leading, supporting, coordinating, supervising, and managing industrial development. For instance, Shenzhen has developed from a small fishing village to a metropolis with prosperous industries and inexhaustible innovation impetus.

Measures to support industrial development are also commonly seen in western countries. For example, the Obama administration's national networks for manufacturing innovation (NNMI) was one of the important measures taken by the United States to implement its "re-industrializing" strategy. Seeing the 2008 international financial crisis, the United States launched the advanced manufacturing partnership (AMP) in June 2011, and NNMI in March 2012, which was composed of multiple interrelated institutes for manufacturing innovation (IMI) with common goals and independent focuses. First, it was guided by national strategic goals and organized relatively independent R&D projects in view of regional and industrial needs. Second, it centered on resource optimization and redistribution, and integrated the existing innovative resources by both the "top-down" and "bottom-up" approaches. Third, it adopted a public-private partnership that the government provided stable early support and universities and private institutions provided follow-up funds. Fourth, it relied on each IMI to source regional and global innovative resources and set up leadership councils to promote overall coordination and cooperation, supported by network governance. In the relationship between government and market, in optimizing government's investment and coordinating the interests of various stakeholders, the government played a guiding and leverage role with its investment, pointed out the direction of industrial R&D, promoted the deployment of high-end manufacturing industries, and speeded up the process of innovation and commercialization. The knowledge transfer partnership (KTP) of UK was another example. KTP is supported by public funds from the government and research institutions as well as supporting funds from enterprises. Since 2003, KTP has realized the transfer of knowledge, technology, and skill from research institutions to enterprises by supporting the partnership between enterprises and research institutions. It has expanded the services provided to enterprises, driven enterprises to increase innovative investment, integrated talent, enterprise, research institution, and innovation resources, and helped upgrade and develop the industrial structure.

明，当时顺德区政府在经济领域开展的引导、调节和预警措施，促进了区域第一产业精细发展、第二产业提升发展、第三产业加快发展，使得传统产业得以改造提升、新兴产业得以培植壮大、高新技术产业得以迅猛成长，同时，大中小企业梯度形成，产业集群优势互补，顺德区保持着在中国2800多个县域经济中排头兵的地位。在中国经济的改革开放中，区域政府规划、引领、扶持、调节、监督、管理产业发展的成功案例比比皆是。例如大家熟悉的深圳市，从一个小渔村发展成为一个勇立潮头的产业铁军，有着源源不竭的创新动力，勇当新时代的"拓荒牛"，最终成为一个蓬勃升腾的创新之都[1]。

在西方国家，扶持产业发展的举措也屡见不鲜。例如，奥巴马政府的美国制造业创新网络建设计划(national network for manufacturing innovation，NNMI)，就是美国实施其"再工业化"战略的重要举措之一。在2008年的国际金融危机后，美国在2011年6月启动了先进制造业伙伴计划(advanced manufacturing partnership，AMP)；2012年3月启动了NNMI，由多个具有共同目标、相互关联，但又各有侧重的制造业创新研究院(institutes for manufacturing innovation，IMI)所组成[2]。其主要特点有以下四个：一是以国家战略目标为导向进行建设，并根据区域和产业需求组织相对独立的研发项目；二是以资源优化和再布局为核心，通过"自上而下"和"自下而上"的结合实现已有创新资源的整合；三是以公私合作为保障，包括政府相对稳定的前期支持和大学、私营机构等的配套资金跟进；四是以网络化治理为支撑，以每个IMI链接区域和国际创新资源，通过建立领导理事会总体推动相互之间的协调合作。在政府与市场的关系中，在优化政府投资与协调多方利益关系中，政府发挥了投资引导作用和杠杆效应，引领了产业研发方向，促进了高端制造业布局，加速了创新和商业化进程。英国知识转移伙伴(knowledge transfer partnership，KTP)计划也是一例。KTP计划的资金既来源于政府和研究机构的公共资金，又来源于企业的配套资金。自2003年以来，KTP计划通过支持企业和研究机构之间的伙伴关系，实现知识、技术、技能从研究机构向企业转移，从而拓展了对企业提供的服务，带动了企业的创新投入，整合了人才、企业、研究机构、创新资源，促进了产业结构的提升与发展。

---

[1] 瞿长福、佘惠敏、刘亮等：《深圳领跑——践行习近平新时代中国特色社会主义经济思想调研记》，《经济日报》2021年5月10日。

[2] IMI是一种产学研合作伙伴关系，由美国联邦、州或者地方政府支持成立。每个IMI都聚焦于特定的领域，重点是将公私资源结合在一起，营造更加有活力的国家创新生态系统，目标是加快把发明转化成产品的速度，同时加速中小企业的发展。

2. Urban construction

Let's take Foshan City of Guangdong Province where the author had served as an example. By the end of 2006, thanks to the momentum of reform and opening up, Foshan City had exchanged 300% of construction land growth for 3000% of economic growth. However, the prominent contradiction between land supply and land demand there was a major bottleneck for its development. In 2007, the government of Foshan issued the *Decision on Accelerating the Renovation of Old Factories and Villages in Old Urban Areas* (referred to as the "Three-Old" Renovation). In 2009, the *Special Plan for the "Three-Old" Renovation in Foshan City (2009—2020)* was issued. Under the market-oriented renovation mode that "government provides policies, owners (users) provide land, and developers provide funds", in the first three years, social funds of RMB 35.7 billion were introduced, 730 "Three-Old" Renovation projects launched, and a construction area of 23.99 million square meters was added. The "Three-Old" Renovation, with the participation of enterprises, and run by the market, bettered the appearance of regional construction rapidly, raised land use efficiency, helped adjust and improve the land use structure and industrial structure. As a result, it was propagandized the "Foshan Experience". Soon later in 2010, the government put forward the construction strategy of "integrating four modernizations to build a smart Foshan", that is, relying on modern information technology to boost industrial development, raise urbanization level, accelerate the process of going global, and enhance the comprehensive competitiveness of Foshan City. Foshan aimed to achieve the goals of making the city safe, efficient, convenient, green, and harmonized by vigorously constructing intelligent transportation, intelligent environmental protection, intelligent land monitoring, intelligent public security, intelligent urban management, intelligent education, intelligent healthcare, intelligent culture, intelligent commerce, and intelligent government affairs. This effective government has promoted industrial upgrading, increased urbanization, and improved global prominence for Foshan City. Let's take a look at western countries. It is repeatedly reported that the German government has achieved the nirvana of Ruhr Industrial Base (known as the capital of industrial pollution) through pollution control and renovation. In view of the industrial pollution in Ruhr Industrial Base, the German government formulated guidelines to adjust industrial structure, developed emerging industries, and carried out ecological transformation, ecological restoration, and environmental improvement for the industrial heritage. As a result, Ruhr Industrial Base managed to inherit its regional culture, achieve industrial transformation and upgrading, and renovate infrastructure, thereby becoming a new type of urban industrial zone that is livable, suitable for business, and prosperous for development.

2. 关于城市建设

笔者仍以曾经从政过的广东省佛山市为例。至 2006 年年底，佛山市借助改革开放之势，用 3 倍的建设用地增加率换取了 30 倍的经济增长，与此同时，佛山市土地供需矛盾凸显，成为发展的主要瓶颈。2007 年，佛山市政府出台《关于加快推进旧城镇旧厂房旧村居改造的决定》(简称"三旧"改造)；2009 年，出台《佛山市"三旧"改造专项规划(2009—2020 年)》，按照"政府出政策、所有者(使用者)出土地、开发商出资金"的市场化改造模式，前三年就成功引入社会资金 357 亿元，启动"三旧"改造项目 730 个，新增建设面积达 2399 万平方米，"政府推动、企业参与、市场运作"的城乡"三旧"改造，迅速改善了区域建设面貌，提升了土地使用效率，促进了土地利用结构和产业结构的调整与完善，被推广为"佛山经验"[1]。紧接着，2010 年，佛山市政府提出"四化融合，智慧佛山"建设，以信息化带动工业化、以信息化提升城镇化、以信息化加快国际化，全面提升佛山城市综合竞争力。通过大力开展智能交通、智能环保、智能土地监控、智能治安、智能城管、智能教育、智能医疗、智能文化、智能商务、智能政务等，全面实现城市安全、高效、便捷、绿色、和谐的目标。政府的有为作用，推动了佛山市的工业化转轨、城市化加速和国际化提升[2]。在西方国家，德国政府通过治污重建，实现了"工业毒都"鲁尔工业区的涅槃，这也是人们津津乐道的话题。针对鲁尔工业区的污染问题，德国政府制定纲要，着手推动产业结构调整，发展新兴产业和工业遗产的生态改造、生态修复、环境改善"三部曲"，使得鲁尔工业区传承了区域文化，实现了产业转型升级，改造了基础设施，最终使城市得以提升发展，成为宜居、宜商、宜发展的新型城市工业区。

---

[1] 陈云贤：《超前引领：对中国区域经济发展的实践与思考》，北京大学出版社，2011，第 128-131 页。

[2] 同上书，第 47-56 页。

3. People's livelihood

The author once served as Vice Governor of Guangdong Province. Since 2012, the government of Guangdong Province has repeatedly put forward the practical matters on people's livelihood that should be handled and carried out every year in its government work report. Specifically, the government has ①consolidated and improved the bottom line of people's livelihood; ②increased the support for disadvantaged groups in need; ③strengthened the housing security for low-income and disadvantaged groups; ④improved production and living conditions in rural areas; ⑤bettered medical and health services at the primary level; ⑥promoted fair and balanced allocation of educational resources; ⑦facilitated entrepreneurship and employment; ⑧enhanced pollution control and ecological construction; ⑨strengthened public security; ⑩intensified disaster prevention and reduction; etc. In the 1960s, the proportion of farmers in Korea was 70%, and its agriculture was on the brink of collapse. In view of this, the Korean government proposed to carry out the Saemaeul Movement to revitalize agriculture. It utilized policy guidance and specific physical objects to support rural construction projects, uphold the self-operated cooperative financing business of the farmers' association, and vigorously promoted the construction of new villages, thus creating the famous "Han-Gang River Miracle" and achieving economic takeoff. It was a typical case of developed country addressing its livelihood issues and serious urban-rural imbalance.

Therefore, the stability and development of a country or region are reflected in its three economic functions: developing industries, conducting urban construction, and safeguarding people's livelihood. It is an epitome of both the "political achievements" and the dual attributes of a country (or regional) government.

The three economic functions of regional government are correlated with the three types of economic resources that can be allocated in a region, as shown in Table 2-1.

Table 2-1 The Three Economic Functions of Regional Government and the Three Types of Economic Resources That Can Be Allocated in a Region

Three economic functions of regional government	Three types of economic resources that can be allocated in a region
Industrial development	Operative resources
People's livelihood	Non-operative resources
Urban construction	Quasi-operative resources

Therefore, a government may essentially manage the region as a resource from an economic perspective. The author summarizes the allocation policies of a regional government on these three types of economic resources as follows: ①allocation policies of operative resources to provide planning, guidance, support, coordinating, supervision, and management; ②allocation policies of non-operative resources to provide general underpinning, maintain

3. 关于社会民生

笔者曾任广东省副省长之职。2012年以来，广东省政府在历年政府工作报告中不断提出每年需要办理和落实的民生实事。它们包括①巩固提升底线民生保障水平；②加大对困难弱势群体帮扶力度；③强化低收入住房困难群体住房保障；④改善农村生产生活条件；⑤改善基层医疗卫生服务；⑥促进教育资源公平均衡配置；⑦促进创业就业；⑧加强污染治理和生态建设；⑨强化公共安全保障；⑩抓好防灾减灾；等等。与之类似，20世纪60年代，韩国政府面对当时农民比例约70%、农业一度处于崩溃边缘的状况，提出开展复兴农业的"新村运动"，运用政策导向和具体实物，扶持农村建设项目，支持农协自办合作金融，全力推进新村建设，创造出闻名遐迩的"汉江奇迹"，实现了经济腾飞，可谓发达国家解决民生问题和城乡严重失衡问题的典型案例。

可见，一个国家或一个区域的稳定与发展，具体体现在其三大经济职能——产业发展、城市建设和社会民生的实现状况上。这既是一国（或区域）政府的"政绩"体现，又是一国（或区域）政府的双重属性的外在表现。

区域政府的三大经济职能，与区域可配置的三类经济资源相联系，见表2-1。

表2-1 区域政府三大经济职能与区域可配置的三类经济资源

区域政府的三大经济职能	区域可配置的三类经济资源
产业发展	可经营性资源
社会民生	非经营性资源
城市建设	准经营性资源

因此，从经济学的视角来分析，政府实质上可以把区域作为一种资源来管理。笔者借此把区域政府对三类经济资源的配置政策概括为①可经营性资源的配置政策：规划、引导、扶持、调节、监督、管理；②非经营性资源的配置政策：

fairness, and make practical improvement; ③allocation policies of quasi-operative resources to provide planning and layout, participating in construction, and achieving orderly management.

In the study and analysis of Chapter I of this book, we have drawn conclusions from the allocation carrier and capital operation of quasi-operative resources that: ①quasi-operative resources are generative resources, that is, resource generation; ②regional government is the first investor in quasi-operative resources and one of the participants in market competition; ③regional government must act in accordance with market rules; ④regional governments at different levels serve as guiders, coordinators, and supervisors of the market economy.

We must distinguish the "political achievements" of government and the "outlook on political achievements" of government officials. "Political achievements" refer to the achievements and contributions of officials in governance, that is, the work achievements and contributions made by officials during their term of office. The "outlook on political achievements" refers to the fundamental understanding and attitude of officials in fulfilling their duties and what political achievements they pursue. The "political achievements" of government and the "outlook on political achievements" of government officials are driven by multiple elements. The "political achievements" pursued by governments around the world (or regions) must not be confused with the "outlook on political achievements" of government officials.

Now, let's review the three economic functions of a regional government, the three types of economic resources that can be allocated, and the allocation policies thereon. They embody the "political achievements" of a regional government and reveal its dual attributes. There are external possibilities and internal inevitability for a regional government to participate in inter-regional competition.

(1) There are external possibilities for a regional government to participate in competition. The core of the economic behaviors conducted by a regional government lies in optimizing the allocation of regional resources or improving the efficiency of regional resource allocation. The investment and development, equity management, and capital operation of quasi-operative resources create external possibilities for a regional government to participate in competition. The allocation of three types of resources in the region will lead to the following objective results that: ①the allocation of operative resources strengthens economic vitality in the region; ②the allocation of non-operative resources betters investment environment in the region; ③ the allocation of quasi-operative resources boosts sustainable economic development in

the region. The theory of "competitive advantage" and its practical results are embodied in the development process between regions.

(2) There is internal inevitability for a regional government to participate in competition. The greatest flaw of market hypothesis in Western Economics is that government, market, and society are viewed as a "trinity", that is, separating government and market. As for the author's

基本托底、公平公正、有效提升；③准经营性资源的配置政策：规划布局、参与建设、有序管理。

在本书第一章的研究分析中，我们已从准经营性资源的配置载体与资本运营中得出结论：①准经营性资源就是生成性资源，即资源生成；②区域政府是准经营性资源的第一投资人，也是市场竞争参与者之一；③区域政府必须按照市场规律办事；④不同层级的区域政府是市场经济的引导者、调节者、监督者。

在此，我们需要界定政府的"政绩"与政府官员的"政绩观"的区别。"政绩"，是从政之绩，施政之绩，指官吏在执政时办事的成绩，即官员在任期内履行相关职务取得的工作成绩和贡献。"政绩观"，是官员对如何履行职责、去追求何种政绩的根本认知和态度。应该说，政府的"政绩"和官员的"政绩观"是多元因素驱动的。但我们一定不能把世界各国（或各区域）政府追求的"政绩"与具体负责实施的政府官员的"政绩观"混为一谈。

现在，我们回溯区域政府的三大经济职能、可调配的三类经济资源及其三类配置政策，它们既是区域政府的外在"政绩"表现，又揭示出区域政府的双重属性。可见，区域政府参与区域与区域之间的竞争，存在着外在的可能性和内在的必然性。

(1) 区域政府竞争具有外在可能性。优化区域资源配置或提升区域资源配置效率，是区域政府经济行为的核心；准经营性资源的投资开发、股权管理和资本运营方式，使区域政府参与竞争具备了外在可能性。区域三类资源配置呈现的客观结果是①对可经营性资源的配置能提升区域经济活力；②对非经营性资源的配置能优化区域投资环境；③对准经营性资源的配置能推动区域经济可持续发展。这里，在区域与区域之间的发展进程中，隐含着"竞争优势"理论与其现实结果。

(2) 区域政府竞争具有内在必然性。西方经济学市场理论的最大的缺陷是，政府、市场、社会"三位一体"，把政府与市场分立。然而，笔者研究分析的结

study and analysis, the government seeks to maximize regional economic benefits, which provides internal inevitability for a regional government to participate in competition. A regional government boasts the dual attributes. On one hand, the "quasi-state" attribute requires the government to maintain stable economic, political, cultural, social, and ecological civilization construction in the region. On the other hand, the "quasi-enterprise" attribute requires it to develop projects, industrial chains, import and export, and their supporting policies in the region. Regional fiscal revenue is the main restraining element for the government to achieve its dual attributes.

III. Objective Function of Government's Economic Activities: the Fiscal Revenue Determination Mechanism

The main reasons why regional governments around the world view the fiscal revenue determination mechanism as the objective function of economic activities include the following facts that: ①they need to be supported by increased fiscal revenue scale as their functions extend and their role in economic coordination intensifies; ②they need to be backed by increased fiscal revenue scale as the population in the region grows and the total demand for regional public services by the public increases; ③they need to be supported by increased fiscal revenue scale as regional urban scale increases and social public investment grows; ④they need to be backed by increased fiscal revenue scale as regional technological level rises, promoting them to keep exploring new fields of technology and production; ⑤they need to be supported by increased fiscal revenue scale as regional social welfare undertakings get expanded. There are another three reasons we have seen in China's economic development process: ①they need to promote and build a modern industrial system; ②they need to safeguard and promote the layout of major regional projects; ③they need to advance and coordinate the development of urban-rural integration. All of these need fiscal revenue to play a more significant role.

Fiscal revenue is usually classified according to the form in which it is obtained by the government at abroad, such as tax revenue, state-owned asset revenue, treasury bond revenue, fee revenue, and other revenues.

When state-owned asset revenue and treasury bond revenue are fixed, the fiscal revenue will mainly come from tax revenue and fee revenue.

(1) Tax revenue. Keynes and Keynesianism referred to a country's tax function and the discretionary approach for applying tax policies as "manual stabilizers". Samuelson believed that tax revenue acts as an "automatic stabilizer", as shown in Figure 2-1.

果是，政府追求区域经济利益的最大化，这使区域政府参与竞争具备了内在必然性。区域政府双重属性呈现的客观结果是：一方面，"准国家"的属性要求区域的经济、政治、文化、社会、生态文明建设呈现出稳定性；另一方面，"准企业"的属性要求区域的项目、产业链、进出口及其政策措施配套呈现出发展性。在此，区域财政收入的多少成为政府实现双重属性的主要制约因素。

三、政府经济活动的目标函数——财政收入决定机制

世界各国区域政府把财政收入决定机制作为经济活动目标函数的主要动因包括：①区域政府职能不断扩张，其经济调控功能扩大，需要财政收入规模作为支撑；②区域人口不断增长，民众对区域公共服务需求总量增加，需要财政收入规模作为支撑；③区域城市规模不断扩大，社会公共投资不断增长，需要财政收入规模作为支撑；④区域科技水平不断进步，推动区域政府不断开拓新的科技领域和生产领域，需要财政收入规模作为支撑；⑤区域社会福利事业不断扩大，需要财政收入规模作为支撑。中国在现实的经济发展进程中补充了三点：①促进和构建现代产业体系；②保障和推动区域重大项目布局；③推动和协调城乡一体化发展。这些都需要财政收入发挥更大作用。[①]

国际上通常按政府取得财政收入的形式对财政收入分类，分为税收收入、国有资产收益、国债收入、收费收入及其他收入等。

在国有资产收益和国债收入既定的情况下，财政收入主要来自税收收入和收费收入。

(1) 税收收入。凯恩斯及凯恩斯主义把一国的税收功能和运用税收政策的相机抉择机制称为"人为稳定器"。萨缪尔森认为，税收具有"自动稳定器"功能[②]，如图2-1所示。

---

① 吕炜：《让财政在新征程中发挥更大作用》，《人民日报》2021年5月21日。
② 张思锋主编，王立剑、张立、张园副主编《公共经济学》，中国人民大学出版社，2015。

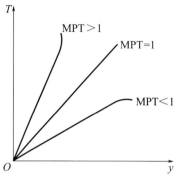

Figure 2-1 Tax Revenue's Role of "Automatic Stabilizer"

In Figure 2-1, T represents the tax revenue; y represents the national income; MPT represents the marginal tax propensity, which is the ratio of the growth rate of tax revenue to the growth rate of national income.

$$\text{MPT} = \frac{\Delta T / T_0}{\Delta y / y_0} = \frac{\Delta T}{\Delta y} \cdot \frac{y_0}{T_0} \qquad 2\text{-}1$$

(2) Fee revenue. According to relevant World Bank documents, the use fee in fee revenue refers to "payments made in exchange for special goods and services provided by the public sector".

The structure of regional tax revenue and fee revenue depends on the regional economic structure. The scale of regional tax revenue and fee revenue mainly depends on the regional economic development level, the regional economic policies, and the regional economic management efficiency. The fiscal revenue determination mechanism of a region is dependent on the fiscal budget expenditure structure of a regional government. The fiscal budget expenditure of a regional government is based on its fiscal revenue for the following year. The way a government maximizes its fiscal revenue by coordinating consumption expenditure, investment expenditure, and transfer expenditure is shown in Equation 2-2.

$$\max_{\{CE, IE, TE\}} \text{FInc} = \tau \text{CumP(IE)} + \omega[\varphi_1(Y_1, Y_0) \cdot \text{CE} + \varphi_2(Y_2, Y_0) \cdot \text{IE} + \varphi_3(Y_3, Y_0) \cdot \text{TE} + \text{Const1}] + \text{Const2}$$

$$\text{s.t. CE+IE+TE=FE} \qquad 2\text{-}2$$

$$\text{FInc} \geq \text{FE}$$

$$0 < \omega < 1$$

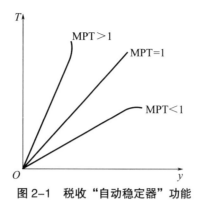

图 2-1　税收"自动稳定器"功能

图 2-1 中，T 为税收收入；y 为国民收入；MPT 为边际税收倾向，即税收收入增长速度与国民收入增长速度之比。

$$\text{MPT} = \frac{\Delta T / T_0}{\Delta y / y_0} = \frac{\Delta T}{\Delta y} \cdot \frac{y_0}{T_0} \qquad 2\text{-}1$$

(2) 收费收入。按世界银行相关文件的表述，收费收入中的使用费是指"为交换公共部门所提供特殊商品和服务而进行的支付"。[①]

区域税收收入和收费收入的结构取决于区域经济结构；区域税收收入和收费收入的规模主要取决于区域经济发展水平、区域经济政策措施及区域经济管理效率。而区域的财政收入决定机制，又首先取决于区域政府的财政预算支出结构。区域政府的财政预算支出基于来年的财政收入。假设政府通过调节社会消费性支出、公共投资性支出和转移性支出使得财政收入最大化，那么优化问题如式 2-2 所示。

$$\begin{aligned}
\max_{\{CE, IE, TE\}} \text{FInc} &= \tau \text{CumP(IE)} + \omega [\varphi_1(Y_1, Y_0) \cdot \text{CE} + \varphi_2(Y_2, Y_0) \cdot \text{IE} + \\
&\quad \varphi_3(Y_3, Y_0) \cdot \text{TE} + \text{Const1}] + \text{Const2} \\
\text{s.t.} \quad & \text{CE} + \text{IE} + \text{TE} = \text{FE} \\
& \text{FInc} \geq \text{FE} \\
& 0 < \omega < 1
\end{aligned} \qquad 2\text{-}2$$

推导过程（补充说明）

---

① 张思锋主编，王立剑、张立、张园副主编《公共经济学》，中国人民大学出版社，2015。

In the equation, CE represents the consumption expenditure; IE represents the investment expenditure; TE represents the transfer expenditure; FE represents the total fiscal expenditure; Y represents the regional economic development level; Const1 represents the economic effects that cannot be affected by fiscal expenditure; φ_1、φ_2、φ_3 is a variable coefficient; FInc represents the total fiscal revenue; $\tau CumP(IE)$ represents the fee revenue obtained by the government from infrastructure projects; $\omega[\varphi_1(Y_1, Y_0) \cdot CE + \varphi_2(Y_2, Y_0) \cdot IE + \varphi_3(Y_3, Y_0) \cdot TE + Const1]$ represents the tax revenue obtained by the government from total economic output; Const2 is the sum of treasury bond revenue, state-owned asset revenue and other revenues, which is assumed to be a constant for a period of time.

According to Equation 2-2, consumption expenditure, investment expenditure, and transfer expenditure are different in their promoting effects on the economic development level. Therefore, at different stages of economic development, a regional government ought to optimize its fiscal expenditure structure with different focuses. In view of the fiscal revenue determination mechanism in the region, a regional government should take measures to enlarge the scale of regional fiscal revenue, implement the fiscal development policy of "determining expenditure scale in view of revenue scale" and "determining revenue scale in view of expenditure scale", and take effective tools from the dynamic changes in the elasticity coefficient of fiscal revenue growth and marginal propensity indicators to coordinate the scale of fiscal revenue and promote its positive growth. Hence, the fiscal revenue determination mechanism and the optimized allocation of fiscal expenditure structure it combines constitute the key or objective function of a regional government's administration and competition.

IV. Indicator Function of Government's Economic Activities: the Regional Competitiveness Determination Mechanism

The indicator function of government's economic activities focuses on reflecting the type of mechanism and policy environment that determine regional competitiveness. Therefore, a government's fiscal expenditure structure and its policies on optimizing allocation of fiscal expenditure structure are the key elements in determining regional competitiveness in different stages of economic development.

For example, since the formulation of the 13th Five Year Plan, China's fiscal expenditure structure has been continuously optimized. In order to use its non-infinite funds in "key areas", China has adhered to maintaining consumer demand and suppressing investment scale, maintaining economic quality and suppressing growth rate, and maintaining government reform and suppressing excessive administrative power, optimized its expenditure structure, and strived to promote consumption, stabilize investment, and unleash the potential of domestic demand.

式中，CE 为社会消费性支出；IE 为公共投资性支出；TE 为转移性支出；FE 为财政总支出；Y 为区域经济发展水平；Const1 为无法由财政支出所影响的其他经济效应；φ_1、φ_2、φ_3 为可变系数；FInc 为财政总收入；$\tau\text{CumP(IE)}$ 为政府从基建项目当中取得的收费收入；$\omega[\varphi_1(Y_1, Y_0) \cdot \text{CE} + \varphi_2(Y_2, Y_0) \cdot \text{IE} + \varphi_3(Y_3, Y_0) \cdot \text{TE} + \text{Const1}]$ 为政府从经济总产出当中取得的税收收入；Const2 为国债收入、国有资产收益和其他收入之和，并假定 Const2 在一段时期内为常量。

根据式 2-2 可知，社会消费性支出、公共投资性支出和转移性支出三者对经济发展水平的促进作用不同，所以，在不同的经济发展阶段，区域政府应该将重点放在不同的财政支出结构优化配置上。即应根据区域财政收入决定机制，采取措施扩大区域财政收入规模，实施"以收定支"兼顾"以支定收"的财政发展方针，并从财政收入增长弹性系数和增长边际倾向指标的动态变化中采取有效手段，调节财政收入规模，促其正常增长。因此，财政收入决定机制和与之结合的不同阶段的财政支出结构优化配置，是区域政府管理和竞争的关键或目标函数。

四、政府经济活动的指标函数——区域竞争力决定机制

政府经济活动的指标函数侧重体现决定区域竞争力的机制类型和政策环境。因此，政府的财政支出结构及其优化配置政策成为区域在不同经济发展阶段中竞争力决定的关键性因素。

比如，自从"十三五"规划以来，中国财政支出结构不断优化——为把有限的资金用在"刀刃"上，坚持有保有压，优化支出结构，着力促消费、稳投资，释放内需潜力。一方面，不断增加中央基建投资规模，优化投资方向和结构，集中支持保障性安居工程、重大基础设施等方面。另一方面，为支持地方稳投资、

On one hand, China keeps increasing the scale of central infrastructure investment, optimizes investment direction and structure, and focuses on supporting affordable housing projects and major infrastructure projects. On the other hand, China permits local governments to issue special bonds to support them to stabilize investment, improve weak links, and leverage their role in driving investment.

The amount and structure of fiscal expenditure by a regional government reflect the scale and depth of the government's intervention in economic and social life, as well as the position and role of the regional government in economic development and social life. In fact, the fiscal expenditure by a regional government is divided into transfer expenditure and purchasing expenditure by its economic nature. The former is incurred by the regional government unilaterally for transferring the ownership of a portion of its revenue. The latter includes consumption expenditure and investment expenditure.

1. Transfer expenditure

Transfer expenditure includes a regional government's fiscal subsidy and social security expenditure.

Fiscal subsidy is mainly used by a regional government to develop industries and economy, including price subsidy, foreign trade subsidy, fiscal interest subsidy, and other cash or in-kind subsidies. It runs through the production, circulation, distribution, and consumption links of industrial economy.

Social security expenditure, as one of the most important transfer expenditure items in the fiscal expenditure by a regional government, represents voluntary payments unilaterally made by the regional government with its fiscal funds.

2. Purchasing expenditure

Purchasing expenditure includes investment expenditure and consumption expenditure.

Investment expenditure is incurred by a regional government in the investment, development, and construction of urban infrastructure in view of elements such as its own financial conditions, the market demand, and how the public accepts it.

Consumption expenditure includes the grants, research costs, and allowances for education, science, culture, health, sports, publishing, earthquakes, and ocean undertakings.

Investment expenditure directly affects the development of industries and fiscal revenue in a region. Figure 2-2 shows the output model of general industrial investment and infrastructure investment. The empirical analysis results of various countries around the world suggest that most developed countries in Europe and America have followed an economic growth path of $Q_1\to C\to Q_2\to D\to Q_3$. Japan and Korea have followed an economic growth path of $Q_1\to A\to Q_2\to B\to Q_3$.

补短板，发行地方政府专项债券，发挥其对拉动投资的杠杆作用[①]。

可见，在区域政府的财政支出中，财政支出的数额和结构反映着区域政府介入经济和社会生活的规模和深度，也反映着区域政府在经济发展和社会生活中所处的地位和发挥的作用。现实中，按不同的经济性质，可将区域政府财政支出分为购买性支出和转移性支出两类，前者包括社会消费性支出和公共投资性支出，后者指区域政府单方面把一部分收入所有权转移出去而发生的支出。

1. 转移性支出

转移性支出包括区域政府财政补贴和社会保障支出。

区域政府财政补贴主要用于促进产业经济发展，包括价格补贴、外贸补贴、财政贴息等，通过采取现金补贴或实物补贴的方式，贯穿于产业经济的生产环节、流通环节、分配环节和消费环节中。

社会保障支出作为区域财政支出中最重要的转移性支出项目之一，直接表现为区域政府财政资金无偿的、单方面的支付。

2. 购买性支出

购买性支出包括公共投资性支出和社会消费性支出。

公共投资性支出，主要包括城市基础设施的投资、开发与建设，由区域政府根据自身的财政状况、市场需求和社会民众的可接受程度等因素来决定。

社会消费性支出，主要包括教育、科学、文化、卫生、体育、出版、防震、海洋保护等方面的经费、研究费和补助费支出。

其中，公共投资性支出直接影响区域的产业发展和财政收入。图2-2为一般产业投资和基础设施投资的产出模型。从世界各国实证分析的结果来看，欧美发达国家的经济增长路径大体是：$Q_1\to C\to Q_2\to D\to Q_3$；而日本、韩国等国家的经济增长路径大体是：$Q_1\to A\to Q_2\to B\to Q_3$。

---

① 曾金华：《积极财政政策护航高质量发展》，《经济日报》2020年10月28日。

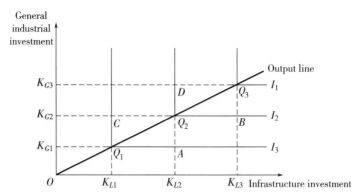

Figure 2-2　The Output Model of General Industrial Investment and Infrastructure Investment

The longitudinal and transverse axes in Figure 2-2 represent general industrial investment and infrastructure investment respectively. The line starting from the origin represents the output line. I_1, I_2, and I_3 are the lines representing the relationship between a certain amount of infrastructure investment and general industrial investment. When infrastructure investment and general industrial investment are K_{L1} and K_{G1} respectively, the output will be Q_1. If general industrial investment increases to K_{G2} and infrastructure investment remains unchanged, there will be an intersection point C, meaning that the output will not be Q_2. In contrast, if infrastructure investment increases to K_{L2} and general industrial investment remains unchanged, there will be an intersection point A, meaning that the output will not be Q_2. To make the output increase to Q_2, infrastructure investment and general industrial investment must increase to K_{L2} and K_{G2} respectively, same for the rest. That is to say, in order to achieve a certain output, a certain ratio must be maintained between infrastructure investment and general industrial investment, and it must increase in a certain proportion.

Therefore, investment expenditure in the fiscal structure of a regional government is directly related to the development of industries and the fiscal revenue. It directly or indirectly affects the objective function and indicator function of the regional government's economic activities at different stages of economic development.

(1) Urban infrastructure features the characteristic of quasi-operative resources, and belongs to the field of resource generation in the economic sense. The investment, development and construction of software and hardware for urban infrastructure can be undertaken by the government, provided by private enterprises, or achieved in the way of mixed economy.

(2) The functional relationship between investment expenditure and fiscal expenditure is:

$$I = \lambda_1 \lambda_2 G \qquad 2\text{-}3$$

Wherein, λ_1 is the proportion of purchasing expenditure in fiscal expenditure, and $1-\lambda_1$ is the proportion of transfer expenditure in fiscal expenditure; λ_2 is the proportion of investment expenditure

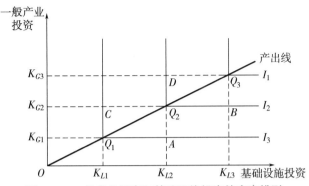

图 2-2 一般产业投资和基础设施投资的产出模型

图 2-2 的纵轴与横轴分别代表一般产业投资与基础设施投资，从原点出发的射线是产出线，I_1、I_2、I_3 为一定数量的基础设施投资和一般产业投资关系的示意线。当基础设施投资和一般产业投资分别为 K_{L1} 和 K_{G1} 时，产出量为 Q_1；如果一般产业投资增加到 K_{G2}，而基础设施投资不增加，那么组合点为 C，即产出量不可能为 Q_2；反之，如果基础设施投资增加到 K_{L2}，而一般产业投资不增加，那么组合点为 A，即产出量不可能为 Q_2。要使产出量增加到 Q_2，必须使基础设施投资和一般产业投资分别增加到 K_{L2} 和 K_{G2}，以此类推。也就是说，为达到一定的产出量，基础设施投资和一般产业投资之间必须保持一定的配比关系，且必须按一定的比例递增。

这就告诉我们，区域政府财政结构中的公共投资性支出与产业发展、财政收入有着直接的关系，它在经济发展的不同阶段，直接或间接地影响着区域政府经济活动的目标函数与指标函数。

(1) 城市基础设施具有准经营性资源的特性，它属于经济学意义上的资源生成领域，其软硬件的投资、开发和建设既可以由政府来承担，又可以由私人企业来提供，也可以采取混合经济方式来提供。

(2) 公共投资性支出与财政支出的函数关系式为：

$$I = \lambda_1 \lambda_2 G \qquad 2\text{-}3$$

其中，λ_1 为购买性支出在财政支出中的占比，$1-\lambda_1$ 为转移性支出在财政支出中的占比；λ_2 为公共投资性支出在购买性支出中的占比，可知社会消费

in purchasing expenditure, and $1-\lambda_2$ is the proportion of consumption expenditure in purchasing expenditure; I and G represent investment expenditure and fiscal expenditure respectively.

When fiscal expenditure is given, the proportion of investment expenditure in fiscal expenditure will be limited by transfer expenditure and consumption expenditure. To increase investment expenditure, we can raise λ_1 or λ_2. Raising λ_1 will reduce the proportion of transfer expenditure, while raising λ_2 will reduce the proportion of consumption expenditure.

(3) Investment expenditure plays an important role in the fiscal expenditure structure as it determines a government's investment in infrastructure construction. Infrastructure construction is a major source of fiscal revenue. Hence, investment expenditure bridges fiscal expenditure and fiscal revenue.

As such, we can use the "government expenditure multiplier" to express the relationship between the fiscal expenditure structure and regional fiscal revenue in regional government economic activities, and even the relationship with regional competitiveness level. The government expenditure multiplier is equal to the investment multiplier. It represents the multiplying relationship between changes in national income and changes in government fiscal expenditure that cause changes in national income. It can be expressed by the following equation:

$$KG = \frac{dy}{dG} \qquad 2\text{-}4$$

Wherein, KG represents the government expenditure multiplier; dG represents the changes in government fiscal expenditure; dy represents the changes in national income caused by dG.

The economic effects caused by government fiscal expenditure vary at different levels of economic development, as shown in Figure 2-3.

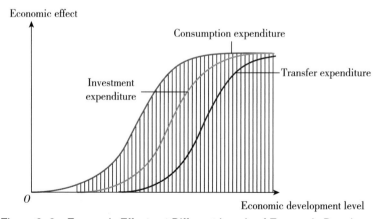

Figure 2–3　Economic Effects at Different Levels of Economic Development

性支出在购买性支出中的占比为 $1-\lambda_2$；I 和 G 分别表示公共投资性支出和财政支出。

在财政支出既定的情况下，公共投资性支出在财政支出中的占比会受到转移性支出的限制，也会受到社会消费性支出的限制。若需要提高公共投资性支出，那么我们可以提高 λ_1 或者 λ_2，前者会降低转移性支出的占比，后者会降低社会消费性支出的占比。

(3) 公共投资性支出在财政支出结构中占据重要地位，决定了政府在基础设施建设上的投资力度，而基础设施建设是财政收入的重要来源，由此公共投资性支出建立了财政支出与财政收入之间的桥梁。

因此，区域政府经济活动中财政支出结构与区域财政收入乃至区域竞争力水平的关系，可以用"政府支出乘数"来阐述。政府支出乘数跟投资乘数相等，指国民收入变化量与引起这种变化量的政府财政支出变化量的倍数关系，用公式表示为：

$$KG=\frac{dy}{dG} \qquad 2-4$$

其中，KG 代表政府支出乘数；dG 代表政府财政支出变化量；dy 代表由 dG 引起的国民收入变化量。

政府财政支出在不同经济发展水平下引起的经济效应将会有所不同，如图 2-3 所示。

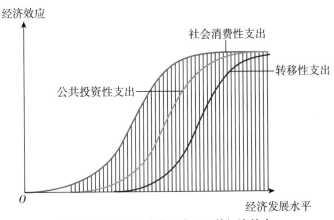

图 2-3 不同经济发展水平下的经济效应

Therefore, a government ought to adopt the discretionary approach in view of the stage of economic and social development where the region is to optimize its fiscal expenditure structure and increase its fiscal revenue, thereby enhancing regional competitiveness.

Hence, it can be concluded as follows.

(1) Regional government has the dual attributes. It means the government seeks profits in "quasi-micro" economic activities and coordinate benefits in "quasi-macro" economic activities, forming a unity of opposites.

(2) "Political achievements" are the manifestation of the dual attributes of a regional government, for which it undertakes two major missions: maintaining stability (including the response to emergency) and achieving development. The economic functions of a regional government include developing industries, conducting urban construction, and safeguarding people's livelihood.

(3) Fiscal revenue determination mechanism is the objective function of regional government economic activities. The determining elements such as tax, types of taxes, and tax rate serve as stabilizers for the objective function.

(4) Regional competitiveness determination mechanism is the indicator function of regional government economic activities. The key for a government to enhancing regional competitiveness lies in taking the discretionary approach to continuously optimize the regional fiscal expenditure structure in different stages of economic development.

(5) National macroeconomy, regional mezzoeconomy, and enterprise microeconomy are linked by total tax revenue. There are external possibilities and internal inevitability for a regional government to participate in competition.

所以，政府应根据经济社会的发展阶段相机抉择，通过优化财政支出结构和提高财政收入水平，来提升区域竞争力。

至此，本章得出如下结论。

(1) 区域政府具有双重属性。它表现在"准微观"的逐利性与"准宏观"的协调性的对立统一的经济活动之中。

(2) "政绩"是区域政府双重属性的外在表现，体现在稳定（包括对突发事件的处置）与发展两大任务上。区域政府的经济职能，体现在产业发展、城市建设和社会民生三项发展事业上。

(3) 区域政府经济发展的目标函数是财政收入决定机制。其中，税收、税种、税率等决定因素起着目标函数稳定器的作用。

(4) 区域政府经济发展的指标函数是区域竞争力决定机制。对区域财政支出结构在不同经济发展阶段的相机抉择与不断优化，成为政府提升区域竞争力的核心要点。

(5) 国家宏观经济、区域中观经济与企业微观经济存在以税收总额大小为聚焦的关联效应。区域政府存在竞争发展的外在可能性与内在必然性。

Chapter III

Regional Government Competition and Government's Foresighted Leading

In Chapter I, we analyze the role of a government in the field of resource generation and clarify that the government can use the troika on the supply side to promote the economic growth of a country or region. In Chapter II, we discuss the dual attributes of a government, and point out that the fiscal revenue determination mechanism is the objective function of regional government economic activities, and that the regional competitiveness determination mechanism is the indicator function of regional government economic activities. In this chapter, we will further discuss the characteristics, features and the policy tools of regional government competition, and point out the necessity for a government to achieve foresighted leading.

I. The Characteristics of Regional Government Competition

Regional competitiveness refers to the strength that supports a region's sustainable survival and development. In particular, regional competitiveness is the strength of a region compared with other regions in attracting, competing for, occupying, coordinating, and transforming resources and competing for, occupying, and coordinating the marketing in the process of competition and development. It is the ability to optimize resource allocation required for the region's own development. In short, regional competitiveness is the ability of a region to develop and attract resources, and to compete for the market.

第三章

区域政府竞争与政府超前引领

第一章分析了政府在资源生成领域的作用,明确了政府可以在供给侧运用三驾马车推动一国或区域的经济增长。第二章研究了政府的双重属性,指出区域政府经济活动的目标函数是区域财政收入决定机制,区域政府经济活动的指标函数是区域竞争力决定机制。本章将进一步深入探讨区域政府竞争的特点、表现及其政策工具选择,指出政府超前引领的必要性。

一、区域政府竞争特点

区域竞争力是指能支撑一个区域持久生存和发展的力量。具体来说,区域竞争力指一个区域在竞争和发展的过程中,与其他区域相比较而言,所具有的吸引、争夺、占有、调控和转化资源的能力,以及争夺、占有和调控市场的能力,也就是其自身发展所需的优化资源配置的能力。简言之,区域竞争力是一个区域发展所需的对资源的开发力、吸引力和对市场的争夺力。

Regional government competition refers to the competition between regional governments in industrial development, urban construction, and people's livelihood. It requires a regional government to create competitive advantages, increase the regional resource allocation efficiency, and advance scientific and sustainable development of regional economy via conceptual innovation, institutional innovation, organizational innovation, and technological innovation.

Regional government competition is different from enterprise competition in the following eight aspects. First, they have different objective functions. The objective function of regional government competition is the fiscal revenue determination mechanism, while that of enterprise competition is the price determination mechanism. Second, different indicator functions. The indicator function of regional government competition is the regional competitiveness determination mechanism, while that of enterprise competition is the enterprise competitiveness determination mechanism. The regional competitiveness determination mechanism functions in mezzoeconomy and seeks to maximize regional resource allocation efficiency. Enterprise competitiveness determination mechanism functions in microeconomy and seeks to maximize enterprise resource allocation efficiency. Third, they use different paths to achieve the indicator function. Regional government competition seeks to strengthen industrial competitiveness in the stage of developing industrial economy, increase investment growth rate in the stage of developing urban economy, raise contribution rate of technological progress in the stage of developing innovative economy, and better the effects of regional government in "9-in-3" Competition in the stage of developing shared economy. Enterprise competition seeks to improve labor productivity, capital productivity, technological progress rate, and total factor productivity in the above four stages respectively. Fourth, they have different fields in which competition is carried out. Regional government competition focuses on the field of resource generation and the contesting for urban economy and allocated urban resources. Differently, enterprise competition focuses on the contesting for industrial economy and allocated industrial resources (occupying more industrial resources will lead to a better position in the industrial economy, vice versa) when resources are scarce. Fifth, they seek different orientations. Regional government competition aims to optimize the supply side, while enterprise competition aims to satisfy the demand side. Sixth, they play different roles in competition. A regional government is a market entity in mezzoeconomy, with "quasi-macro" and "quasi-micro" attributes. These dual attributes make it play both the roles of competition participant and cooperation facilitator in regional economic development. Differently, an enterprise acts as the microeconomic entity in market economy. Seventh, they practice different management modes. Regional governments adopt the DRP model, while enterprises take the ERP model. Eighth, they produce different effects. A balance should be struck between fairness and efficiency when it comes to regional government competition. Enterprise competition mainly pursues profitability and efficiency.

区域政府竞争是指区域政府与区域政府之间，在产业发展、城市建设、社会民生等方面的竞争。它通过理念创新、制度创新、组织创新和技术创新，创造竞争优势，优化区域资源配置效率，推动区域经济科学可持续发展。

区域政府竞争与企业竞争之间的区别主要有以下八点。第一，竞争的目标函数不同。区域政府竞争的目标函数是财政收入决定机制；企业竞争的目标函数是价格决定机制。第二，竞争的指标函数不同。区域政府竞争的指标函数是区域竞争力决定机制；企业竞争的指标函数是企业竞争力决定机制。前者作用在中观经济领域，追求区域资源配置效率最大化；后者作用在微观经济领域，追求企业资源配置效率最大化。第三，实现指标函数的路径不同。区域政府竞争在产业经济导向阶段以提高产业竞争力为路径，在城市经济导向阶段以提高投资增长率为路径，在创新经济导向阶段以提高科技进步贡献率为路径，在共享经济导向阶段以提高"三类九要素"作用力为路径；企业竞争在经济发展四个阶段则依次以提高劳动生产率、资本生产率、技术进步率和全要素生产率为路径。第四，竞争的领域不同。区域政府竞争侧重在资源生成领域，及对城市经济、城市资源配置的争夺上；企业竞争则侧重在资源稀缺条件下对产业经济、产业资源配置的争夺上，两者相辅相成。第五，竞争的导向不同。区域政府竞争以优化供给侧为导向；企业竞争则以满足需求侧为导向。第六，竞争的角色不同。区域政府是中观经济市场主体，具备"准宏观"和"准微观"两种属性，双重属性使其在区域经济发展中发挥着竞争与合作的双重作用；企业则属于微观经济领域，在市场经济中发挥微观经济主体的作用。第七，管理的模式不同。区域政府采用区域资源配置系统的DRP模型；企业则主要采用企业资源配置系统的ERP模型。第八，竞争的效应不同。区域政府竞争需兼顾公平与效率，企业竞争则以盈利性和效率为主。

Frankly speaking, enterprise competition is the foundation of all forms of competition in market economy as it drives regional governments to compete. Regional government competition mainly pursues optimized resource allocation efficiency in terms of system, policy, environment, and project. It is above enterprise competition but affects, supports, and promotes the competition among enterprises. Regional government competition and enterprise competition are two competition systems at different levels. They are both separated and correlated. Regional governments and enterprises carry out competition in their own realms but they are intertwined. Therefore, a country or a regional economy should follow the rules of market competition to achieve sustainable growth, optimize the allocation of resources, and realize the harmonized development of macro, mezzo, and microeconomic operations.

II. The Manifestation of Regional Government Competition

Fiscal revenue determination mechanism is the objective function of regional government competition. It refers to the functional relationship between the goal (a certain variable) of concern to a regional government and related elements (some other variables).

The indicator function of regional government competition is the regional competitiveness determination mechanism. It is not a statistical term. It requires us to analyze and identify the type, applicable environment, and conditions of the indicator in a certain indicator system of the regional government, as well as the effectiveness of the restraining elements of such indicator.

Regional governments compete in the mezzoeconomic field and use the troika on the supply side to promote economic development, as shown in Table 3-1.

Table 3-1 The Troika Boosts Economic Development

	The troika		Boosting effect
Supply side	Supply of factor	Tangible factors	Promoting economic growth (economic development level)
		Intangible factors	
	Supply of environment	Hard environment	Improving the business environment (economic policies)
		Soft environment	
	Supply of market	Transverse system	Improving the development level (efficiency of economic management)
		Longitudinal system	

The core influencing elements and key supporting conditions for the objective and indicator functions of regional government competition stem from three aspects (the troika on the supply side that promotes regional economic development), so this theory is called "9-in-3"

可以说，企业竞争是市场经济中一切竞争的基础。企业竞争带动了区域政府间的竞争。区域政府竞争主要是在制度、政策、环境、项目等方面优化资源配置效率的竞争，它属于企业竞争层面之上的另一种竞争，但又反过来影响、支撑和促进着企业的竞争。区域政府竞争和企业竞争是两个不同层面的竞争体系，二者既互相独立，又互相联系，在各自相对独立的领域竞争，却又彼此交融。因此，一个国家或一个区域经济要可持续增长，就应遵循市场竞争规则，优化资源配置，实现宏观、中观、微观经济运行的协调发展。

二、区域政府竞争表现

区域政府竞争的目标函数为财政收入决定机制。它指区域政府所关心的目标（某一变量）与相关因素（某些变量）的函数关系。

区域政府竞争的指标函数为区域竞争力决定机制。它不是一个统计学专用术语，而是从区域政府的某个指标体系中分析和确定该指标的类型、适用环境、条件及其制约因素的有效性。

区域政府从中观经济领域开展竞争，在供给侧运用三驾马车推动经济发展，如表3-1所示。

表3-1 三驾马车推动经济发展

	三驾马车		推动效应
供给侧	要素供给	有形要素／无形要素	促进经济增长（经济发展水平）
	环境供给	硬环境／软环境	改善营商环境（经济政策措施）
	市场供给	横向体系／纵向体系	提升发展水平（经济管理效率）

在此，区域政府竞争目标函数和指标函数的核心影响因素和关键支持条件主要来自三个方面，即供给侧三驾马车推动区域经济发展形成的效应，称为"三类

Competition theory or sheep horn competition theory, as shown in Figure 3-1.

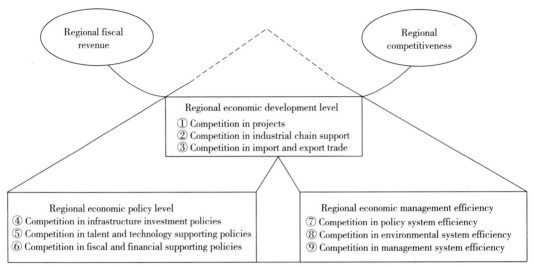

Figure 3-1 "9-in-3" Competition Theory or Sheep Horn Competition Theory

"9-in-3" Competition theory or sheep horn competition theory is summarized as follows.

(1) The first class is regional economic development level, which is determined by three factors of development.

① Competition in projects, including national major projects, social investment projects, and foreign investment projects.

② Competition in industrial chain support, which is carried out in factor of production and industrial cluster and support.

③ Competition in import and export trade, which is embodied in four aspects: development of processing trade and general trade; overseas investment; export of capital; import.

(2) The second class is regional economic policy level, which is determined by three factors of policy.

④ Competition in infrastructure investment policies, including urban infrastructure policies, policies on the software and hardware investment and construction for various economic and technological development zones, and policies on the development and application of modern smart cities.

⑤ Competition in talent and technology supporting policies, which adhere to the concept that talent resource is the primary resource and science and technology are the primary productive force, and focus on the measures to provide support for talent and technology.

⑥ Competition in fiscal and financial supporting policies. The competition in fiscal supporting policies centers on the investment by government, such as infrastructure investment, technology R&D investment, and policy funding for industries in urgent need of development. The competition in financial supporting policies refers to actively building

九要素"竞争理论或羊角竞争理论，如图 3-1 所示。

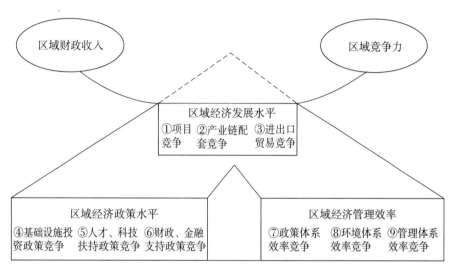

图 3-1 "三类九要素"竞争理论或羊角竞争理论

"三类九要素"竞争理论或羊角竞争理论可以概括表述为如下内容。

(1) 第一类是区域经济发展水平，主要由三大发展要素决定。

① 项目竞争，主要包括国家重大项目、社会投资项目和外资引进项目。

② 产业链配套竞争，主要从两个方面展开：一是在生产要素方面；二是在产业集群、产业配套方面。

③ 进出口贸易竞争，主要体现在四个层面：一是在加工贸易与一般贸易的发展中；二是在对外投资上；三是在资本输出上；四是在进口方面。

(2) 第二类是区域经济政策水平，主要由三大政策要素决定。

④ 基础设施投资政策竞争，主要包括城市基础设施、各类经济技术开发区平台的软硬件投资建设和现代化智能城市的开发运用等政策。

⑤ 人才、科技扶持政策竞争，其竞争最根本点是确立人才是第一资源、科技是第一生产力的理念，以及对人才、科技的扶持措施。

⑥ 财政、金融支持政策竞争。财政支持政策竞争最主要的措施是政府投资，

various investment and financing platforms to mobilize and attract regional, domestic, and even overseas financial institutions, funds, talented people, information, and other financial resources as much as possible, and have them serve the industrial development, urban construction, and people's livelihood in the region.

(3) The third class is regional economic management efficiency, which is determined by three factors of efficiency.

⑦ Competition in policy system efficiency, including the internal and external policy systems of a regional government.

⑧ Competition in environmental system efficiency, which refers to the construction of economic, political, cultural, social, and ecological environments.

⑨ Competition in management system efficiency, mainly in improving macro efficiency, micro efficiency, organizational efficiency, and individual efficiency in the activity, speed, quality, and effectiveness of a regional government's administrative management.

Here are some cases.

◎ **Case 3-1   Make the Project an "Engine" for Transformation and Development**

The government of Shanxi Province, China, has stated that it will place project construction in a prominent position and dare to make decisions on major and key issues, in order to drive the majority of cadres to play a role in project construction.

(1) Work should be adapted to the project by centering on the project to guide development and promote transformation.

(2) Funds should be granted for the project to seize the initiative and support with high-quality projects.

(3) Factors should be provided for the project to accelerate the implementation of projects with efficient guarantees.

(4) Services should be offered where the project is located to create a first-class environment to lure investment and store energy.

◎ **Case 3-2   Use Precise Policies to Enhance the Modernization Level of Industrial Chain and Supply Chain**

Economic experts believe that industrial and supply chains are dynamic, diversified, networked, and complex. It is necessary to obtain insights into various industries, identify different governance structures, industrial advantages and differences in driving forces, grasp the main contradictions, capture where efforts should be made, and implement precise policies, thereby continuously improving

包括基础设施投资、科技研发投资、向急需发展产业的政策性资金投资等。金融支持政策竞争指积极搭建各类投融资平台，最大限度地动员和吸引区域、国内乃至国际各类金融机构、资金、人才、信息等金融资源，为本区域产业发展、城市建设、社会民生服务。

(3) 第三类是区域经济管理效率，主要由三大效率要素决定。

⑦ 政策体系效率竞争，包括区域政府对内和对外的政策体系。

⑧ 环境体系效率竞争，主要指经济、政治、文化、社会、生态环境的建设。

⑨ 管理体系效率竞争，主要是指区域政府的行政管理活动、行政管理速度、行政管理质量、行政管理效能，包括宏观效率、微观效率、组织效率、个人效率四类主体。

下文是几个具体案例。

◎ 案例 3-1　让项目成为转型发展的"引擎"①

中国山西省发声，要把项目建设摆在十分突出的位置，在重大关键问题上敢于决策拍板，示范带动广大干部在项目建设主战场上展身手、见真章、论英雄。

(1) 工作跟着项目走，以项目为重引领发展、促进转型。

(2) 资金跟着项目走，以优质项目抢占先机、争取支持。

(3) 要素跟着项目走，以高效保障加快落地、早日见效。

(4) 服务跟着项目走，以一流环境吸引投资、储能蓄势。

◎ 案例 3-2　提升产业链、供应链的现代化水平要精准施策②

经济专家认为，产业链、供应链具有动态化、多样化、网络化、复杂性等特点。要分行业摸清底数，区分治理结构类型、产业优势基础、驱动力量差异，抓

---

① 胡健：《让项目成为转型发展的"引擎"》，《人民日报》2020年6月22日。
② 张其仔：《提升产业链供应链现代化水平要精准施策》，《经济日报》2021年1月21日。

the modernization level of industrial chain and supply chain. First, it is necessary to identify different governance structures of industrial chain and supply chain, and implement differentiated strategies to optimize the structures. Second, it is necessary to identify the types of industrial advantages that support the modernization of industrial chain and supply chain, and adopt differentiated strategies to leverage these advantages. Third, it is wise to identify different paths to modernized industrial chain and supply chain, and select the right area for efforts to be made, thereby raising regional competitiveness with industrial chain.

◎ **Case 3-3　Better the Regulatory System That Integrates Domestic Trade and Foreign Trade**

On December 30, 2021, the *Opinions of the General Office of the State Council on Promoting the Integration of Domestic Trade and Foreign Trade* put forward to establish a "dual circulation" development pattern in which domestic economic cycle plays a leading role while international economic cycle remains its extension and supplement. Work must be done to promote the transformation from the development mode of "focusing on foreign raw materials and foreign sales markets" and "acting as the world factory" to the mode of relying on the domestic circulation and giving play to comparative advantages. To better the regulatory system that integrates domestic trade and foreign trade, we must fully utilize domestic and overseas markets and resources, and actively promote the harmonized development of domestic and overseas demand, import and export, investment attraction, and foreign investment. It is wise seek to align the trade laws and regulations, regulatory systems, business qualifications, quality standards, inspection and quarantine, certification and recognition at home and abroad, urge export enterprises to produce export and domestic products according to the same standards on the same production line, improve the quality of Chinese goods and services in an all-round way, strengthen China's export competitiveness, and import more high-quality products.

Therefore, the author divides the competition between regional governments into general regional government competition and special regional government competition.

General regional government competition includes the competition for operative resources, non-operative resources, and quasi-operative resources. In essence, it represents regional governments using fiscal revenue for industrial development, urban construction, and people's livelihood.

Special regional government competition is mainly reflected in quasi-operative resources, namely regional governments providing urban infrastructure and supporting policies. In essence, it represents regional governments' investment expenditure in urban infrastructure and other related fields.

住主要矛盾点，找准发力点，精准施策，不断提升产业链、供应链的现代化水平。第一，要区分不同的产业链、供应链治理结构，实施差异化的优化结构策略。第二，要区分支撑产业链、供应链现代化水平提升的产业优势类型，采取差异化的优势发挥策略。第三，要区分驱动产业链、供应链现代化的不同路径，选准发力点，用产业链条串起区域竞争力[①]。

◎ 案例 3-3　完善内外贸一体化调控体系

2021 年 12 月 30 日，《国务院办公厅关于促进内外贸一体化发展的意见》提出，要构建国内、国际双循环相互促进的新格局，必须推动从"两头在外""世界工厂"的发展模式向立足国内大循环发挥比较优势转变。完善内外贸一体化调控体系，充分利用国内、国际两个市场、两种资源，积极促进内需和外需、进口和出口、引进外资和对外投资协调发展。促进内外贸法律法规、监管体制、经营资质、质量标准、检验检疫、认证认可等相衔接，推进同线同标同质，全面提升中国商品和服务质量，增强出口竞争力，增加优质产品进口。

为此，笔者把区域政府与区域政府之间的竞争概括为广义的区域政府竞争和狭义的区域政府竞争。

广义的区域政府竞争包括了对可经营性资源、非经营性资源和准经营性资源的竞争。广义区域政府竞争的实质就是区域政府运用财政收入在产业发展、城市建设、社会民生中的竞争。

---

① 乔文江:《产业链条串起区域竞争力》，《经济日报》2021 年 8 月 26 日。

In another sense, general regional government competition and special regional government competition embody the pursuit of objective function and indicator function respectively by a regional government.

We herein introduce a specific model of the regional government competitiveness determination mechanism: the DRP model.

First, the entire process of the regional government competitiveness determination mechanism is analyzed, as shown in Figure 3-2.

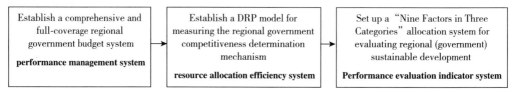

Figure 3-2 The Entire Process of the Regional Government Competitiveness Determination Mechanism

Second, establish the function expression of the "9-in-3" Competition theory.

At a specific time and in a specific range, a regional government may adjust the fiscal expenditure(FE) structure (the proportions of fiscal expenditure in different aspects) while adjusting its total fiscal expenditure, in order to maximize benefits. A regional government's fiscal expenditure is divided into consumption expenditure (CE), which is mainly used to improve the level of environmental support, management system support, and policy support in the region with a view to influencing the economic management efficiency of a regional government; investment expenditure (IE), which is mainly used to improve the level of regional infrastructure construction, such as roads, bridges, power grids and so on, with a view to influencing the economic policy level of a regional government; transfer expenditure (TE), which is mainly used to improve the level of talent, technology, and fiscal and financial support in the region with a view to influencing the economic policy level of a regional government.

As mentioned in Chapter II, these three classes of expenditures are always consistent with the following relational expression:

$$CE+IE+TE=FE \qquad 3-1$$

By introducing the variable coefficient φ_i, the following relational expression can be obtained:

$$Y=\varphi_1(Y_1, Y_0) \cdot CE+\varphi_2(Y_2, Y_0) \cdot IE+\varphi_3(Y_3, Y_0) \cdot TE+Const1 \qquad 3-2$$

We further introduce the variable λ ($0<\lambda<1$) to represent the proportion of social quasi-operative resources in the public sector. The value of λ affects the infrastructure products

狭义的区域政府竞争主要体现在区域政府对准经营性资源，即城市基础设施建设及其政策的配套与落实上。狭义区域政府竞争的实质就是区域政府运用公共投资性支出政策在城市基础设施等方面的竞争。

广义的区域政府竞争和狭义的区域政府竞争又共同表现为区域政府在追求目标函数与指标函数方面的竞争。

在此，我们引入区域政府竞争力决定机制的具体模型——DRP模型。

首先，对决定区域政府竞争力机制的全流程进行分析，如图3-2所示[①]。

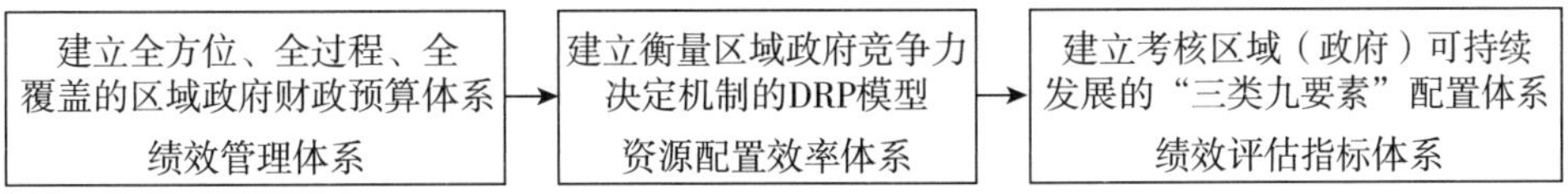

图 3-2 决定区域政府竞争力机制的全流程

其次，对"三类九要素"竞争理论的函数表达进行推导。

在特定时间和特定区间内，区域政府在调节其财政支出(FE)的总量时，也可以同时调整其结构，即财政支出在不同方面的分配比例，以获得最大效益。已知区域政府的财政支出主要包括三类：一是社会消费性支出(CE)，主要用于提升区域的环境配套、管理体系配套和政策配套水平，其核心是影响区域政府的经济管理效率；二是公共投资性支出(IE)，主要用于提升区域的基础设施建设水平，如道路、桥梁、电网等，其核心是影响区域政府的经济政策水平；三是转移性支出(TE)，主要用于提升区域的人才水平、科技水平、财政及金融的支撑水平，其核心也是影响区域政府的经济政策水平。

如第二章所述，三者总是满足以下关系：

$$CE+IE+TE=FE \qquad 3-1$$

引入可变系数 φ_i 后，又有如下关系：

$$Y=\varphi_1(Y_1, Y_0) \cdot CE + \varphi_2(Y_2, Y_0) \cdot IE + \varphi_3(Y_3, Y_0) \cdot TE + Const1 \qquad 3-2$$

进一步，我们再次引入变量$\lambda(0<\lambda<1)$，来表示社会上准经营性资源在公共

[①] 这里，我们可以引申研究区域人均GDP和人均财政收入增长对区域经济增长的拉动作用(目标函数角度)；也可以引申研究区域制度(政策)创新的变量在经济发展不同阶段中对人均GDP和人均财政收入增速的影响(指标函数角度)，但本书先暂且不论。

that fiscal expenditure can actually bring about, and then the actual effectiveness of investment expenditure. As such, by introducing λ, Equation 3-3 can be obtained. As mentioned above, λ is affected by the development level of market economy (Y), the fiscal revenue and expenditure including fiscal budget (B) and fiscal expenditure (FE), and the cognitive degree of residents or society (γ). By taking the assumptions and conclusions in the previous text, we can obtain the following expression:

$$\lambda = e^{-\left(aY + b^{\frac{FE}{B}}\right)} \left(\frac{Y}{Y^*}\right)^{-c\gamma} \qquad 3-3$$

By using λ to adjust Equation 3-2, Equation 3-4 can be obtained:

$$Y = \varphi_1(Y_1, Y_0) \cdot CE + \varphi_2(Y_2, Y_0) \cdot \frac{IE}{\lambda} + \varphi_3(Y_3, Y_0) \cdot TE + Const1 \qquad 3-4$$

A government's fiscal revenue is related to the tax revenue and the fee revenue from infrastructure projects as follows:

$$FInc = \tau CumP(IE) + \omega Y + Const2 \qquad 3-5$$

Wherein, FInc represents the fiscal revenue; τ represents the proportion of fee revenue; ω represents the proportion of tax revenue; $\tau CumP(IE)$ is the fee revenue obtained by the government from infrastructure projects and a function of IE; Const2 represents other revenues.

Therefore, fiscal surplus (FS) can be expressed as follows:

$$FS = FInc - FE = \tau CumP(IE) + \omega Y + Const2 - FE \qquad 3-6$$

We can discuss the functional expression of the "9-in-3" Competition theory on the basis of the above equations.

First, regional output level (DEV) can be expressed by the development level of market economy (Y):

$$DEV = Y = \varphi_1(Y_1, Y_0) \cdot CE + \varphi_2(Y_2, Y_0) \cdot \frac{IE}{\lambda} + \varphi_3(Y_3, Y_0) \cdot TE + Const1 \qquad 3-7$$

Second, regional economic management efficiency (EME) refers to the policy system support, environmental system support, and management system support provided by a regional government, and is determined by the proportion of consumption expenditure in the government's fiscal revenue. As such, we define EME as:

$$EME = \omega \varphi_1(Y_1, Y_0) \cdot CE / FInc \qquad 3-8$$

部门当中的配置比例。λ 的大小会影响财政支出所能实际撬动的基础设施产品，进而影响公共投资性支出的实际效果，因此我们加入 λ 进行调整，得到式3-3。如前文所述，λ 受到市场经济发展程度 (Y)、财政收支状况——包括财政预算 (B) 和财政支出 (FE)，以及居民或社会认知程度 (γ) 的影响。沿用前文中的假设和结论，我们有如下表达式：

$$\lambda = e^{-\left(aY + b\frac{FE}{B}\right)} \left(\frac{Y}{Y^*}\right)^{-c\gamma} \qquad 3\text{-}3$$

用 λ 来调整式3-2，得到式3-4：

$$Y = \varphi_1(Y_1, Y_0) \cdot CE + \varphi_2(Y_2, Y_0) \cdot \frac{IE}{\lambda} + \varphi_3(Y_3, Y_0) \cdot TE + Const1 \qquad 3\text{-}4$$

政府的财政收入与税收收入、基建项目中取得的收费收入有如下关系：

$$FInc = \tau CumP(IE) + \omega Y + Const2 \qquad 3\text{-}5$$

这里，FInc 为财政收入，τ 为收费比例，ω 为税收比例，$\tau CumP(IE)$ 为政府从基建项目中取得的收费收入，且为 IE 的函数，Const2 为其他收入。

因此，财政盈余 (FS) 可用下式表达：

$$FS = FInc - FE = \tau CumP(IE) + \omega Y + Const2 - FE \qquad 3\text{-}6$$

在以上公式的基础上，我们来讨论"三类九要素"竞争理论的函数表达。

第一，区域产出水平 (DEV) 可以用市场经济发展程度 Y 来表示：

$$DEV = Y = \varphi_1(Y_1, Y_0) \cdot CE + \varphi_2(Y_2, Y_0) \cdot \frac{IE}{\lambda} + \varphi_3(Y_3, Y_0) \cdot TE + Const1$$

$$3\text{-}7$$

第二，区域经济管理效率 (EME) 主要是指区域政府的政策体系、环境体系和管理体系的配套，由社会消费性支出在政府财政收入中的比重所决定，于是，我们可以将 EME 定义为：

$$EME = \omega \varphi_1(Y_1, Y_0) \cdot CE / FInc \qquad 3\text{-}8$$

Third, regional economic policy level (POL) refers to the infrastructure construction, talent quality, technological level, and fiscal and financial support in a region, and is determined by the proportion of investment expenditure and transfer expenditure in the government's fiscal revenue. So, we define POL as:

$$POL = \omega \varphi_2(Y_2, Y_0) \frac{IE}{\lambda} / FInc + \omega \varphi_3(Y_3, Y_0) TE / FInc \qquad 3\text{-}9$$

To sum up, in the short-term development stage, the resource allocation efficiency (SYN) in a region mainly depends on the following five indicators: fiscal expenditure elasticity (ELA) and fiscal surplus (FS) in the dimension of total amount; regional output level (DEV), regional economic management efficiency (EME), and regional economic policy level (POL) in the dimension of structure. A regional government may increase its fiscal revenue for the year by raising the level of annual fiscal expenditure and optimizing the annual fiscal expenditure structure. The regulated variable is fiscal expenditure (FE), which includes consumption expenditure (CE), investment expenditure (IE), and transfer expenditure (TE). We can set up the function expression for resource allocation efficiency thereon.

The key questions are how do we constitute SYN based on the above five indicators (ELA, FS, DEV, EME, and POL) and how do we maximize SYN by adjusting the four dependent variables (FE, CE, IE, and TE)?

The indicators in the dimension of total amount measure the input end of policy, and focus on whether a policy can take effect in an efficient and continuous manner. The indicators in the dimension of structure measure the output end of policy, and focus on whether a policy can bring about actual improvement for the economy.

$$SYN = \omega_1 Q(ELA, FS) + \omega_2 G(DEV, EME, POL) \qquad 3\text{-}10$$

$$SYN = \frac{ELA}{ELA + \overline{ELA}} FS + \frac{\overline{ELA}}{ELA + \overline{ELA}} G(DEV, EME, POL) \qquad 3\text{-}11$$

Wherein, $\overline{ELA}$ represents the mean of ELA within all historical time ranges.

$$G(DEV, EME, POL) = DEV(\omega_3 EME + \omega_4 POL) \qquad 3\text{-}12$$

We can use the variable coefficient φ_i in Equation 3-2 to assign weights, i.e.:

$$\omega_3 = \frac{\varphi_1}{\varphi_1 + \varphi_2 + \varphi_3}, \quad \omega_4 = \frac{\varphi_2 + \varphi_3}{\varphi_1 + \varphi_2 + \varphi_3} \qquad 3\text{-}13$$

第三，区域经济政策水平 (POL) 主要是指区域的基础设施建设，人才、科技水平，财政、金融支撑水平，由公共投资性支出和转移性支出在政府财政收入中的比重所决定，于是，我们可以将 POL 定义为：

$$POL=\omega\varphi_2(Y_2, Y_0)\frac{IE}{\lambda}/FInc+\omega\varphi_3(Y_3, Y_0)TE/FInc \qquad 3-9$$

综上所述，在区域的短期发展阶段，区域的资源配置效率 (SYN) 主要依赖于以下五个指标：总量维度上的财政支出弹性 (ELA) 和财政盈余 (FS)，结构维度上的区域产出水平 (DEV)、区域经济管理效率 (EME) 和区域经济政策水平 (POL)。区域政府主要通过提高年度财政支出水平、优化年度财政支出结构来提高当年的财政收入，调控变量主要是财政支出 (FE)，具体包括社会消费性支出 (CE)、公共投资性支出 (IE) 及转移性支出 (TE)。据此可得资源配置效率的函数表达式。

引申出的问题是：如何基于上述五个指标 (ELA、FS、DEV、EME、POL) 构造 SYN？如何通过调整四大因变量 (FE、CE、IE、TE)，使 SYN 最大化？

其中，总量维度的指标考量的是政策的输入端，侧重于政策能否高效且持续地发挥效应；而结构维度的指标考量的是政策的输出端，侧重于政策能否带来实际的经济改善。

$$SYN=\omega_1 Q(ELA, FS)+\omega_2 G(DEV, EME, POL) \qquad 3-10$$

$$SYN=\frac{ELA}{ELA+\overline{ELA}}FS+\frac{\overline{ELA}}{ELA+\overline{ELA}}G(DEV, EME, POL) \qquad 3-11$$

其中，$\overline{ELA}$ 是历史各时间区间内 ELA 的均值。

$$G(DEV, EME, POL)=DEV(\omega_3 EME+\omega_4 POL) \qquad 3-12$$

我们可以利用式 3-2 中的可变系数 φ_i 来赋予权重，即：

$$\omega_3=\frac{\varphi_1}{\varphi_1+\varphi_2+\varphi_3}, \quad \omega_4=\frac{\varphi_2+\varphi_3}{\varphi_1+\varphi_2+\varphi_3} \qquad 3-13$$

By substituting it into Equation 3-12, we can obtain:

$$G(DEV, EME, POL) = DEV\left(\frac{\varphi_1}{\varphi_1+\varphi_2+\varphi_3}EME + \frac{\varphi_2+\varphi_3}{\varphi_1+\varphi_2+\varphi_3}POL\right) \quad 3\text{-}14$$

As such, we can obtain the expression for SYN:

$$SYN = \frac{ELA}{ELA+\overline{ELA}}FS + \frac{\overline{ELA}}{ELA+\overline{ELA}}DEV\left(\frac{\varphi_1}{\varphi_1+\varphi_2+\varphi_3}EME + \frac{\varphi_2+\varphi_3}{\varphi_1+\varphi_2+\varphi_3}POL\right) \quad 3\text{-}15$$

In the case of limited budget, a regional government may maximize SYN by adjusting the proportion of three types of fiscal expenditures.

We can define the DRP model that the objective function satisfies as follows.

$$\max_{\{CE, IE, TE\}} \frac{ELA}{ELA+\overline{ELA}}FS + \frac{\overline{ELA}}{(ELA+\overline{ELA})}DEV\left(\frac{\varphi_1}{\varphi_1+\varphi_2+\varphi_3}EME + \frac{\varphi_2+\varphi_3}{\varphi_1+\varphi_2+\varphi_3}POL\right) \quad 3\text{-}16$$

$$\text{s.t.} \quad CE+IE+TE=FE$$

$$FS>0$$

$$\varphi_1+\varphi_2+\varphi_3 \neq 0$$

This DRP model indicates that by adjusting three types of fiscal expenditures, a regional government is able to identify the most competitive fiscal expenditure structure for the region, thus achieving the optimal regional economic development level (maximizing the scale of fiscal revenue) at a specific stage.

What's mentioned above represents our way to maximize the efficiency of regional resource allocation in the DRP model and the fiscal revenue of a regional government by optimizing the fiscal expenditure structure at different stages from the perspective of the objective function of regional government competition. Now we can try to raise regional competitiveness and promote regional sustainable economic growth by optimizing the paths and methods adopted by a regional government performance evaluation system from the perspective of the indicator function of regional government competition.

By utilizing the results of regional "9-in-3" Competition and assuming relevant elements and weights, we can constitute a regional government performance evaluation and assessment system, as shown in Table 3-2. It should be noted that the weight of each element is changeable. At different economic stages, we ought to adjust the focus or value of each weight.

将其代入式 3-12，可得出：

$$G(\text{DEV}, \text{EME}, \text{POL}) = \text{DEV}\left(\frac{\varphi_1}{\varphi_1+\varphi_2+\varphi_3}\text{EME} + \frac{\varphi_2+\varphi_3}{\varphi_1+\varphi_2+\varphi_3}\text{POL}\right) \quad 3\text{-}14$$

综上，我们可以得到 SYN 的表达式：

$$\text{SYN} = \frac{\text{ELA}}{\text{ELA}+\overline{\text{ELA}}}\text{FS} + \frac{\overline{\text{ELA}}}{\text{ELA}+\overline{\text{ELA}}}\text{DEV}\left(\frac{\varphi_1}{\varphi_1+\varphi_2+\varphi_3}\text{EME} + \frac{\varphi_2+\varphi_3}{\varphi_1+\varphi_2+\varphi_3}\text{POL}\right) \quad 3\text{-}15$$

在满足预算约束的条件下，区域政府可以通过调整三种财政支出的比例，使 SYN 最大化。

可以定义目标函数所满足的 DRP 模型如下。

$$\max_{\{CE, IE, TE\}} \frac{\text{ELA}}{\text{ELA}+\overline{\text{ELA}}}\text{FS} + \frac{\overline{\text{ELA}}}{(\text{ELA}+\overline{\text{ELA}})}\text{DEV}\left(\frac{\varphi_1}{\varphi_1+\varphi_2+\varphi_3}\text{EME} + \frac{\varphi_2+\varphi_3}{\varphi_1+\varphi_2+\varphi_3}\text{POL}\right) \quad 3\text{-}16$$

$$\text{s.t.} \quad CE+IE+TE=FE$$
$$FS>0$$
$$\varphi_1+\varphi_2+\varphi_3 \neq 0$$

这一 DRP 模型表明，通过对三大类财政支出进行调整，能够找到使得该区域最具备竞争优势的财政支出结构，从而促使其在特定阶段中的区域经济发展水平达到最优（财政收入规模最大化）。

以上是我们从区域政府竞争的目标函数的角度出发，通过对不同阶段的财政支出结构进行优化，来实现 DRP 模型中区域资源配置效率的最大化，从而实现区域政府的财政收入最大化的方法。现在，我们从区域政府竞争的指标函数的角度出发，尝试通过优化区域政府绩效评估体系的路径和方式，来提升区域的竞争力，从而推动区域经济的可持续增长。

运用区域"三类九要素"竞争的作用力结果，假设相关因素和权重，可以构建出下面的区域政府绩效评估考核体系，如表 3-2 所示。需要注意的是，各因素的权重设置是个动态的概念，随着经济阶段的发展，需要不断调整其权重的侧重点或比重。

Table 3-2 Regional Government Performance Evaluation and Assessment System

Class	Factor	S/N	Indicator	Positive/negative indicator	Weight	
Regional economic development level	Project	1	Quantity of national major science and technology projects	Positive	7	17
		2	Quantity of social investment projects	Positive	6	
		3	Quantity of foreign investment protects	Positive	4	
	Industrial chain support	4	Soundness of industries with regional resource advantages	Positive	6	13
		5	Development level of industrial clusters	Positive	4	
		6	Introduction and development status of high-tech industries	Positive	3	
	Import and export trade	7	Proportion of foreign investment in local enterprises	Positive	4	12
		8	Year-on-year growth of total import and export trade	Positive	5	
		9	Investment structure of foreign-funded enterprises	Positive	3	
Regional economic policy level	Infrastructure investment policies	10	Degree of intelligence in cities	Positive	5	15
		11	Convenient level of public transportation	Positive	3	
		12	Educational infrastructure	Positive	3	
		13	Development level and coverage of medical facilities	Positive	4	
	Talent and technology support policies	14	Local employment rate of higher education graduates (including the number of introduced high-end talented people)	Positive	5	10
		15	Patent index	Positive	3	
		16	Proportion of R&D investment of enterprises	Positive	2	
	Fiscal and financial support policies	17	Growth rate of circulating market value of local listed companies	Positive	4	9
		18	Financing subsidies for MSMEs	Positive	3	
		19	Industrial support structure	Positive	2	
Regional economic management efficiency	Policy system	20	Social security system	Positive	4	8
		21	Popularization of legal education	Positive	2	
		22	Residential satisfaction of urban and rural residents	Positive	2	
	Environmental system	23	Residents' happiness index	Positive	4	9
		24	Environmental index	Positive	2	
		25	Frequency of resident complaint	Negative	3	
	Management system	26	Residents' satisfaction with government affairs	Positive	3	7
		27	Cumbersomeness of government affairs	Negative	3	
		28	Social evaluation of emergency response	Positive	1	

表 3-2　区域政府绩效评估考核体系

类别	要素	序号	指标	正/负指标	权重	
区域经济发展水平	项目	1	国家重大科技项目数	正	7	17
		2	社会投资项目数	正	6	
		3	外资合作项目数	正	4	
	产业链配套	4	区域资源优势产业健全程度	正	6	13
		5	产业集群发展程度	正	4	
		6	高科技产业引进程度及发展状况	正	3	
	进出口贸易	7	外资在本地企业投入占比	正	4	12
		8	进出口贸易总额同比增速	正	5	
		9	外资企业投资结构	正	3	
区域经济政策水平	基础设施投资政策	10	城市智能化程度	正	5	15
		11	公共交通便捷程度	正	3	
		12	基础教育设施完善程度	正	3	
		13	医疗设施发展水平及覆盖度	正	4	
	人才、科技扶持政策	14	受高等教育毕业生本地就业率（含高端人才引进数量）	正	5	10
		15	专利指数	正	3	
		16	企业研发经费投入占比	正	2	
	财政、金融支持政策	17	本地上市公司流通市值增速	正	4	9
		18	中小微企业融资补贴优惠程度	正	3	
		19	产业扶持结构	正	2	
区域经济管理效率	政策体系	20	社会福利保障制度	正	4	8
		21	法治教育普及程度	正	2	
		22	城乡居民居住满意度	正	2	
	环境体系	23	居民生活幸福指数	正	4	9
		24	绿色环保指数	正	2	
		25	居民投诉频次	负	3	
	管理体系	26	居民公务办事满意度	正	3	7
		27	政府办公繁复程度	负	3	
		28	紧急事态应对的社会评价	正	1	

To better utilize the regional government performance evaluation and assessment system, we may evaluate the indicators with basic score, quality score, and adjusting score. The highest basic values for basic score, quality score, and adjusting score are 50, 30, and 20 respectively.

Regions may vary in economic development stages and levels, for which different evaluation criteria can be set for different regions. To make up for this difference, we may give tiered basic scores (B_i).

For example, we may set the following four tiers for a certain indicator. If none of the set goals is achieved, a basic score of 20 will be given; if part of the set goals is achieved, a basic score of 30 will be given; if all of the set goals are achieved, a basic score of 40 will be given; if all of the set goals are achieved excessively, a basic score of 50 will be given.

We introduce positive and negative indicators to calculate the relative quality score.

Positive indicator: $$Q_i = \frac{x_i - x_{min}}{x_{max} - x_{min}} \times 30 \qquad 3\text{-}17$$

Negative indicator: $$Q_i = \frac{x_{max} - x_i}{x_{max} - x_{min}} \times 30 \qquad 3\text{-}18$$

Wherein, Q_i represents the quality score of the i-th indicator; x_i represents the value of the i-th indicator; x_{max} represents the maximum value of the indicator in all comparable regions; and x_{min} represents the minimum value of the indicator in all comparable regions.

According to Equations 3-17 and 3-18, the quality score measures the comparative advantage of a region in competition with other regions. In Equation 3-17, the closer the value of the i-th indicator is to its maximum value, the higher the score will be. If the value of the i-th indicator is equal to its maximum value, a maximum score of 30 will be given. On the contrary, the farther the value of the i-th indicator is from the maximum value, the higher the negative indicator score will be. If the value of the i-th indicator is equal to its minimum value, a maximum negative indicator score of 30 will be given.

We introduce positive and negative indicators to calculate the adjusting score.

Positive indicator: $$L_i = 20 \times I_{\{S_i > S_{med}\}} \qquad 3\text{-}19$$

Negative indicator: $$L_i = 20 \times I_{\{S_i < S_{med}\}} \qquad 3\text{-}20$$

Wherein, L_i represents the adjusting score of the i-th indicator; S_i represents the value of the i-th indicator; and S_{med} represents the median of historical indicator of the region (the current period is included in the calculation, the same below). In the positive indicator equation,

$I_{\{S_i>S_{med}\}}$ is the indicative function. When the current performance is higher than the median of historical indicator values, it will be taken as 1, otherwise as 0. In the negative indicator

为了更好地使用这一区域政府绩效评估考核体系，我们可以采用基础评分、质量评分、调整评分对指标进行评价。其中基础评分总分为50，质量评分总分为30，调整评分总分为20。

由于不同区域所处的经济发展阶段和经济发展水平不同，因此不同区域设定的评估目标标准可以有所区别。这种区别可以用区域的基础评分进行弥补，即通过设置目标完成情况的等级，我们可以得到相应的基础评分 (B_i)。

举个例子，对于某个指标，我们可以设置如下四个等级：一个既定目标都未完成，获得基础评分20；完成部分既定目标，获得基础评分30；完成所有既定目标，获得基础评分40；超额完成目标，获得基础评分50。

为了衡量质量评分，我们引入正指标、负指标，正指标和负指标皆可用来计算相对的质量得分。

正指标：
$$Q_i = \frac{x_i - x_{\min}}{x_{\max} - x_{\min}} \times 30 \qquad 3\text{-}17$$

负指标：
$$Q_i = \frac{x_{\max} - x_i}{x_{\max} - x_{\min}} \times 30 \qquad 3\text{-}18$$

其中，Q_i 表示第 i 个指标的质量得分，x_i 表示第 i 个指标值，$x_{\max}$ 表示在所有可对比的区域中该指标值的最大值，$x_{\min}$ 则是在所有可对比的区域中该指标值的最小值。

由式 3-17 和式 3-18 可知，质量得分衡量的主要是该区域在与其他区域竞争中的比较优势。式 3-17 中，第 i 个指标值超过最小值越多，越接近最大值，则其得分越高。最好的情况是第 i 个指标值等于最大值，它就可得到最高的 30 分。反之，如果区域比较优势越差，即第 i 个指标值离最大值越远，则负指标得分越高。最差的情况是第 i 个指标值等于最小值，则负指标得分达到最高的 30 分。

为了衡量调整得分，我们同样引入正负两个指标。

正指标：$\qquad L_i = 20 \times I_{\{S_i>S_{med}\}} \qquad 3\text{-}19$

负指标：$\qquad L_i = 20 \times I_{\{S_i<S_{med}\}} \qquad 3\text{-}20$

其中，L_i 表示第 i 个指标的调整得分，S_i 表示第 i 个指标值，S_{med} 表示该区域该指标历史数值的中位数（计算时包含了本期，下同）。在正指标公式中，$I_{\{S_i>S_{med}\}}$ 为示性函数，当本期表现超越历史指标的中位数时，它取值为1，否则为0；

equation, $I_{\{S_i>S_{med}\}}$ is the indicative function. When the current performance is lower than the median of historical indicator values, it should be taken as 1, otherwise as 0.

According to Equations 3-19 and 3-20, the adjusting score measures the comparative advantages of a region between its current performance and its historical performance. When the current performance of a positive indicator is higher than the median of historical performance, the adjusting score of the indicator for the region will be 20; when the current performance of a positive indicator is lower than the median of historical performance, the adjusting score of the indicator for the region will be 0. On the contrary, when the current performance of a negative indicator is lower than the median of historical performance, the adjusting score of the indicator for the region will be 20; otherwise, it will be 0. We can choose a positive or negative indicator to calculate the adjusting score as necessary.

In summary, we can obtain the score of indicator i as follows:

$$V_i = B_i + Q_i + L_i \qquad 3\text{-}21$$

Therefore, when evaluating a certain factor, its total score can be calculated according to Equation 3-22:

$$\text{Factor}_k = \sum_{i=1}^{n} \left[V_i \cdot \left(\frac{w_i}{\sum_{j=1}^{n} w_j} \right) \right] \qquad 3\text{-}22$$

Wherein, Factor_k represents the total score of the k-th factor, which includes n indicators; w_i represents the weight of the i-th indicator in the k-th factor.

With the evaluation or score of factor, we can obtain the overall performance evaluation score of a region [1]:

$$\text{Score}_p = \sum_{k=1}^{l} \left[\text{Factor}_k \cdot \left(\frac{w_k}{\sum_{j=1}^{l} w_j} \right) \right] \qquad 3\text{-}23$$

Wherein, Score_p represents the total performance evaluation score of the p-th region, which includes l factors; w_k represents the weight of the k-th factor in the p-th region.

The DRP model focuses on studying the efficiency of regional resource allocation from

---

[1] Performance can be evaluated by both superior government agencies and third-party institutions. The author believes that third-party institutions in the market can play a greater role.

the perspective of a regional government's optimizing its fiscal revenue and expenditure structure in stages. The performance evaluation and assessment system takes the perspective of

在负指标公式中，$I_{\{S_i<S_{\text{med}}\}}$ 为示性函数，当本期表现低于历史指标的中位数时，它取值为 1，否则为 0。

由式 3-19 和式 3-20 可知，调整得分衡量的主要是该区域本期与历史表现的相对优势。在正指标体系中，当本期表现超越了历史指标的中位数表现时，在该指标上，该区域的调整得分为 20；当本期表现低于历史指标的中位数表现时，在该指标上，该区域不获得调整得分，即调整得分为 0。负指标与之相反，如果本期表现较差，低于历史表现，则调整得分为 20，反之为 0。根据具体需要，我们可选择正指标或负指标来计算调整得分。

综上，我们可以得到指标 i 的得分：

$$V_i = B_i + Q_i + L_i \qquad 3\text{-}21$$

因此，要评估某一要素，其总得分可以用式 3-22 计算：

$$\text{Factor}_k = \sum_{i=1}^{n} \left[V_i \cdot \left(\frac{w_i}{\sum_{j=1}^{n} w_j} \right) \right] \qquad 3\text{-}22$$

其中，Factor_k 表示第 k 个要素的总得分，此要素包含了 n 个指标，w_i 表示第 k 个要素中的第 i 个指标的权重。

在此，基于要素的评估或得分，可以最终获得对该区域的总绩效评价得分[①②]：

$$\text{Score}_p = \sum_{k=1}^{l} \left[\text{Factor}_k \cdot \left(\frac{w_k}{\sum_{j=1}^{l} w_j} \right) \right] \qquad 3\text{-}23$$

其中 Score_p 表示第 p 个区域的总绩效评估得分，此区域内有 l 个要素，w_k 表示第 p 个区域中第 k 个要素的权重。

至此，可以说，DRP 模型侧重从区域政府阶段性的财政收支结构优化的角度出发去研究区域的资源配置效率；绩效评估考核体系侧重从区域政府推动经济

---

① 陈云贤：《市场竞争双重主体论：兼谈中观经济学的创立与发展》，北京大学出版社，2020，第 120–124 页。

② 绩效评价，既可以由上级政府机构来考核，也可以由市场第三方机构来评估。笔者认为市场第三方机构能够发挥更大作用。

a regional government's promoting sustainable economic development. Finally, it comes to an evaluation and assessment system that centers on the effects of regional government in "9-in-3" Competition (i.e. regional economic development level, regional economic policy level, and regional economic management efficiency).

The comparison between regional resource allocation efficiency and enterprise resource allocation efficiency in different stages of a country's economic development is shown in Figure 3-3.

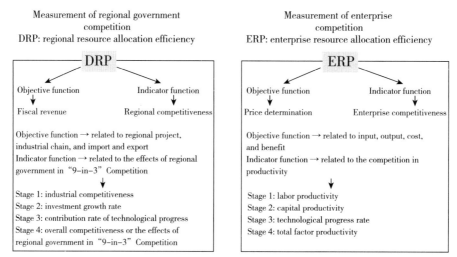

Figure 3–3   Comparison of Regional Resource Allocation Efficiency and Enterprise Resource Allocation Efficiency

The policy systems of various countries around the world include at least the following six connotations, so does the competition policy system of a regional government.

(1) Subject of competition policy. The subject of regional policy is its maker and implementer. Regional government is the only subject of regional competition policy.

(2) Content of competition policy. Competition policy refers to the policy on planning, guiding, supporting, coordinating, supervising, and managing the operative resources in the economic development of a region; the fair and equitable policy on providing general underpinning of and making a practical improvement of the non-operative resources; the policy on coordinating, engaging in, and maintaining order of the quasi-operative resources. In essence, competition policy is the connotation of the effects of regional government in "9-in-3" Competition.

(3) Objectives of competition policy. The specific objective of a regional government in guiding, coordinating, and pre-alarming the industrial economy is to promote the mechanism of "fairness and efficiency". The specific objective in coordinating, engaging in, and maintaining order of the urban economy is to facilitate growth and better the economic environment.

可持续发展的角度进行研究；最后集中到对区域经济发展水平、区域经济政策水平、区域经济管理效率三方面的评估考核上，形成以"三类九要素"作用力为核心的评价体系。

在一国经济发展的不同阶段，区域资源配置效率与企业资源配置效率的比较如图 3-3 所示。

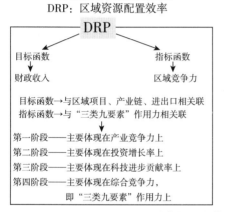 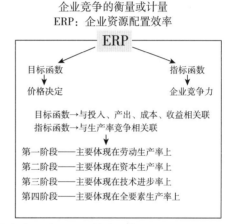

图 3-3 区域资源配置效率与企业资源配置效率比较

世界各国的政策体系，至少包括以下六大方面内涵，区域政府竞争政策体系也是如此。

(1) 竞争政策主体。区域政策的制定者和执行者就是政策主体，而区域竞争政策主体只能是区域政府。

(2) 竞争政策内容。竞争政策就是在区域经济发展中对可经营性资源进行规划、引导、扶持、调节、监督、管理的政策；对非经营性资源进行基本托底、有效提升的公平公正的政策；对准经营性资源进行调配、参与、维序相关的政策。其实质就是一个区域的"三类九要素"作用力的内涵。

(3) 竞争政策目标。区域政府对产业经济进行导向、调节、预警的具体目标是推进"公平与效率"机制运行；区域政府对城市经济进行调配、参与、维序的

The specific objective in providing general underpinning, maintaining fairness, and making practical improvement of the livelihood economy is to achieve the stable and harmonious development of society. The objective of competition policy is reflected in the objective function of as well as the indicator function at different stages of regional government competition. A policymaker sets up long-term, medium-term, and short-term objectives successively. A policy implementer manages to achieve these objectives the other way around.

(4) Means of competition policy. The means of competition policy involves the selection of policy tools after policy formulation, such as fiscal means, financial means, environmental means, efficiency means, and legal means. The environmental means includes at least three layers. The first layer refers to the construction and improvement of infrastructure; the second layer refers to improvement and enhancement of education, science, culture, health, and social security conditions; the third layer refers to the construction and improvement of a social credit system. The efficiency means is reflected in the functional efficiency brought by the policy system, and the time efficiency brought by the innovated management mechanism. The legal means centers on the modern property protection laws, including those on property rights and intellectual property rights.

(5) Effect of competition policy.

$$Y=f(T)+f(E)+f(P)+f(L)+f(R) \qquad 3\text{-}24$$

Wherein, Y represents the effect of competition policy; $f(T)$ represents the effect of competition policy brought by fiscal means; $f(E)$ represents the effect of competition policy brought by financial means; $f(P)$ represents the effect of competition policy brought by environmental means; $f(L)$ represents the effect of competition policy brought by efficiency means; $f(R)$ represents the effect of competition policy brought by legal means.

(6) Delay of competition policy. Overcoming policy delay is a key point in improving regional economic management efficiency. The delay in selecting competition policy is shown in Figure 3-4.

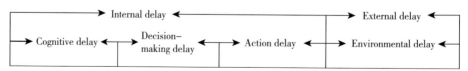

Figure 3-4　Delay in Selecting Competition Policy

具体目标是促进增长、改善环境；区域政府对民生经济进行保障、托底、提升的具体目标是促进社会稳定、和谐发展。竞争政策目标具体体现在区域政府竞争的目标函数与不同阶段的指标函数上，有长期、中期、短期之分。其中，政策制定者按从长期到中期、短期的顺序来确立目标；政策执行者按从短期到中期、长期的顺序来落实目标。

(4) 竞争政策手段。竞争政策手段是政策制定之后的政策工具选择问题，包括财政手段、金融手段、环境手段、效率手段和法治手段。环境手段至少包括三个层次：第一层次是基础设施的建设与完善；第二层次是教科文卫和社会治安条件的改善与提升；第三层次是社会信用体系和制度的建设与健全。效率手段主要体现在两个方面：一是政策体系配套带来的功能效率；二是管理机制创新带来的时间效率。法治手段中最核心的是现代产权制度保护法案，包括财产权和知识产权保护法等。

(5) 竞争政策效应。

$$Y=f(T)+f(E)+f(P)+f(L)+f(R) \qquad 3-24$$

其中，Y 表示竞争政策效应；$f(T)$ 表示财政手段带来的竞争政策效应；$f(E)$ 表示金融手段带来的竞争政策效应；$f(P)$ 表示环境手段带来的竞争政策效应；$f(L)$ 表示效率手段带来的竞争政策效应；$f(R)$ 表示法治手段带来的竞争政策效应。

(6) 竞争政策时滞。克服政策时滞是提高区域经济管理效率的一个关键点。相机抉择竞争政策的时滞如图3-4所示。

图3-4　相机抉择竞争政策的时滞

III. The Spillover Effect of Competition Policy and "Voting with Feet" to Select a Regional Government

There is external economic influence or external economy in a region, that is, the economic externality or the spillover effect. Spillover effect refers to the favorable or unfavorable effect that a micro unit in the industrial economy (an enterprise or a consumer) creates in its own decision-making activities on other enterprises or consumers. It is the "non-market" influence of one economic force on the other. Marshall once took the concepts of "internal economy" and "external economy" to explain how changes in the fourth type of factor of production lead to an increase in output. In *The Economics of Welfare*, Pigou elaborated on positive and negative external effects. Coase believed that external effects often involve mutual infringement by both parties; Pigovian Tax is unnecessary when the transaction cost is zero; when the transaction cost is not zero, it is necessary to weigh the costs and benefits of various policies to address the internalized external effects.

According to various economic explanations, the spillover effect can be classified as follows. First, from the perspective of influence, it can be divided into external economy (or positive external economic effect or positive externality) and external diseconomy (or negative external economic effect or negative externality). Second, in terms of the field where it is generated, it can be divided into external economy of production, external economy of consumption, external diseconomy of production, and external diseconomy of consumption. Third, in terms of time when it is generated, it can be divided into intra-generation externality and inter-generation externality. Fourth, according to its preconditions, it can be divided into externality under competitive conditions and externality under monopoly conditions. Fifth, it can be divided into stable externality and unstable externality. Sixth, it can be divided into one-way externality and interactive externality. Seventh, from the perspective of its source, it can be divided into institutional externality and technological externality.

In terms of competition among regional governments, there are spillover effect of competition policies, namely the spillover effect of fiscal means, financial means, environmental means, efficiency means, and legal means.

The above-mentioned spillover effect of regional government competition is reflected in the following three aspects.

The first aspect is the externality of regional supply-side and demand-side effects, namely the scale effect. Pareto's Law begins to manifest for inter-regional economic growth and effects.

三、竞争政策溢出效应与"用脚投票"选择区域政府

一个区域,存在着经济的外部影响,即经济的外部性,又称溢出效应。溢出效应原指产业经济中微观单位(一个企业或一个消费者)在自己的行为决策活动中对其他企业或其他消费者产生一些有利或不利的影响。这种溢出效应是一种经济力量对另外一种经济力量的"非市场性"的影响。马歇尔曾用"内部经济"和"外部经济"这一对概念,来说明第四类生产要素的变化如何导致产量的增加。庇古在《福利经济学》中,阐述了正外部效应与负外部效应的问题。科斯则认为:第一,外部效应往往不是一方侵害另一方的单向问题,而具有相互性;第二,在交易费用为零的情况下,庇古税根本没有必要;第三,在交易费用不为零的情况下,解决外部效应的内部化问题要对各种政策手段的成本和收益进行权衡比较。

纵观各经济学说的不同阐述,可以把溢出效应从以下七种角度进行分类。第一,从影响效果来说,可以分为外部经济(或称正外部经济效应、正外部性)和外部不经济(或称负外部经济效应、负外部性);第二,从产生领域来说,可以分成生产的外部经济性、消费的外部经济性、生产的外部不经济性和消费的外部不经济性四种类型;第三,从产生的时空来说,可以分为代内外部性与代际外部性;第四,从产生前提条件来说,可以分为竞争条件下的外部性与垄断条件下的外部性;第五,从稳定性来说,可以分为稳定的外部性与不稳定的外部性;第六,从方向性来说,可以分为单向的外部性与交互的外部性;第七,从根源来说,可以分为制度外部性和科技外部性。

回到区域政府之间的竞争,现实中也存在竞争政策的溢出效应问题,它表现为财政手段、金融手段、环境手段、效率手段和法治手段的溢出效应。

区域政府竞争的上述溢出效应,具体体现在以下三方面。

第一,区域供给侧与需求侧效应的外部性,即规模效应,区域间经济增长和经济效应的二八效应开始形成。

The second aspect is the externality of regional economic stock and increment effects, namely the agglomeration effect. The pattern of inter-regional economic development gradually forms a gradient structure.

The third aspect is the externality of regional equilibrium and disequilibrium effects, namely the neighborhood effect. As the advantages of living, business, and tourism in the region increase, the contradiction between the growing demand of residents in the region for a better life and the unbalanced and insufficient development of the region will be gradually alleviated.

The spillover effect of regional government competition policy are shown in Figure 3-5.

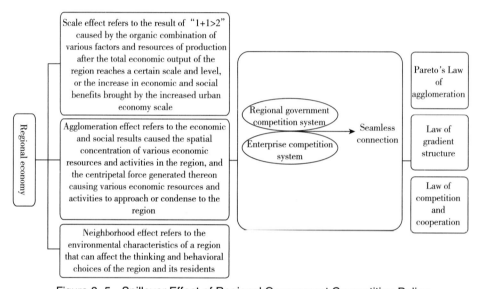

Figure 3–5 Spillover Effect of Regional Government Competition Policy

The Pareto's Law of agglomeration (Pareto's Law), or 80/20 Law, is shown in Figure 3-6.

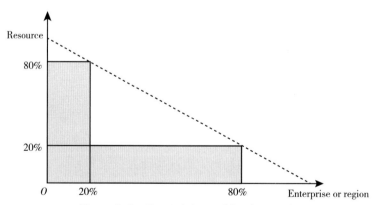

Figure 3–6 Pareto's Law of Agglomeration

第二，区域经济存量与增量效应的外部性，即集聚效应，区域间经济发展格局不断推移，逐步形成梯度结构状况。

第三，区域均衡与非均衡效应的外部性，即邻里效应，区域内宜居、宜业、宜游的环境优势不断确立，区域间人民日益增长的美好生活需要与不平衡、不充分的发展之间的矛盾逐步得到缓解。

区域政府竞争政策溢出效应的具体体现如图 3-5 所示。

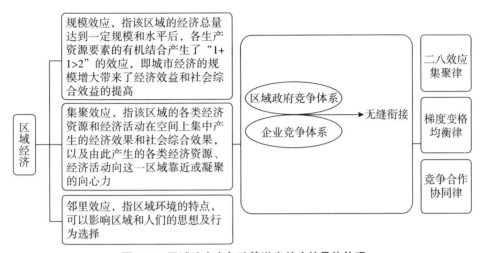

图 3-5　区域政府竞争政策溢出效应的具体体现

其中，二八效应集聚律简称二八定律，又名 80/20 定律，如图 3-6 所示。

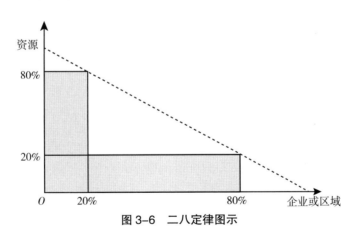

图 3-6　二八定律图示

In regional government competition, externality leads to Pareto's Law of inter-regional economic development. Pareto's Law is not only an inevitable law for regional economic growth that we should use for reference, but also an important topic that economists should focus on in order to promote the harmonized development of regional economy.

According to Tiebout's Model, as long as residents can choose the jurisdiction to live in, there will be competition among governments of jurisdictions. This is because a key factor for individuals to choose the jurisdiction is the tax and service (expenditure) structure and level available therein. To attract more residents, a jurisdiction must provide attractive public services. As residents are different in appetite, jurisdictions may adopt differentiated competitive strategies. When the results are balanced, there may be differences among various jurisdictions and may not in a jurisdiction. In this ideal case, the "voting with feet" by residents will be enough to bring hard constraints to the government of the jurisdiction. The author believes that this hypothesis only involves seeming issues such as regional public environment and public services, and fails to dive into the underlying reasons for the flow of talent and other factors among regions.

In fact, in an open economic and social system, the competition among regional governments will generate spillover effect of regional competition policies, resulting in the scale effect, agglomeration effect, and neighborhood effect among regions in terms of project, industrial chain support, import and export trade, as well as related factors such as talent, capital, and technology. As such, investors will choose where their factor of production should flow to. They will choose the regional government by "voting with feet". This approach enables investors to choose urban areas and high-quality economic development circles that are more suitable for living, business and tourism via the flow of factor of production.

Therefore, the author believes that the spillover effect of competition among regional governments and the phenomenon of "voting with feet" in choosing regional governments are also important topics for the economic community study.

IV. Government's Foresighted Leading

To gain a predominant advantage in regional competition and achieve sustainable economic growth, a government must carry out foresighted leading.

That is, enterprises do what they should do and let the government do what enterprises cannot do or cannot do well. Both enterprises and the government are indispensable, but should function where they should function. Government's foresighted leading should

在区域政府竞争中，其外部性带来区域间经济发展的二八定律，二八定律既是区域经济增长不可避免和需要借鉴的定律，又是需要经济学家们重视和研究，从而推动区域间经济协调发展的重要课题。

根据蒂伯特模型，只要居民可以择区而居，那么各辖区的政府之间就会出现竞争。这是因为个人选择辖区的一个关键要素是辖区可供选择的税收和服务(支出)结构及水平。如果一个辖区试图吸引更多的居民进驻，就必须提供具有吸引力的公共服务，由于居民的偏好不同，辖区之间可以采取差异化的竞争策略，结果均衡的时候，辖区之间存在差异，但辖区内部可能没有差异。在这种理想状况下，居民的"用脚投票"足以给辖区政府带来硬约束。笔者认为，该假说只涉及区域公共环境和公共服务等表层问题，并没有深入探讨区域人才等要素流动的深层原因。

现实中，在开放型的经济社会体系里，区域政府之间的竞争，会产生区域竞争政策的溢出效应，形成区域与区域之间在项目、产业链配套、进出口贸易，以及与之相连的人才、资本、技术等要素方面的规模效应、集聚效应和邻里效应，由此产生投资者生产要素流向选择的问题。这使得投资者"用脚投票"，选择区域政府。"用脚投票"使投资者的生产要素通过流动去选择更加宜居、宜业、宜游的城市区域和优质经济发展圈。

所以，笔者认为，区域政府之间竞争的溢出效应及其产生的"用脚投票"选择区域政府的现象，也是经济学界需要重视和研究的课题。

四、政府超前引领

要在区域竞争中取得领先优势，实现经济上的可持续增长，政府需要进行超前引领。

政府超前引领，即让企业做企业该做的事，让政府做企业做不了和做不好的事。二者都不能空位、越位。政府超前引领需要政府遵循市场规则、依靠市场力

follow market rules, rely on market's invisible hand, and play its guiding, coordinating, and pre-alarming roles in the industrial economy, its allocating, participating, and marshoulding roles in the urban economy, and its providing general underpinning, maintaining fairness, and making practical improvement roles in the livelihood economy. It is also necessary for a government to take policies on planning, investment, consumption, pricing, tax, interest rate, and exchange rate, innovate concepts, institutions, organizations, and technologies, and promote the supply side to boost structural reform on the demand side, thereby forming predominant advantages in economic growth and achieving scientific and sustainable economic development.

To sum up, from the perspective of concept, regional government's foresighted leading should focus on emancipating the mind and seeking truth from facts; from the perspective of institution, it should focus on integrating various systems and rules; from the perspective of organization, it should focus on reforming management methods and modes; from the perspective of technology, it should focus on developing policies and selecting policy tools. A regional government's foresighted leading is conducive to making it stand out in developing the economy in competition with other regional governments and become a key minority specified in the Pareto's Law.

Theoretically, conceptual innovation, institutional innovation, organizational innovation, and technological innovation are the cores of regional government's foresighted leading and the keys to regional government competition.

It should be noted that regional government's technological innovation is different from enterprise's one.

The latter is conducted in the micro field. In the micro market, technological-innovation-driven development is characterized by ①strengthening the dominant position of entrepreneurs in innovation in the operation of microeconomy; ②utilizing talent, technological achievement, R&D institution and other mechanisms to unblock channels for the transformation of technological innovation achievements; ③advancing the integration and development of technological factor and capital factor.

Regional government's technological innovation is conducted in the mezzo field. In the mezzo market, technological-innovation-driven development is characterized by ①increasing the investment in fundamental research in the region and supporting fundamental research and original innovation; ② building innovation-driven platforms to strengthen the leading role of innovation in the region; ③implementing the strategy of strengthening the region with talented people and promoting the innovations to be applied; ④strengthening intellectual property right protection and relevant rules, and aligning the standard systems on innovation at home and abroad.

Now, let's define in detail the specific connotations of government's conceptual innovation, institutional innovation, organizational innovation, and technological innovation.

量,发挥对产业经济的导向、调节、预警作用,对城市经济的调配、参与、维序作用,对民生经济的保障、托底、提升作用。政府超前引领也需要政府运用规划、投资、消费、价格、税收、利率、汇率等政策手段,开展理念、制度、组织、技术的创新,有效推动供给侧带动需求侧结构性改革,形成经济增长领先优势,促进经济科学、可持续发展。

可以这样概括,区域政府在理念上的超前引领,应该侧重解放思想、实事求是;在制度上的超前引领,应该侧重制度集成、规则集成;在组织上的超前引领,应该侧重管理方式、管理模式的变革;在技术上的超前引领,应该侧重政策制定与政策工具的选择。区域政府超前引领有利于使其在区域政府竞争经济的发展中脱颖而出,成为二八定律中的关键少数。

在理论上,理念创新、制度创新、组织创新、技术创新为区域政府超前引领的核心和区域政府竞争的关键。[①]

这里,需要我们阐明的是,区域政府技术创新与企业技术创新是有区别的。

企业技术创新是在微观领域。在该领域,市场科技创新驱动发展的特点是:①强化企业家在微观经济运行中的创新主体地位;②运用人才、成果、机构等机制,打通科技创新成果转化通道;③促进技术要素与资本要素融合发展。

区域政府技术创新是在中观领域。在该领域,市场科技创新驱动发展的特点是:①加大区域基础研究投入,支持基础研究、原始创新;②建设创新驱动平台,强化区域创新引领作用;③实施人才强区战略,推动创新成果应用;④加强知识产权和制度规则保护,推进国内、国际创新标准体系对接。

现在,我们来细化和界定政府理念创新、制度创新、组织创新、技术创新的具体内涵。

---

① 郑延冰:《坚持以创新破解发展难题》,《人民日报》2021年8月24日。

A regional government should carry out conceptual innovation by constructing new development patterns in view of the stages where its economic development is in. New development concepts must be grasped in a comprehensive and systematic manner. In other words, we should grasp conceptual innovation in terms of development stage, issue orientation, and competition pattern.

When carrying out institutional innovation, a regional government ought to focus on fundamental and significant innovative measures, unify the orientation of different policies, and implement the policies on a mutually promoted basis, thereby integrating institutions and rules to enhance the overall efficiency and effectiveness of innovation. Institutional innovation should be the innovation of systems and institutions in all aspects, the systematic improvement that covers various fields and levels, and the organic agglomeration centering on institutions and rules.

Regional government's organizational innovation should focus on making breakthroughs in management mode. Management model involves management structure, management system, management behavior, management efficiency, etc. A regional government ought to raise its ability to carry out innovative management on its own and advocate collaborative innovation and open innovation, so as to build an innovation highland in the region and a high-quality innovation platform for the region.

Regional government's technological innovation essentially refers to innovating the policies it develops and the policy tools it selects. In practice, both regional government's foresighted leading and regional government competition focus on forming, applying, and bettering the policy tools for regional governments to compete, which drives a regional government to crystallize its conceptual innovation, institutional innovation, organizational innovation, and technological innovation.

Regional government's foresighted leading is theoretically reflected in the objective function of the effects of regional government in "9-in-3" Competition that we have established for regional government and the indicator functions we have established for different stages. The result of regional government's foresighted leading stands for the regional resource allocation efficiency that is embodied in the economic development level, economic policy, and economic management efficiency achieved by a regional government at a certain time.

V. Disruptive Innovations in the Theory of Government's Foresighted Leading

The author proposes that a government's keeping up with the times, competing in all aspects, and making government affairs public are the conditions for it to achieve foresighted leading.

　　区域政府的理念创新要结合经济发展的不同阶段，构建不同阶段的新发展格局。新发展理念需要整体性和系统性，从发展阶段把握理念创新，从问题导向把握理念创新，从竞争格局把握理念创新。

　　区域政府的制度创新要聚焦基础性和具有重大牵引作用的创新举措，在政策取向上相互配合，在实施举措上相互促进，促进制度集成、规则集成，提升创新整体效能。制度创新是各个方面体制与制度的创新；是各个领域、各个层次的系统推进；是着眼于制度与规则的有机聚合。

　　区域政府的组织创新的核心在于管理模式上的突破。管理模式包括管理结构、管理体制、管理行为、管理效率等，既要提升自主创新管理能力，又要倡导协同创新和开放式创新，构筑区域创新高地，打造优质创新平台。

　　区域政府的技术创新，实质就是政策制定与政策工具选择的创新。在实践中，区域政府超前引领和区域政府竞争的焦点，在于区域政府竞争政策工具的形成、应用与完善。它推动着区域政府理念创新、制度创新、组织创新和技术创新的具体化。

　　区域政府超前引领的目标即理论上已经确立的区域政府"三类九要素"作用力的目标函数，以及不同阶段确立的指标函数；其效果即在一定时点上，区域政府实际推动的经济发展水平、经济政策措施、经济管理效率等综合反映的区域资源配置效率。

五、政府超前引领理论的颠覆性创新

　　笔者提出，政府超前引领的条件包括与时俱进、全方位竞争和政务公开。

A government's relying on market rules and market mechanism is the prerequisite for it to achieve foresighted leading.

The principle for a government's foresighted leading is to let the market determine resource allocation and let the government play its guiding, coordinating, and pre-alarming roles in the industrial economy, its allocating, participating, and marshalling roles in the urban economy, and its providing general underpinning, maintaining fairness, and making practical improvement roles in the livelihood economy.

To achieve foresighted leading, a government should take planning, investment, consumption, price, tax, interest rate, exchange rate, law, and other policies and carry out innovation in terms of concept, institution, organization, and technology.

The purpose of government's foresighted leading is to utilize the supply-side troika to boost economic growth and scientific and sustainable economic development.

The key to government's foresighted leading lies in innovation and the selection of policy tools.

The theory of government's foresighted leading is fundamentally different from Keynesianism. First, they have different behavioral nodes. The former is a pre-event behavior, while the latter is mid-event and post-event interventions. Second, they have different focuses of coordinating and policy means. The former focuses on guiding, coordinating, and supervising the three types of resources in the region with comprehensive and thorough policy means. Differently, the latter focuses on the demand side and utilizing fiscal policy means. Third, they see a different role for government. The former explains that a government has dual attributes, and believes that the competitive role a government plays is non-negligible in the market economy. Differently, the latter peels off the government from the market. Fourth, they practice different operation modes. The former takes a mode of government leading and supply-side coordination, lays emphasis on expanding the field of resource generation, and values the effect of competition policy, for which it operates in all aspects and the entire process. Differently, the latter takes a mode of government intervention and demand-side coordination. Therefore, the theory of government's foresighted leading should not be confused with Keynesianism.

"Supply-side boost" mentioned in the theory of government's foresighted leading is also different from the supply-side economics in the western world. Although they both start with the supply side and analyze the economic effect of government policy, they exhibit essential differences. First, they are supported by different theoretical foundations. The former is built on the theory of resource generation, which advocates for the interdependence and coordinated operation of supply-side and demand-side economic activities in the region. Differently, the latter utilizes Say's Law, which claims a complete break from demand management. Second, the government plays different roles. The former advocates to fully leverage the role of the government provided that supply-side boost is performed and resources are allocated by the

政府超前引领的前提为依靠市场规则和市场机制。

政府超前引领的原则包括市场决定资源配置；政府对产业经济发挥导向、调节、预警作用，对城市经济发挥调配、参与、维序作用，对民生经济发挥保障、托底、提升作用。

政府超前引领的手段为运用规划、投资、消费、价格、税收、利率、汇率、法律等政策，开展理念、制度、组织、技术的创新。

政府超前引领的目的为运用供给侧三驾马车，推动经济增长领先优势和科学可持续发展。

政府超前引领的关键为创新与政策工具的选择。

政府超前引领理论与凯恩斯主义理论有着本质区别。第一，行为节点不同。政府超前引领属事前行为；凯恩斯主义属事中、事后干预。第二，调节侧重点或政策手段不同。政府超前引领，侧重点在对区域三类资源的引导、调节和监督，主要政策手段是全方位、全过程的；凯恩斯主义，侧重点在需求侧，主要运用财政政策手段。第三，政府的作用不同。政府超前引领理论阐述了政府具有双重属性，认为政府在市场经济中的竞争作用不可忽视；而在凯恩斯主义理论中，政府与市场是剥离的。第四，运行模式不同。政府超前引领表现为：政府引领+供给侧调节，政府超前引领注重开拓资源生成领域，重视竞争政策效应，作用于全方位、全过程；而凯恩斯主义则表现为：政府干预+需求侧调节。因此，政府超前引领理论与凯恩斯主义理论不能混为一谈。

政府超前引领理论中的"供给侧推动"与西方经济学中的供给学派也不是一回事。虽然二者都将供给侧作为理论的主要出发点，都重视对政府政策的经济效应分析，但二者仍有本质区别。第一，理论基础不同。政府超前引领理论运用资源生成理论，促使区域经济活动的供给与需求相互依存、协调运行；供给学派运用萨伊定律，宣称与需求管理彻底决裂。第二，政府作用不同。政府超前引领理

market. On the contrary, the latter ignores or even denies the role of government intervention. Third, they have different policy goals. The former aims to boost sustainable economic development by optimizing the allocation of the three types of resources in the region, while the latter aims to govern stagflation. Fourth, they use different policy means. The former fully utilizes fiscal policy means, financial policy means, environmental policy means, efficiency policy means, and legal policy means. Differently, the latter only values tax policy.

Hence, the author believes that the economic operation mode of "government's foresighted leading and supply-side troika" represents a reform of the mode of production for the following reasons.

(1) It extends the scope of influence of the market economy. The government develops, utilizes, and manages the three types of resources in the field of resource generation according to market rules, thus extending the scope of influence of the market economy from the field of industrial economy to the field of resource generation.

(2) It builds a new multi-layer market system. In the transverse market system, enterprise and government are dual entities of market economy. They jointly explore, construct, and develop in the market field that is divided into industrial economy, urban economy, international economy and other layers. In the longitudinal market system, market factor system, market organization system, market law system, market supervision system, market environment system, and market infrastructure function operate in a unified and orderly manner.

(3) It expounds the comprehensive role of a government in the market economy. Government plays a role in allocating the three types of resources, providing supporting policies, and achieving goals.

The Chinese government has taken substantial steps in carrying out foresighted leading by developing its "14th Five Year Plan" and Long-Range Objectives through 2035. ①Entering a new development stage. Building a socialist modern country in an all-round way and basically realizing socialist modernization are not only required by China's development in the primary stage of socialism, but also for China to move on from the primary stage to a higher stage of socialism. ②Implementing the new development concepts. It is wise to grasp the new development concepts in terms of fundamental purpose, issue orientation, and consciousness of risk, and provide support for innovative development, coordinated development, green development, open development, and shared development. ③Building a new development pattern. We will speed up the formation of a new development pattern in which the domestic circulation acts as the mainstay and the dual circulations at home and overseas promote each other. All of these set an example for all countries around the world to jointly build a community with a shared future for mankind.

论主张在供给侧推动的前提下，在市场配置资源的基础上，充分发挥政府的作用；供给学派忽视甚至否认政府干预的作用。第三，政策目标不同。政府超前引领的政策目标是通过对区域三类资源的优化配置，促进经济的可持续发展；供给学派的政策目标是治理滞胀。第四，政策手段不同。政府超前引领是对财政政策手段、金融政策手段、环境政策手段、效率政策手段、法治政策手段等的全面运用；供给学派只关注税收政策。

因此，笔者认为，"政府超前引领＋供给侧三驾马车推动"的经济运行模式，是生产方式的一场变革。

(1) 它扩大了市场经济的作用范围。政府在遵循市场规律的基础上开发、利用和管理资源生成领域的三类资源，从而把市场经济的作用范围从产业经济领域拓展到了资源生成领域。

(2) 它构建了全新的、多层次的市场体系。在市场横向体系中，企业与政府是市场经济的双重主体。它们共同在产业经济、城市经济、国际经济等多层次的市场领域中开拓、建设与发展。在市场纵向体系中，市场要素体系、市场组织体系、市场法治体系、市场监管体系、市场环境体系、市场基础设施六大功能正在统一、有序地发挥着作用。

(3) 它阐明了政府在市场经济中的全方位作用。政府的作用不断体现在对三类资源的调配、政策的配套和目标的实现上。

可以说，中国政府已经在超前引领的实践中迈出实质步伐，制定了"十四五"规划和2035年远景目标纲要。①进入新发展阶段。全面建设社会主义现代化国家、基本实现社会主义现代化，既是中国特色社会主义初级阶段发展的要求，也是中国特色社会主义从初级阶段向更高阶段迈进的要求。②贯彻新发展理念。从根本宗旨把握新发展理念，从问题导向把握新发展理念，从忧患意识把握新发展理念，支持创新发展、协调发展、绿色发展、开放发展、共享发展。③构建新发展格局。加快构建以国内大循环为主体、国内和国际双循环相互促进的新发展格局。这些，为世界各国共同构建人类命运共同体做出了示范。

Hence, it can be concluded as follows.

(1) Regional government competition and enterprise competition are different in eight characteristics.

(2) Regional government competition is reflected in the effects of regional government in "9-in-3" Competition on the region.

(3) The DRP model of the regional government competitiveness determination mechanism and the indicators of the regional government performance evaluation and assessment system measure the goals and results of regional government's foresighted leading.

(4) Theoretically, government's foresighted leading is centered on conceptual innovation, institutional innovation, organizational innovation, and technological innovation. In practice, the key lies in attaching importance to policy innovation and scientific selection of policy tools.

(5) In the market economy, investors choose a regional government through "voting with feet", namely the flow of talent, wealth, supply, and information.

(6) The economic operation mode of "government's foresighted leading and supply-side troika" represents a reform of the modes of production taken by various countries.

至此，本章得出如下结论。

(1) 区域政府竞争与企业竞争具有八大不同特征。

(2) 现实中，区域政府竞争表现在对区域"三类九要素"的作用力上。

(3) 区域政府竞争力决定机制的 DRP 模型和区域政府绩效评估考核体系指标就是区域政府超前引领目标与效果的衡量测度。

(4) 在理论上，政府超前引领的核心是理念创新、制度创新、组织创新和技术创新；在实际工作中，最关键的是政府应充分重视政策的创新及对政策工具的科学选择。

(5) 在市场经济中，投资者及其人、财、物、信息流等，将"用脚投票"选择区域政府。

(6) "政府超前引领＋供给侧三驾马车推动"的经济发展模式，是世界各国生产方式的一场变革。

Chapter IV

Regional Resource Allocation Efficiency and New Engine for Economic Growth

Effective government actions start with the exploration, construction, and development in the field of resource generation. The dual attributes constitute an important motivation for the regional government to take economic actions. Regional government competition brings scale effect, agglomeration effect, and neighborhood effect for regional economy. Government's foresighted leading is required by a country's or a region's sustainable economic development. In this chapter, we will analyze the characteristics of different stages of economic development and studying new engines that boost economic growth in a region or even a country.

I. Comparison of Regional Resource Allocation Efficiency and Enterprise Resource Allocation Efficiency

As we know, the objective function of regional government competition is the fiscal revenue determination mechanism, while the indicator function is the regional competitiveness determination mechanism. The objective function of enterprise competition is the price determination mechanism; the indicator function of enterprise competition is the enterprise competitiveness determination mechanism.

第四章

区域资源配置效率与经济增长新引擎

对资源生成领域的开拓、建设和发展,是政府有为行为的重要切入点。区域政府的双重属性,是政府经济行为取向的重要动因。区域政府竞争将带来区域经济的规模效应、集聚效应和邻里效应。一个国家或一个区域经济的可持续发展,需要政府超前引领。在此章,我们侧重分析不同经济发展阶段的特征,研究推动一个区域乃至一国经济增长的新引擎。

一、区域资源配置效率与企业资源配置效率比较

我们已经知道,区域政府竞争的目标函数是财政收入决定机制;指标函数是区域竞争力决定机制。而企业竞争的目标函数是价格决定机制;指标函数是企业竞争力决定机制。

Now, the author compares the objective and indicator functions of regional government competition and enterprise competition at different stages of economic development, as shown in Figure 4-1.

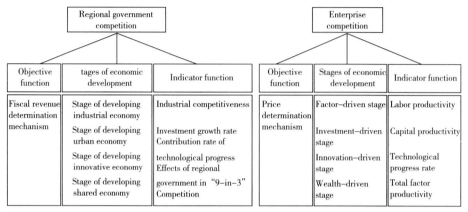

Figure 4-1　Objective and Indicator Functions of Regional Government Competition and Enterprise Competition at Different Stages of Economic Development

Accordingly, there are four combinations of regional resource allocation efficiency and enterprise resource allocation efficiency, as shown in Figure 4-2.

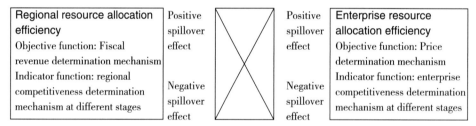

Figure 4-2　Four Combinations of Regional Resource Allocation Efficiency and Enterprise Resource Allocation Efficiency

According to Figure 4-2, regional government regulates resource allocation efficiency in the field of mezzoeconomy, while enterprise adjusts resource allocation efficiency in the field of microeconomy. Both of them are correlated and form four combinations: the interaction between positive spillover effect and positive spillover effect (positive effect plus positive effect); the interaction between positive spillover effect and negative spillover effect (positive effect plus negative effect); the interaction between negative spillover effect and positive spillover effect (negative effect plus positive effect); the interaction between negative spillover effect and negative spillover effect (negative effect plus negative effect). We can learn from the correlation between regional government's economic behaviors in the field of mezzoeconomy and enterprise's economic behaviors in the field of microeconomy that the economic behaviors of a government should comply with objective market rules and the economic behaviors of an enterprise should be consistent with market development trends and the government's long-range

现在，笔者将区域政府竞争与企业竞争在不同经济发展阶段的目标函数、指标函数进行比较，如图 4-1 所示。

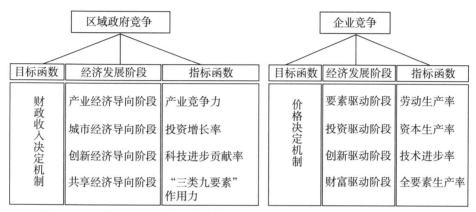

图 4-1 区域政府竞争与企业竞争在不同经济发展阶段的目标函数、指标函数

据此，区域资源配置效率与企业资源配置效率存在四种组合，如图 4-2 所示。

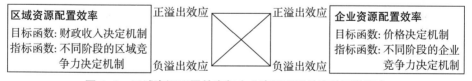

图 4-2 区域资源配置效率与企业资源配置效率的四种组合

根据图 4-2 可知，区域政府从中观经济领域调节资源配置效率，企业从微观经济领域调节资源配置效率，它们共同作用，产生关联效应，形成不同结果的四种组合：正溢出效应与正溢出效应关联互动（正正叠加）；正溢出效应与负溢出效应关联互动（正负叠加）；负溢出效应与正溢出效应关联互动（负正叠加）；负溢出效应与负溢出效应关联互动（负负叠加）。区域政府在中观经济领域的经济行为与企业在微观经济领域行为的关联效应告诉我们，政府的经济行为应符合客观市场规则，企业的经济行为应与市场发展趋势和政府长远规划相一致，否则二

planning. Otherwise, both economic behaviors will collide and cause a delay or even stasis in the economic development efficiency of a region or country. Economists ought to study and seek to realize "positive effect plus positive effect" of regional resource allocation efficiency and enterprise resource allocation efficiency. In this way, we will achieve the optimal mode of a country's economic development.

II. The Growth Stage Dominated by Industrial Economy

The growth stage dominated by industrial economy represents the first stage of regional economic development, namely the factor-driven stage. In this stage, the debate on improving regional resource allocation efficiency mainly revolves around whether industrial policy is needed. Also, the core of regional development lies in the industrial competitiveness of the region, or in other words, the development of and competition for primary resources.

Industrial competitiveness refers to the competitiveness of a certain industry in a country or region in terms of production efficiency, satisfied market demand, and sustained profitability compared with other countries or regions. The connotation of industrial competitiveness involves the content of comparison and the scope of comparison. In particular, the content of comparison of industrial competitiveness is exactly the competitive advantage of a certain industry, which is ultimately reflected in how products, enterprises, and the industry itself are realized in the market. In essence, industrial competitiveness is the comparative productivity of an industry. Comparative productivity refers to the overall ability of a company or industry to continuously produce products that are acceptable to consumers in a more effective manner than its competitors and obtain satisfactory economic benefits therefrom. The scope of comparison of industrial competitiveness covers countries or regions, so we should regard industrial competitiveness as a regional concept. Therefore, the analysis of industrial competitiveness ought to focus on various elements that affect regional economic development, such as industrial agglomeration, industrial transfer, geographical advantages, etc.

In essence, industrial chain support and agglomerated development of industries in a region stand for the competition for factors of production, and the allocation and competition among regional governments for primary resources. The growth stage dominated by industrial economy is a factor-driven stage essentially, which follows three steps: ①the region relies on local resources for entrepreneurship; ②the region makes all efforts in attracting investment, enterprises, and talented people; ③the region competes by providing supporting policies and optimizing business environment.

者行为结果将产生冲撞现象，并导致一个区域或一个国家经济发展效率出现延缓甚至停滞的状况。经济学家需要研究并力图推动区域资源配置效率与企业资源配置效率的"正正叠加"，实现一国经济发展的最优目标模式。

二、产业经济驱动主导的增长阶段

产业经济驱动主导的增长阶段，是区域经济发展的第一阶段，即要素驱动阶段。在该阶段，如何提高区域的资源配置效率，主要围绕着是否需要产业政策展开争论。此阶段区域发展的核心或焦点是区域产业竞争力。其实质或特征是对原生性资源的一种开发与争夺。

产业竞争力，指某国或某一区域的某个特定产业相对于他国或其他区域同一产业来说，在生产效率、满足市场需求、持续获利等方面所体现的竞争能力。产业竞争力的内涵涉及两个基本方面的问题：一个是比较的内容，另一个是比较的范围。具体来说，产业竞争力比较的内容就是产业竞争优势，而产业竞争优势最终体现在产品、企业及产业的市场实现能力上。因此，产业竞争力的实质是产业的比较生产力。所谓比较生产力，是指企业或产业能够以比其他竞争对手更有效的方式持续生产出消费者愿意接受的产品，并由此获得满意的经济收益的综合能力。产业竞争力比较的范围是国家或地区，产业竞争力是一个区域的概念。因此，产业竞争力分析应重点关注影响区域经济发展的各种因素，包括产业集聚、产业转移、区位优势等。

区域产业链配套或产业集群发展的实质是区域生产要素配置的竞争，特别是区域政府对原生性资源的一种调配与争夺。区域产业经济驱动主导的增长阶段，本质是区域经济增长的要素驱动阶段，其发展路径有三个步骤：①区域依赖本地资源创业发展；②区域全力开展招商引资、招才引智；③区域展开政策配套和优化环境的竞争。

The focus of market-economy-related debates in this stage falls on regional industrial policy. The debate revolves around three aspects: ①whether industrial policy is needed; ②what kind of industrial policy is the key or how to objectively evaluate the industrial policies of various countries around the world; ③what is the theoretical framework behind industrial policy.

The debate over the preservation or abolition of industrial policy mainly involves the following ten key points: ①free market or industrial policy; ②is industrial policy a gamble; ③whether there is an "efficient market"; ④who is the market player; ⑤should the first person who eat crabs be encouraged; ⑥whether industrial policy will lead to power's rent-seeking; ⑦what drives technological innovation; ⑧how to leverage comparative advantages; ⑨is "entrepreneurial spirit" exclusive to entrepreneurs; ⑩does corner overtaking really exist.

Porter described industrial policy in his book *The Competitive Advantage of Nations* as follows: ①productivity is the main purpose; ②there are prerequisites for a government to formulate industrial policy; ③a government faces challenges in formulating industrial policy; ④industrial policy affects factor of production. The author summarizes Porter's viewpoints on industrial policy as follows: ①Porter basically affirms industrial policy; ②Porter identifies the basic content of industrial policy; ③Porter puts forward the prerequisites and potential challenges for formulating industrial policy; ④Porter believes the purpose of formulating industrial policy is to develop and improve productivity; ⑤Porter believes that in promoting industrial development, the positive impact of tax reduction is greater than that of subsidy policy, and indirect subsidy is better than direct subsidy.

After studies, the author believes that first, the theoretical framework behind industrial policy stems from the existing demand for economic growth driven by industrial economy. Second, the objective reality requires three layers of industrial policies to overcome market failure: ①the industrial policy at the planning and guidance layer is used to overcome the failure caused by "market mechanism defects"; ②the industrial policy at the supporting and coordination layer is used to overcome the failure caused by "market mechanism gaps"; ③the industrial policy at the supervision and management layer is used to overcome the failure caused by "market mechanism obstacles". Third, industrial policy should not only provide industrial subsidies, but also oppose interventions that deviate from market rules.

Hence, the author summarizes the main characteristics of the factor-driven stage as follows: ①this stage stands for the development and competition for primary resources; ②both industrial transfer and labor transfer exist among regions; ③the "extensive" management of industry turns into "intensive" management; ④a modern property right system takes shape; ⑤the modern industrial system gets improved. In this stage, a regional government may increase regional resource allocation efficiency by playing its roles of planning, guiding, supporting, coordinating, supervising, and managing.

区域产业政策的匹配，是该阶段市场经济争论的焦点。争论的内容主要有三方面：①要不要产业政策；②什么样的产业政策才是核心，即如何对世界各国的产业政策做出客观评价；③支撑产业政策的理论框架是什么。

产业政策存废之争主要涉及以下十个要点：①自由市场与产业政策之争；②产业政策是不是一场豪赌；③"有效市场"是否存在；④谁是市场的主角；⑤是否该鼓励第一个吃螃蟹的人；⑥产业政策会否导致权力寻租；⑦技术创新靠谁驱动；⑧如何发挥比较优势；⑨"企业家精神"是否为企业家的专利；⑩弯道超车是否真的存在。

波特在《国家竞争优势》一书中对产业政策的表述是：①生产力是主要目标；②政府制定产业政策存在前提；③政府制定政策存在挑战；④政策对生产要素存在影响。笔者将波特的产业政策观点概括如下：①基本肯定了产业政策；②确定了产业政策的基本内容；③提出了制定产业政策的前提和可能遇上的挑战；④认为制定产业政策的目标是发展和提高生产力；⑤认为在促进产业发展方面，减税的正面影响大于补贴政策，间接的补贴行为也会比直接补贴的效果更佳。

笔者的研究认为，第一，支撑产业政策的理论框架来源于现实存在的产业经济驱动主导的经济增长需求。第二，客观现实需要三个层面的产业政策克服市场失灵：①规划与引导层面的产业政策用于克服"市场机制缺陷性"失灵；②扶持与调节层面的产业政策用于克服"市场机制空白性"失灵；③监督与管理层面的产业政策用于克服"市场机制障碍性"失灵。第三，产业政策不只是产业补贴，还必须反对脱离市场规则的干预行为。

因此，笔者把要素驱动阶段的主要特征概括为：①此阶段是对原生性资源的一种开发与争夺；②在区域之间会出现产业和劳动力双转移状况；③产业的"粗放式"经营逐渐向"集约式"经营转化；④现代产权制度逐步形成；⑤现代产业体系逐步完善。区域政府在此阶段对产业政策进行规划、引导、扶持、调节、监督和管理，能促进区域资源的配置效率。

III. The Growth Stage Dominated by Urban Economy

The growth stage dominated by urban economy represents the second stage of regional economic development, namely the investment-driven stage. In this stage, it is necessary for a regional government to practically "provide planning and layout, participate in construction, and achieve orderly management" for urban areas in order to improve regional resource allocation efficiency. Also, the core of regional development lies in the investment growth rate of the region, or in other words, the development of and competition for secondary resources.

This investment growth rate refers to the one determined by a country or region after overall arrangement and comprehensive balance in view of the demands for national economy and society to develop, as well as its financial, material, and human resources. It is calculated as annual investment growth rate or annual average investment growth rate: ①annual investment growth rate, namely the ratio between the increase in annual planned investment and the actual investment amount of the previous year; ②annual average investment growth rate, namely the ratio between the increase in investment during the planned period (five years) and the actual investment amount in the previous period (five years).

Like the definition of urban infrastructure specified in Chapter I, the investment growth in urban infrastructure involves three layers.

Layer 1: ①urban hardware infrastructure, namely the engineering infrastructure such as urban energy supply system, water supply and drainage system, transportation system, post and communication system, environmental protection and sanitation system, and defense and disaster prevention system; ②urban software infrastructure, including administration, culture and education, healthcare, commercial service, finance and insurance, social welfare, and other social infrastructure.

Layer 2: as urban-rural integration gets advanced, urban and rural infrastructure will include rural productive infrastructure, rural living infrastructure, ecological infrastructure construction, and rural social development infrastructure.

Layer 3: the engineering infrastructure for urban and rural intelligent management, as well as the specific implementation of the connotation of "new infrastructure" at present.

Let's take the *Plan of Chicago* in the early 20th century as an example. This book was divided into sections: Origin of Plan of Chicago Ancient and Modern Urban Planning; Chicago: Capital of the Midwest; Chicago's Park System, Transportation, and Urban Street System; The

三、城市经济驱动主导的增长阶段

城市经济驱动主导的增长阶段，是区域经济发展的第二阶段，即投资驱动阶段。在该阶段，是否提高了区域资源配置效率，将由区域政府是否有实质推动城市的"规划布局、参与建设、有序管理"来体现。此阶段区域发展的核心或焦点是区域投资增长率。其实质或特征是对次生性资源的一种开发与争夺。

投资增长率，指某国或某一区域根据国民经济与社会发展的需要和国家（或区域）的财力、物力、人力的可能，经统筹安排、综合平衡后，确定的投资增长率。其计算方法有两种：①年投资增长率，即年度计划投资增加额与上年实际投资额的比率；②年平均投资增长率，即计划时期（五年）投资增加额与上个时期（五年）实际投资额的比率。

在城市基础设施中的投资增长，正如本书第一章详细阐述的城市基础设施定义一样，包括以下三个层次。

第一层次：①城市硬件基础设施，即城市能源供应系统、供水排水系统、交通运输系统、邮电通信系统、环保环卫系统和防卫防灾安全系统六大方面的工程性基础设施；②城市软件基础设施，即行政管理、文化教育、医疗卫生、商业服务、金融保险和社会福利等社会性基础设施。

第二层次：随着城乡一体化的进程，城乡基础设施还包括乡村生产性基础设施、乡村生活性基础设施、生态环境设施建设和乡村社会发展基础设施四大类。

第三层次：城乡智能管理的系列开发和建设工程性基础设施等，也包括对现阶段"新基建"内涵的具体实施运用。

这里我们首先列举20世纪初美国的《芝加哥规划》。该规划方案中涉及的内容有芝加哥规划的起源；古代和现代的城市规划；芝加哥：中西部区之都会；芝加哥的公园系统，交通运输，城市街道系统；芝加哥的心脏；最终结

Heart of Chicago; and Final Conclusion. To date, the regional economic development driven by Chicago's urban planning and construction still has a profound impact on the development of urban planning and construction in the United States and even the world.

Let's turn to China's urban-rural integrated development. The Central Committee of the Communist Party of China and the State Council have issued the *Strategic Plan for Rural Revitalization (2018—2022)*, the *Opinions of the Central Committee of the Communist Party of China and the State Council on Establishing and Improving the System, Mechanism, and Policy for Urban-Rural Integrated Development*, the *Opinions of the Central Committee of the Communist Party of China and the State Council on Comprehensively Promoting Rural Revitalization and Accelerating Agricultural and Rural Modernization*, and other documents. These documents require us to vigorously implement rural construction, including speeding up the planning of villages, preserving the countryside characteristics, and avoiding reckless demolition and construction; to strengthen the construction of public infrastructure and basic public services in rural areas; to speed up the urban-rural integrated development in counties and promote a new type of people-centric urbanization. These documents embody the progress and orientation of China's urban-rural integrated development.

The last example falls on the development and construction of intelligent society. Intelligent service revolves around intelligent education, intelligent healthcare, intelligent health and elderly care, etc. Intelligent social governance includes intelligent government affairs, intelligent court, intelligent city, intelligent transportation, intelligent environmental protection, using artificial intelligence to enhance public safety and security capabilities, social interaction, sharing, and mutual trust, etc. Intelligent infrastructure involves network infrastructure, big data infrastructure, high-performance computing infrastructure, etc.

Therefore, the development, changes, and trends driven by urban economy are manifested in the following aspects.

(1) In different stages of regional economic development, continuous changes are seen in the total investment amount and the investment structure. As the per capita income of a region significantly increases, the residents will begin to pursue a high-quality life, urging the regional government to provide a better environment, more developed transportation, faster communication, and better education, sanitation, and healthcare services.

(2) Changes in the total amount and structure of regional government investment depend

on the structure and elasticity of the demands of investors and general people for public goods in the region, which are dynamic in different stages of economic development.

(3) Bettering urban infrastructure and developing intelligent city will allow us to improve the investment environment of a region and breach the bottleneck of regional economic growth driven by factors of production, thereby turning to the investment-driven stage and moving on to a growth stage dominated by urban economic competition.

论。时至今日，芝加哥城市规划建设所带动的区域经济发展成就，仍然对美国乃至世界的城市规划建设发展产生着深远影响。

其次，我们列举中国的城乡一体化发展。中共中央、国务院印发了《乡村振兴战略规划 (2018—2022 年)》《中共中央　国务院关于建立健全城乡融合发展体制机制和政策体系的意见》《中共中央　国务院关于全面推进乡村振兴加快农业农村现代化的意见》等文件。其中，大力实施乡村建设行动，包括：加快推进村庄规划工作，保留乡村特色风貌，不搞大拆大建；加强乡村公共基础设施建设，提升农村基本公共服务水平；加快县域内城乡融合发展，推进以人为核心的新型城镇化；等等。它体现了中国城乡一体化的进程和发展走向。

最后，我们来列举智能社会的开发、建设事项。服务智能化包括：智能教育、智能医疗、智能健康和养老等。社会治理智能化包括：智能政务、智慧法庭、智慧城市、智能交通、智能环保、运用人工智能提升公共安全保障能力、社会交往共享互信等。基础设施智能化包括：网络基础设施、大数据基础设施、高效能计算基础设施等。

因此，城市经济驱动主导的发展、变化与趋势表现在以下几个方面。

(1) 在区域经济发展的不同阶段，投资总量和投资结构呈现不断变化的趋势。一旦区域人均收入水平大幅上升，人们就会开始追求高品质的生活，这在客观上会迫使区域政府提供更好的环境、更发达的交通、更快捷的通信，以及更高水平的教育、卫生、保健服务等。

(2) 区域政府投资总量和投资结构的变化，取决于投资者和社会民众对区域公共物品的需求结构和需求弹性，而这又是随着经济发展的不同阶段而不断变化的。

(3) 城市基础设施的完善以及智能城市的开发，既能改善区域经济的投资环境，又能突破区域以生产要素驱动经济增长的瓶颈，转向以投资驱动发展，进入由城市经济竞争主导的增长阶段。

(4) The formation of city cluster. City cluster is the supreme form of spatial organization when urban economy goes mature. Generally, at least 3 large cities, which act as constituent units, center on 1 or more extra-large cities and rely on a developed network of transportation, communication, and other infrastructure to form a compact, economically connected, and highly integrated city cluster within a specific geographical area. For example, the "14th Five-Year Plan" of Guangdong Province of China has clearly put forward that it will cultivate and enlarge Guangzhou Metropolitan Circle, Shenzhen Metropolitan Circle, the metropolitan circle of the west bank of the Pearl River Estuary, Shantou-Chaozhou-Jieyang Metropolitan Circle, and Zhanjiang-Maoming Metropolitan Circle to form a "city cluster of five circles" and make city cluster a source of force for development. The *Proposal of the Central Committee of the Communist Party of China on Formulating the 14th Five-Year Plan for National Economic and Social Development and the Long-Range Goals Through 2035* proposed that it is necessary to exert the driving role of central cities and city clusters to build modern metropolitan circles.

The role of government in urban economic development and its policies must not be underestimated. The regional government will play its tri-role in "providing planning and layout, participating in construction, and achieving orderly management" and constitute the main characteristics of a region or country in the investment-driven stage: ①essentially competing for secondary resources; ②urban economy shifts from investing in urban software and hardware infrastructure to carrying out urban-rural integration and regional intelligent management; ③the framework system of city cluster emerges and metropolitan circles take shape; ④domestic and international industrial clusters and consumption centers are generated; ⑤urbanization shows a trend of gradient structured transference, and the modernization of social governance gets improved.

IV. The Growth Stage Dominated by Innovative Economy

The growth stage dominated by innovative economy represents the third stage of regional economic development, namely the innovation-driven stage. In this stage, improving regional resource allocation efficiency will be reflected by a regional government's substantial promotion of innovation in terms of concept, institution, organization, and technology. The core of regional development lies in the contribution rate of technological progress of the region, or in other words, the regulation and containment of retrograde resources.

The contribution rate of technological progress (or technological progress rate) refers to the contribution share of technological progress to economic growth. It is a comprehensive

(4) 城市群的形成。城市群是城市经济发展到成熟阶段的最高空间组织形式，是指在特定地域范围内，一般以 1 个以上特大城市为核心，以至少 3 个大城市为构成单元，依托发达的交通通信等基础设施网络所形成的空间组织紧凑、经济联系紧密，最终实现高度同城化和高度一体化的城市群体。比如，中国广东"十四五"规划明确提出，要培育壮大广州、深圳、珠江口西岸、汕潮揭、湛茂五大都市圈，构建"一群五圈"，让城市群变动力源。《中共中央关于制定国民经济和社会发展第十四个五年规划和二〇三五年远景目标的建议》提出，要发挥中心城市和城市群的带动作用，建设现代化都市圈。①

在此，政府在城市经济发展中的角色及其政策措施不容小觑。它将由区域政府"规划布局、参与建设、有序管理"的三重角色来体现，并由此形成一个区域或一个国家投资驱动阶段的主要特征：①实质是对次生性资源的一种开发与争夺；②城市经济从城市软硬件基础设施投资开始，向城乡一体化和区域智能管理转化；③城市群框架体系出现，都市圈形成；④产生国内、国际产业集群和消费中心城市经济；⑤城市化呈现梯度结构推移的趋势，社会治理现代化逐渐完善。

四、创新经济驱动主导的增长阶段

创新经济驱动主导的增长阶段，是区域经济发展的第三阶段，即创新驱动阶段。在此阶段，如何提高区域资源配置效率，将由区域政府是否有实质性推动理念、制度、组织和技术的创新来体现。此阶段区域发展的核心和焦点是区域科技进步贡献率。其实质或特征是对逆生性资源的一种调控与遏制。

科技进步贡献率亦称技术进步率，是指科技进步对经济增长的贡献份额，

---

① 熊丽：《为什么强调都市圈建设》，《经济日报》2021 年 2 月 28 日。

indicator for measuring regional technological competitiveness and the transformation of technology into real productivity. Production function methods are widely adopted by theorists at home and abroad to calculate the contribution rate of technological progress, including the production function simulation method, the method of Solow Residual, the CES production function method, the growth rate method, the method of Dennison's Factor Analysis, etc. Generally, we can obtain the equation of technological progress rate based on the C-D production function:

$$Y = A + \alpha K + \beta L \qquad 4-1$$

Wherein, Y represents the growth rate per annum of output; A represents the growth rate per annum of technology; K represents the growth rate per annum of capital; L represents the average growth rate of labor; α represents the elasticity of capital output; β represents the elasticity of labor output. It is assumed that α and β are constants in a certain period of time, and $\alpha + \beta = 1$, meaning the scope effect remains unchanged.

We make $E = A/Y \times 100\%$, in which E represents the contribution rate of technological progress. According to the equation of technological progress rate, we can obtain the general formula for calculating the contribution rate of technological progress:

$$E = 1 - \frac{\alpha K}{Y} - \frac{\beta L}{Y} \qquad 4-2$$

According to *China Statistical Yearbook on Science and Technology: 2021*, China's contribution rate of technological progress in 2020 was 60.2%, while that of major developed countries such as the United States and Germany was over 80%.

In the innovation-driven stage, conceptual innovation is where a regional government makes breakthroughs in regional competition. What's more, regional government's technological innovation is the key to competition in this stage; organizational innovation is the impetus for competition in this stage; institutional innovation is the necessary guarantee for regional competition in this stage.

For example, China must reduce its carbon dioxide emissions by 90% over the next 40 years from 2020. In view of this, China may promote technological innovation via re-valuation and industrial restructuring. Carbon neutrality will be the battlefield for technological innovation.

Therefore, the significance of China's proposal for carbon peaking and carbon neutrality is no less than the previous three industrial revolutions. We ought to avoid "one size fits all" and ineffective investment, speed up the development of new energy technologies that are energy-saving and in line with the direction of low-carbon transformation and development, and construct a technological innovation supporting system in a faster manner.

它是衡量区域科技竞争实力和科技转化为现实生产力的综合性指标。对科技进步贡献率的测算，主要采取生产函数法。这是目前国内外理论界广泛采取的一种方法，如生产函数模拟法、索洛余值法、CES 生产函数法、增长速度方法、丹尼森经济增长因素分析法等。一般根据 C-D 生产函数得出科技进步速率方程：

$$Y=A+\alpha K+\beta L \quad\quad 4-1$$

其中，Y 为产出的年均增长速度；A 为科技的年均增长速度；K 为资本的年均增长速度；L 为劳动的平均增长速度；α 为资本产出弹性；β 为劳动产出弹性，通常假定在一定时期内 α、β 为常数，并且 $\alpha+\beta=1$，即范围效应不变。

令 $E=A/Y\times 100\%$，E 为科技进步贡献率。由科技进步速率方程可导出科技进步贡献率测算的一般公式：

$$E=1-\frac{\alpha K}{Y}-\frac{\beta L}{Y} \quad\quad 4-2$$

根据《中国科技统计年鉴：2021》测算，2020 年中国的科技进步贡献率为 60.2%，但美国、德国等主要发达国家的科技进步贡献率超过了 80%。

在创新驱动阶段，区域政府理念创新成为区域竞争的突破点；区域政府技术创新是此阶段竞争的关键；区域政府组织创新是此阶段竞争的推动力；区域政府制度创新是此阶段区域竞争的必要保障。

比如，从 2020 年开始的 40 年，中国的二氧化碳排放量须减少 90%，可以通过价值重估、产业重构推动技术创新。碳中和是科技创新的竞争。[①]

于是，中国提出，碳达峰、碳中和的意义不亚于三次工业革命，要防止"一刀切"和无效投资，加快发展既有节能效果又符合低碳转型发展方向的用能新技术，要加快构建科技创新支撑体系。[②]

---

① 李禾：《贺克斌院士：碳中和是科技创新的竞争》，《科技日报》2021 年 6 月 16 日。
② 刘垠：《碳达峰碳中和要加快构建科技创新支撑体系》，《科技日报》2021 年 6 月 21 日。

China should mobilize comprehensive innovation via technological innovation. There are three objectives to improve overall efficiency by utilizing the technological innovation governance system: allowing diverse entities to equally participate in technological innovation governance; forming a diversified governance mode for technological innovation; and constructing a diversified innovation governance structure.

Therefore, the author believes that China responses to retrograde resources, namely carbon emissions by taking policy systems and measures that facilitate the coordinated and mutual promotion of technology, industry, and finance, such as ①taking "carbon emission permit trading" as an institutional innovation to optimize China's regional allocation of industries; ②promoting the organizational innovation of China's Maritime Silk Road in the 21st century by building a standardized carbon market system; ③using the technological innovation of "carbon emission permit trading bundled with RMB settlement" to realize the "corner overtaking" of RMB internationalization.

If innovative economy plays a dominant role, innovative cities will be formed. An innovative city mainly relies on innovative factors such as technology, knowledge, manpower, culture, and system to drive its development, and lead other regions by radiating development achievements. The connotation of innovative cities is generally reflected in the innovations in ideological concept, development mode, mechanism and system, opening-up, enterprise management, urban management, etc.

The author summarizes the main characteristics of the innovation-driven stage as follows. ①This stage is highlighted by regulating and containment of retrograde resources. ②This stage aims to form an innovative development system in an all-round way via conceptual innovation, institutional innovation, organizational innovation, and technological innovation. ③Intensive development, carbon neutrality, and digital economy are the main themes of this stage. ④Talent is the key to win in this stage. ⑤Technological innovation will lead to comprehensive innovation and in-depth integration with the economy and society, thereby forming a new growth pole for a country's economic development.

V. The Growth Stage Dominated by Shared Economy

The growth stage dominated by shared economy represents the fourth stage of regional economic development, namely the wealth-driven stage. In this stage, a regional government embarks on a transition from prioritized competition to competition and cooperation and then to win-win cooperation.

中国要用科技创新带动全面创新。利用科技创新治理体系提升整体效能有三个目标：一是多元主体平等参与科技创新治理；二是探索形成多元化科技创新治理模式；三是推动构建多样化创新治理结构。[1]

因此，笔者认为，中国对逆生性资源——碳排放应对方式的构思是，应构建科技、产业、金融协同互促的政策体系和措施：①以"碳排放权交易"作为一种制度创新，优化中国产业区域配置；②以标准化的碳市场体系建设作为中国21世纪海上丝绸之路组织创新的重要切入点；③以"碳排放权交易捆绑人民币结算"的技术创新作为演绎人民币国际化"弯道超车"的新路径。

创新经济驱动主导将推动创新型城市的形成。创新型城市是主要依靠科技、知识、人力、文化、体制等创新要素驱动发展的城市，对其他区域具有高端辐射与引领作用。创新型城市的内涵一般体现在思想观念创新、发展模式创新、机制体制创新、对外开放创新、企业管理创新和城市管理创新等方面。

至此，笔者把创新驱动阶段的主要特征概括为：①此阶段突出表现为对逆生性资源的一种调控与遏制；②以理念创新、制度创新、组织创新、技术创新和全方位创新构成创新发展体系；③集约型、碳中和、数字经济是此阶段的主旋律；④人才成为制胜关键；⑤科技创新带动全面创新与经济社会深度融合，形成一国经济发展新增长极。

五、共享经济驱动主导的增长阶段

共享经济驱动主导的增长阶段，是区域经济发展的第四阶段，即财富驱动阶段。区域政府在此阶段从以竞争为主，向竞争合作，再向合作共赢的方向发展。

---

[1] 金凤：《研发作产业　技术作商品　江苏积极引导创新资源配置》，《科技日报》2021年6月23日。

The core or focus of regional development falls on the effects of regional government in "9-in-3" Competition. Its essence or feature is the creation and sharing of the four types of common wealth or public goods of human society by countries (or regions) around the world, including ideological public goods, material public goods, organizational public goods, and institutional public goods.

In this stage, the objective function of regional government development is still the fiscal revenue determination mechanism; the indicator function of regional government competition is still the regional competitiveness determination mechanism. The core influencing elements and key supporting conditions of the objective and indicator functions that support a regional government to develop still come from the following three aspects.

(1) Regional economic development level: projects, industrial chain support, and import and export trade.

(2) Regional economic policy level: infrastructure investment policy, talent and technology supporting policy, and fiscal and financial supporting policy.

(3) Regional economic management efficiency: policy system efficiency, environmental system efficiency, and management system efficiency.

However, in this stage, a regional government's economic behavior embarks on a transition from prioritized competition to competition and cooperation and then to win-win cooperation.

A modern industrial system with regional competitiveness has been built.

A fully functional infrastructure network with intra-regional interconnectivity and unblocked external channels has been constructed.

An open and collaborative innovation community that gathers innovative resources in the region has been formed.

In this stage, the regional industrial chain level and technological development are marching towards the global forefront of technology, technological achievements are constantly transformed into real productivity, and innovation is creating new highlands for industrial chain and supply chain as a new engine.

In this stage, the means, mode, and concept of regional urban governance have been innovated; economic governance, social governance, and urban governance have been coordinated; urban areas have become beautiful homes where people and nature coexist harmoniously.

In this stage, the supply of high-quality products, efficient capital supply, and high-level institutional supply boost the openness of rules, regulations, management, and standards, and facilitate win-win international cooperation in the process of international competition and cooperation.

此阶段区域发展的核心或焦点为区域"三类九要素"作用力。其实质或特征是世界各国(或各区域)对人类社会四种共同财富或四类公共产品的一种创造与共享，分别是思想性公共产品、物质性公共产品、组织性公共产品和制度性公共产品。

此阶段，区域政府发展的目标函数仍然是财政收入决定机制，区域政府发展的指标函数仍然是区域竞争力决定机制。支撑区域政府发展目标函数和指标函数的核心影响因素和关键支持条件仍然主要来自以下三方面。

(1) 区域经济发展水平：项目、产业链配套、进出口贸易。

(2) 区域经济政策水平：基础设施投资政策，人才、科技扶持政策，财政、金融支持政策。

(3) 区域经济管理效率：政策体系效率，环境体系效率，管理体系效率。

然而，此阶段区域政府的经济行为已由以竞争为主，向竞争合作与合作共赢的方向发展。

此阶段的区域产业体系，已培育成为具有区域竞争力的现代产业体系。

此阶段的区域基础设施，已建设成为区内互联互通、区外通道顺畅的功能完善的基础设施网络。

此阶段的区域技术创新，已构建成为集聚创新资源的开放型区域协同创新共同体。

此阶段的区域产业链水平与科技发展，正在向着世界科技前沿推进，科技成果持续转化为现实生产力，创新作为一种新引擎，创建着产业链供应链新高地。

此阶段的区域城市治理，其治理手段、治理模式、治理理念已经创新；经济治理、社会治理、城市治理已经统筹；城市成为人与人、人与自然和谐共生的美丽家园。

在此阶段的国际竞争与合作进程中，高质量产品供给、高效率资金供给、高水平制度供给，推动着规则、规制、管理、标准等制度型开放，推动着国际合作共赢。

The author summarizes the main characteristics of the growth stage dominated by the shared economy as follows: ①the four types of public goods in human society have taken shape and are constantly enriching; ②the regional government embarks on a transition from prioritized competition to competition and cooperation and then to win-win cooperation; ③the consensus on regional multi-polarization and economic integration is being co-constructed; ④mankind and nature coexist harmoniously; ⑤a higher level of global economic governance system and the community with a shared future for mankind are being constantly promoted.

VI. Gradient Transference of Regional Economic Competition

The author has revealed the results of regional economic competition after studies and established a gradient transference model of regional economic competition, as shown in Figure 4-3.

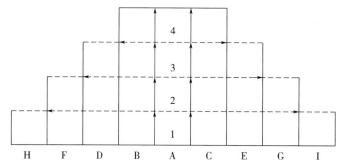

Figure 4–3 Gradient transference model of regional economic competition

In Figure 4-3, the letters A to I represent different regions, and the numbers 1 to 4 represent the four stages of regional economic development. This model describes the following four characteristics of the gradient transference of regional economic competition.

First, transverse extension. Regional economic competition stems from economically developed regions with leading industrial, urban, and innovative economies. As time goes on and the internal elements and external conditions of economic development in various regions change, regional economic competition gradually will extend from developed regions to underdeveloped regions, as shown by the transverse extension from A to I in Figure 4-3.

Second, longitudinal transference. As the economic development level goes higher and the economic growth stage gets deeper, the field where regional economic competition occurs will shift from industrial economy to urban economy, and then to innovative economy, as shown by the longitudinal transference from 1 to 4 in Figure 4-3.

笔者把共享经济驱动主导的增长阶段的主要特征概括为：①此阶段的人类社会四种类型公共产品已经形成并且正不断丰富；②区域政府从以竞争为主向竞争合作与合作共赢的方向发展；③区域多极化、经济一体化，已从共识走向共建；④人与自然和谐共生；⑤更高水平的全球经济治理体系和人类命运共同体正在不断推进。

六、区域经济竞争梯度推移

笔者经过研究揭示出区域经济竞争的结果，形成区域经济竞争梯度推移模型，如图4-3所示。

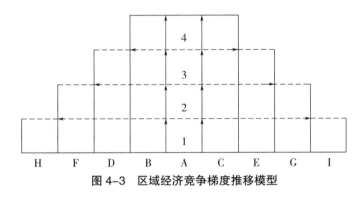

图4-3 区域经济竞争梯度推移模型

图4-3中，A至I表示不同的区域，1至4表示区域经济发展的四个阶段。该模型描述出区域经济竞争梯度推移的以下四个特点。

一是横向拓展。区域经济竞争源于产业经济、城市经济、创新经济领先的经济发达区域，随着时间的推移及各个区域经济发展内在因素和外在条件的作用与变化，区域经济竞争从发达区域逐渐向欠发达区域横向拓展，如图4-3中从A、B、C向D、E、F、G、H、I等区域横向推移的过程。

二是纵向推移。随着经济发展水平的不断成熟和经济增长阶段的不断深入，区域经济竞争的领域不断从产业经济进入城市经济、再逐步进入创新经济等，如图4-3中从1向2、3、4的推移就是纵向推移的过程。

Third, the gradient structure or the 80/20 phenomenon. In the competitive development of regional industrial economy, urban economy, and innovative economy, a region that takes the lead in implementing relevant policies will endow its economic development with leading and guiding advantages, for which it will become the vanguard or high-gradient region in terms of regional economic gradient development. The implementation strength and differences of competition policies in other regions make them located in different medium-gradient or low-gradient zones in the gradient structure, as shown by A, B and C in Figure 4-3.

Fourth, the formation of shared economy. The transference of regional economy from industrial economic competition orientation to urban economic competition orientation, and then to innovative economic competition orientation is a long historical process. However, all kinds of public goods jointly created and provided by our economy and society will eventually make the shared economy popularized and economic growth coordinated among regions. As shown in Figures 4-3, although competition and cooperation mutually drive economic growth and there are differences in the economy of different regions, the orderly transverse extension and the coordinated longitudinal transference will eventually make win-win cooperation mainstream.

There are four economic theories corresponding to the gradient transference model of regional economic competition.

First, the theory of industrial effect. In the growth stage dominated by industrial economy, a region with internal elements and external conditions will be the first to achieve industrial development, and then establish industrial agglomeration effects and regional competitive advantages.

Second, the theory of urban extension. In the growth stage dominated by urban economy, the driving force for regional economic growth mainly comes from investment, development, and construction in terms of urban infrastructure, urban-rural integration, and intelligent city.

Third, the theory of innovation-driven development. In the growth stage dominated by innovative economy, a region may establish its innovative advantages by taking the lead in timely and effectively carrying out various innovations.

Fourth, the theory of coordinated development. In the growth stage dominated by shared economy, regional economy follows the trajectory from "prioritized competition to competition and cooperation and then to win-win cooperation", facilitating various regions to realize coordinated development.

The author would like to clarify the following viewpoints.

(1) The theory of four stages of competitive economic growth is both correlated with and different from Porter's theory of "four stages of economic development". The author draws on Porter's theory of "four stages of economic development" in methodology. However, these two theories involve different competition entities. The competition entity elaborated by the author is not the micro entity: enterprise, but the mezzo entity: regional government.

三是梯度结构或二八现象。在区域产业经济、城市经济和创新经济的竞争发展中，先行推动相关政府政策措施的区域，其经济发展具有领先优势和导向优势，为区域经济梯度发展的前锋或高梯度区域，各个区域竞争政策措施的力度和差异，使其在梯度结构中居于不同的中梯度区域或低梯度区域。例如图4-3中A、B、C区域就不同于其他区域的格局。

四是共享经济的形成。区域经济从产业经济竞争导向向城市经济竞争导向推移，再向创新经济竞争导向推移，是个漫长的历史进程，但人类经济社会共同创造和提供的各类公共产品，终将能驱动共享经济的普及并促成区域间经济增长的协同发展。如图4-3所示，竞争与合作相互推动经济增长，区域经济存在差异，但其横向推移有序，纵向扩展协同，最终合作共赢逐渐成为主流方向。

与区域经济竞争梯度推移模型相对应，存在四种经济学说。

第一，产业效应说。在产业经济驱动主导的增长阶段，具备产业发展内在因素和外在条件的区域率先发展，形成产业集聚效应和区域竞争优势。

第二，城市扩展说。在城市经济驱动主导的增长阶段，区域经济增长的动力主要来自城市基础设施、城乡一体化和智能城市这三个层次的投资、开发和建设。

第三，创新驱动说。在创新经济驱动主导的增长阶段，区域率先、及时、有效地开展各种创新，形成创新优势。

第四，协同发展说。在共享经济驱动主导的增长阶段，区域经济沿着"以竞争为主→竞争合作→合作共赢"的轨迹，促使各区域协同发展。

至此，笔者想说明以下几点。

(1) 竞争型经济增长四阶段论与波特的"经济发展四个阶段"理论，既有联系又有区别。笔者在方法论上借鉴了波特的"经济发展四个阶段"理论；但二者涉及的竞争主体截然不同，笔者阐述的竞争主体不是微观领域的活动主体——企业，而是中观领域的活动主体——区域政府。

(2) To note that the division of the four stages is theoretically feasible, but difficult to fully implement in practice.

(3) The "competitive advantage theory" advocated by the author is the fundamental path to overcome the "comparative advantage trap".

Therefore, the author believes that guided by competition and driven by innovation, we can create a "coordinated, cooperative, and innovative" development path by transforming comparative advantages into integrated advantages.

Here are some cases.

◎ **Case 4-1**

The Guangdong Provincial Party Committee and Provincial Government have issued the *Opinions on Promoting Coordinated Regional Development in the Whole Province by Building a New Pattern of Regional Development of the "One Core, One Belt, and One Zone"*, which emphasizes that we should strive to enhance the radiating and driving capabilities of the Pearl River Delta region and the endogenous development momentum of its eastern and western wings and its northern ecological development zone, achieve coordinated regional economic development, equalize basic public services, provide relatively balanced access to infrastructure, realize roughly equivalent basic living standards and beautiful and safe ecological environment for the people, make development more balanced and coordinated, and strive to "be at the forefront of China in four aspects".

◎ **Case 4-2**

China's national economic layout and regional development strategies can be summarized as the "three regions", the "two basins", and the "Belt and Road". The "three regions" refer to the Beijing-Tianjin-Hebei coordinated development strategy, the integration strategy of Yangtze River Delta, and the strategy of Guangdong-Hong Kong-Macao Greater Bay Area. The "two basins" refer to the ecological protection and high-quality development of the Yangtze River Economic Belt and the Yellow River Basin. The "Belt and Road" refer to the Silk Road Economic

Belt and the Maritime Silk Road. China has proposed new development concepts for the new development stage, thus constituting new development patterns: ①a trend of going towards the development of new industries and industrial-urban complexes occurs; ②a trend of developing mega urban areas and city clusters occurs; ③a trend of regional and virtual clusters occurs; ④a trend of integrated development of special economic regions and important carriers of global economic enclaves occurs.

(2) 要注意，四阶段的划分在理论上是可行的，但在实践中是难以完全实现的。

(3) 笔者倡导的"竞争优势理论"，是克服"比较优势陷阱"的根本路径。

所以，笔者认为，以竞争为引领，以创新为驱动，将比较优势转为集成优势，将能开创出一条"协同合作创新"的发展之路。

下文是几个具体案例。

◎ 案例 4-1

中国广东省委和省政府印发《关于构建"一核一带一区"区域发展新格局促进全省区域协调发展的意见》，强调要着力增强珠三角地区辐射带动能力及东西两翼地区和北部生态发展区内生发展动力，实现区域经济协调发展、基本公共服务均等化、基础设施通达程度比较均衡、人民基本生活保障水平大体相当、生态环境美丽安全，提高发展平衡性和协调性，奋力实现"四个走在全国前列"。

◎ 案例 4-2

中国的国家经济布局与区域发展战略，可简略归结为三区、两流域和"一带一路"等。三区为京津冀协同发展战略、长三角一体化战略、粤港澳大湾区战略；两流域为长江经济带和黄河流域生态保护和高质量发展；"一带一路"为丝绸之路经济带和海上丝绸之路。中国立足新发展阶段，贯彻新发展理念，构建新发展格局：①出现了新产业发展和产城综合体趋势；②出现了巨型城市区域和城市群发展趋势；③出现了区域化集群和虚拟化集群演化趋势；④出现了特殊经济区域与全球经济飞地重要载体融合发展趋势。

VII. New Engine for Economic Growth

The author has repeatedly called for a region or a country to play a major role in the field of resource generation. Taking secondary resources in the field of resource generation, namely the investment, development, and construction of urban infrastructure at three levels, as an example, the author believes that the growth stage dominated by urban economy has arrived for the following reasons.

First, the construction of an interconnected transportation infrastructure network in rural areas is forming an orderly structure, thereby promoting the development of urban-rural integration. The construction of transportation infrastructure, municipal infrastructure, energy infrastructure, water conservancy infrastructure, information infrastructure, and environmental protection infrastructure is laying a solid foundation for cultivating new economic growth points and will keep generating significant economic and social effects.

Second, the construction of new infrastructure will also boost a new round of growth in the real economy. It is reflected in the following three aspects. ①Information infrastructure. It mainly refers to the infrastructure generated in the evolution of information technology, such as the communication network infrastructure represented by 5G, IoT, industrial internet and satellite internet, the new technology infrastructure represented by artificial intelligence, cloud computing and blockchain, and the computing infrastructure represented by data center and intelligent computing center. ②Converged infrastructure. It mainly refers to the converged infrastructure, such as intelligent transportation infrastructure and intelligent energy infrastructure, that is formed by transforming and upgrading conventional infrastructure through in-depth application of Internet, big data, artificial intelligence and other technologies. ③Innovative infrastructure. It mainly refers to the infrastructure with public welfare attributes that support scientific research, technological development, and product development, such as major science and technology infrastructure, science and education infrastructure, and industrial technology innovation infrastructure.

Third, the global population has been converging on large cities for over half a century. City size has obvious positive correlations with economic efficiency, per capita urban output, and urban population. This is the case for the United States, Japan, Korea, Singapore, Australia, and Canada, whose economic activities are concentrated in large metropolitan circles and economic output is greater in large cities.

Meanwhile, countries around the world have introduced the market mechanism to the field of infrastructure investment and financing. Public-private partnership is a typical case.

七、经济增长新引擎

本书中，笔者反复呼吁，一个区域或一个国家，应在资源生成领域大有作为。仍以资源生成领域的次生性资源，即对城市基础设施三个层次的投资、开发、建设为例，笔者认为城市经济驱动主导的增长阶段已经来临。

第一，互联互通的农村交通基础设施网络建设，正在形成有序的结构，推动城乡一体化的发展。交通基础设施建设、市政基础设施建设、能源基础设施建设、水利基础设施建设、信息基础设施建设、环保基础设施建设等，正为培育新的经济增长点奠定牢固的基础，并将持续产生巨大的经济效应和社会效应。

第二，新型基础设施建设也将带动实体经济新一轮增长。新型基础设施建设主要包括三个方面内容。一是信息基础设施。主要是指基于新一代信息技术演化生成的基础设施，比如，以5G、物联网、工业互联网、卫星互联网为代表的通信网络基础设施，以人工智能、云计算、区块链等为代表的新技术基础设施，以数据中心、智能计算中心为代表的算力基础设施等。二是融合基础设施。主要是指深度应用互联网、大数据、人工智能等技术，支撑传统基础设施转型升级，进而形成的融合基础设施，比如，智能交通基础设施、智慧能源基础设施等。三是创新基础设施。主要是指支撑科学研究、技术开发、产品研制的具有公益属性的基础设施，比如，重大科技基础设施、科教基础设施、产业技术创新基础设施等。

第三，从世界范围看，近半个多世纪，全球人口在向大城市集聚。城市规模和经济效率、人均城市产出、城市人口规模有明显的正相关关系。美国、日本、韩国、新加坡、澳大利亚、加拿大等都是如此，其经济活动聚集在大的都市圈，大城市的经济产出更大。

同时，世界各国已将市场机制引入基础设施的投融资领域，其中公共私营

First, it introduces the competitive mechanism and promotes the construction of government credibility. Second, it alleviates the funding shortage caused by insufficient government fiscal resources, and speeds up infrastructure construction and utility development. Third, it fully stimulates the initiative and creativity of foreign and private enterprises, and improves projects' operational efficiency and service quality. Fourth, it significantly advances the improvement of market laws and regulations. Fifth, it boosts technology transfer. Sixth, it helps cultivate professionals. Seventh, it stimulates the financial market to develop. Eighth, it has reduced the capital expenditure of foreign and private enterprises, helping them "launch big projects with small amount of investment". Ninth, it utilizes the characteristics of off-balance-sheet financing to reduce investors' debt burden. Tenth, it makes use of the characteristics of limited recourse to reasonably allocate risks, strengthen the control of project benefits, and maintain a high rate of return on investment (compared with full recourse). Currently, there are three modes of urban development in various countries around the world: TOD, namely transit-oriented development; SOD, namely service-oriented development; EOD, namely ecology-oriented development. It is particularly worth discussing that the "PPP+EOD" mode will boost urban innovative development.

The *Development Report on G20 (2016—2017)* mentions that the significant highlight of economic operation is infrastructure investment and construction and believes that it is an important engine to drive global economic recovery and sustainable growth for the following reasons. First, there is a current huge gap caused by insufficient supply of infrastructure in emerging and developing economies, while the existing infrastructure in developed economies is aging, for which there is a significant demand for infrastructure construction in all countries. Second, in a period of global economic downturn and lack of investment efficiency, strengthening infrastructure investment, especially promoting and optimizing high-quality investment, will provide a strong driving force for economic growth in the short and long term, and help create jobs and raise productivity. Third, as part of the new growth strategy, increasing infrastructure investment is a common focus of the G20 and a key issue at the G20 summit. Fourth, the World Bank announced the establishment of the Global Infrastructure Facility in October 2014, aiming to promote complex PPP infrastructure projects and drive the private sector to play a role in infrastructure investment. Fifth, in recent years, the economic cooperation among BRICS and in Asia has attached great importance to joint infrastructure construction and achieved practical cooperation results, such as BRICS New Development Bank, Asian Infrastructure Investment Bank, etc. Sixth, GIH predicts that by 2030, there will be an investment gap of USD 10 trillion to USD 20 trillion in the infrastructure investment market, which will cause a negative impact on the global economic development prospects. As

合作制方式就是一个典型的案例。第一，它引入竞争机制，促进了政府诚信建设；第二，它缓解了政府财力不足导致的资金短缺困境，加快了基础设施建设和公共事业发展；第三，它充分发挥了外商及民营企业的能动性和创造性，提高了项目运营效率和服务质量；第四，它有效促进了市场法律法规制度的完善；第五，它促进了技术转移；第六，它培养了专业人才；第七，它促进了金融市场的发展；第八，对外商及民营企业而言，它减少了他们的资本金支出，实现了"小投入做大项目"；第九，它利用表外融资的特点，减轻了投资者的债务负担；第十，它利用有限追索权的特点，合理分配风险，加强了对项目收益的控制，保持了较高的投资收益率（对比完全追索权）。现阶段，世界各国城市的发展呈现出三种模式：TOD——公交导向型发展模式；SOD——公共服务导向型发展模式；EOD——生态环境导向型发展模式。尤其值得探讨的是，"PPP+EOD"模式将推动城市创新发展。

《二十国集团(G20)经济热点分析报告(2016—2017)》也提到经济运行的显著亮点是基础设施的投资建设，认为它是驱动世界经济复苏和可持续增长的重要引擎。原因有以下几个。第一，当前新兴经济体和发展中经济体的基础设施供给明显不足，存在巨大缺口，而发达经济体的现有基础设施又逐步老化，各国都有很大的基础设施建设需求；第二，在全球经济不景气、缺乏投资效率的时期，加强基础设施投资，尤其是推动并优化高质量投资，无论在短期还是在长期，都将为经济增长提供强大的动力支持，也有利于创造就业和提高生产力；第三，作为新增长战略的一部分，增加基础设施投资也是二十国集团共同关注的焦点，是二十国集团峰会的重点议题；第四，世界银行2014年10月宣布建立全球基础设施基金，旨在促进复杂的公私合作经营的基础设施项目实施，同时推动私营部门在基础设施投资中发挥作用；第五，近年来金砖国家、亚洲区域的经济合作也都非常重视基础设施领域的共同建设，并取得了务实合作成果，建立了金砖国家新开发银行、亚洲基础设施投资银行等；第六，据全球基础设施中心预测，到2030年，基础设施投资市场将存在10万亿美元至20万亿美元的投资缺口，对全球经

a result, GIH called on various governments in 2016 to refocus on infrastructure investment and exploring development opportunities with great investment potential, so as to boost the global economy. It is foreseeable that global infrastructure construction is ushering in a new round of development opportunities and will become an important engine for global economic recovery and sustainable growth.

As such, the author puts forward the following suggestions.

(1) We should create a new engine for global investment. First, promote supply-side structural reform and new industrialization, and speed up agricultural modernization. Second, increase the investment in infrastructure construction, advance new urbanization and modernization of infrastructure, and boost the development and construction of intelligent cities. Third, increase the investment in scientific and technological projects. Fourth, strengthen ancillary businesses of finance.

(2) We should create a new engine for global innovation. First, promote the innovation in ideological public goods or concepts. Second, promote the innovation in material public goods or technology. Third, promote the innovation in organizational public goods or management. Fourth, promote the innovation in institutional public goods or rules.

(3) We should create a new engine for global regulations. First, establish rules for a peaceful and stable international security order. Second, establish rules for fair and efficient international economic competition. Third, establish rules for international common governance based on win-win cooperation. We ought to construct the community with a shared future for mankind in the process of safeguarding and practicing multilateralism.

Hence, it can be concluded as follows:

(1) A region or a country should put into practice the theory of competitive advantage in different development stages of market economy as it is the fundamental path to overcome the trap of comparative advantage.

(2) Regional government competition has different indicator functions in the four different stages. Regional government's behaviors should not only have different focuses in different stages, but also strive to form a "positive effect plus positive effect" with the indicator functions of enterprises in different stages.

(3) Regional economic competition has shown gradient transference. The author believes that the "equilibrium" of regional development highly valued by economists

should not be a planar "equilibrium", but a gradient "equilibrium".

(4) If a region or a country intends to achieve great success in the field of resource generation, it should strive to create new engines for investment, innovation, and rules, and jointly help human society march towards a stage driven by win-win cooperation.

济发展前景将带来不利影响。因此，在 2016 年，全球基础设施中心发出了倡议，号召各国政府重新把注意力放在基础设施投资领域，开拓极具投资潜力的发展机遇，提振全球经济。可以预见，全球基础设施建设正迎来一轮新的发展机遇，并将成为驱动世界经济复苏和可持续增长的重要引擎。

为此，笔者提出以下几点倡议。

(1) 应构建全球投资新引擎。第一，推进供给侧结构性改革，推动新型工业化并加快农业现代化；第二，加大基础设施投资建设，推进新型城镇化、基础设施现代化，同时推进智能城市开发建设；第三，加大科技项目投入；第四，提升金融配套能力。

(2) 应构建全球创新新引擎。第一，推进思想性公共物品即理念的创新；第二，推进物质性公共物品即技术的创新；第三，推进组织性公共物品即管理的创新；第四，推进制度性公共物品即规则的创新。

(3) 应构建全球规则新引擎。第一，构建和平、稳定的国际安全秩序规则；第二，构建公平、有效率的国际经济竞争规则；第三，构建合作、共赢的国际共同治理规则。在维护和践行多边主义的进程中，推动构建人类命运共同体。

至此，本章得出如下结论。

(1) 一个区域或一个国家，在市场经济发展的不同阶段，应践行竞争优势理论，它是克服比较优势陷阱的根本路径。

(2) 区域政府竞争在四个不同阶段有不同的指标函数，区域政府行为取向既应在不同阶段有不同侧重，又应力争与企业不同阶段的指标函数形成"正正叠加"效应。

(3) 区域经济竞争形成梯度推移状况。对于经济学界高度重视的区域发展"均衡"，笔者认为它不可能是一种平面性的"均衡"，而应该是一种梯度结构的"均衡"。

(4) 一个区域或一个国家，在资源生成领域大有作为，应努力开创投资新引擎、创新新引擎和规则新引擎，共同推动人类社会朝着合作共赢的共享驱动阶段迈进。

Chapter V

Dual Entities of Market Economy and Three Mezzoeconomic Laws

Chapter I elaborates on resource generation or generative resources, including primary resources, secondary resources, and retrograde resources. The government has formed the supply-side troika (supply of factor, supply of environment, and supply of market) through investment and development in the field of resource generation, thereby promoting the market economy to develop. The behaviors and roles of a government in the field of resource generation have increased the connotation of micro-enterprise factor of production, thus promoting the reform of industrial factor of production; increased the connotation of the mezzo-regional business environment, thus promoting the reform of regional business environment; expanded the scope and space of a country's market, thus constructing a brand new multi-layer market system. This chapter discusses government investment and development in the field of carbon emissions and carbon market, which are global hot topics now. The expansion and improvement of this field require the interaction among countries, regions, and enterprises, as well as the dual efforts of governments and enterprises in the market.

I. Carbon Emissions and Carbon Market (Case)

In the field of resource generation, six greenhouse gases including carbon dioxide are referred to as retrograde resources.

第五章
市场经济双重主体与中观经济三大定律

在第一章，我们已经阐述，资源生成，即生成性资源，至少包括原生性资源、次生性资源和逆生性资源三大类。政府在资源生成领域的投资开拓，形成了供给侧三驾马车——要素供给、环境供给、市场供给，助推着市场经济发展。政府在资源生成领域的行为作用，扩大了微观企业生产要素的内涵，引申了产业生产要素的变革；扩大了中观区域营商环境的内涵，推动了区域营商环境的变革；扩大了一国市场作用的领域和空间，构建了全新的多层次市场体系。本章以当前世界各国热门议题——碳排放、碳市场为例，探讨政府对该领域的投资开拓。对该领域的拓展与完善，需要国家、区域、企业三者关联互动，需要政府与企业在市场中的双重作用力。

一、碳排放与碳市场（案例）

在资源生成领域，二氧化碳等六种温室气体被称为逆生性资源。

In December 1997, the third meeting of the members of the United Nations Framework Convention on Climate Change was held in Kyoto, Japan, and formulated the *Kyoto Protocol to the United Nations Framework Convention on Climate Change*. In order to urge various countries to achieve the target of reducing greenhouse gas emissions, *Kyoto Protocol to the United Nations Framework Convention on Climate Change* sets up three flexible cooperation mechanisms for this purpose, allowing developed countries to complete their emission reduction tasks by taking flexible measures such as the carbon emission permit trading market, and helping developing countries obtain relevant technical and financial support, as shown in Figure 5-1.

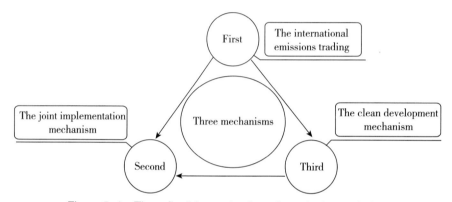

Figure 5-1 Three flexible mechanisms for reducing emissions

Carbon emission permit targets at carbon emissions generated by both the public sector and the private sector. The purpose of issuing carbon emission permits is to effectively curb the emissions of six harmful GHGs, and more importantly, maintaining living standards and ecological environment for the public.

Carbon emission permit trading market can be divided into mandatory trading market and voluntary trading market in view of its legal basis; quota trading market and project trading market in view of the traded object; floor trading market and OTC market in view of the organizational form; the initial allocation market of carbon quota, the spot trading market of carbon quota, and the trading market of carbon futures and carbon financial derivatives in view of its hierarchy.

Carbon emission permit trading system is divided into the following levels, as shown in Table 5-1.

1997年12月，联合国气候变化框架公约参加国三次会议在日本京都制定了《联合国气候变化框架公约》京都议定书。为了促进各国完成温室气体减排目标，该议定书建立了旨在减排的三个灵活合作机制，允许发达国家通过碳排放权交易市场等灵活措施完成减排任务，而发展中国家可以获得相关的技术和资金支持，如图5-1所示。

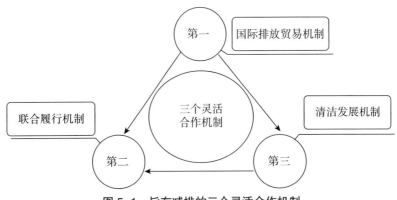

图5-1 旨在减排的三个灵活合作机制

在此，碳排放权发放的对象不仅包括公共部门产生的碳排放量，还包括私人部门产生的碳排放量；碳排放权发放的目的不仅在于有效遏制以二氧化碳为主的六种有害气体的排放量，更重要的是保障社会民众的生活水准和生态环境。

根据建立的法律基础，碳排放权交易市场可以划分为强制交易市场与自愿交易市场；根据交易对象，碳排放权交易市场可以划分为配额交易市场与项目交易市场；根据组织形式，碳排放权交易市场可以划分为场内交易市场与场外交易市场；根据交易市场层次，碳排放权交易市场可以划分为碳配额初始分配市场、碳配额现货交易市场、碳期货和碳金融衍生品交易市场。

根据碳排放权交易的市场层次，可将碳市场体系分为以下层次，如表5-1所示。

Table 5-1   Hierarchy of Carbon Market System

Market level	Traded object	Participant	Main functions
Initial allocation market	Initial allocation of quotas	Governments and emission control enterprises (including new projects)	Creation of carbon quotas
Spot trading market	Spot trading of quotas	Emission control enterprises and other qualified investors	Basic price discovery and resource circulation
The trading market for futures and financial derivatives	Carbon futures, carbon options, and other carbon financial derivatives	Emission control enterprises, financial institutions, and other qualified investors	Price discovery, hedging, and risk avoidance

Currently, the initial allocation markets for carbon emission permits in China is generally handled by the provincial development and reform commissions for quota distribution through free allocation and paid allocation. Paid allocation follows the principle of "pay for quotas, equal rights and prices", and is carried out with a closed bidding mechanism.

Various countries around the world determine "carbon pricing" or "carbon price" in two ways. One is a "carbon tax", which is a tax on carbon dioxide emissions. The other is requiring enterprises to obtain carbon dioxide emission permits and allowing them to transfer carbon dioxide emission permits, that is, total quantity control and emission permit.

The author believes that the following three types of pricing methods in finance can be used for quota allocation of carbon emission permits in the initial allocation market.

First, the average cost pricing method. Regional government may adopt the pricing method that maximizes economic benefits while maintaining a balance of income and expenditure among various carbon emitting entities.

Second, the two-part pricing method. The pricing system consists of two factors: the basic fee paid on a monthly or annual basis unrelated to carbon emissions, and the fee paid for carbon emissions.

Third, the load pricing method. Set different prices in view of the needs of different time periods. Set the highest charge at the peak of carbon emissions, and the lowest when carbon emissions hit bottom.

Therefore, the market area and space of a region or country should be expanded, developed and bettered. The development path of the carbon market is: carbon emissions → issuance of carbon emission permit → trading of carbon emission permit → carbon commodities → carbon market → development and improvement of the carbon market system hierarchy.

Paris Agreement is a stronger and newer agreement based on the *United Nations Framework Convention on Climate Change* and the *Kyoto Protocol to the United Nations Framework Convention on Climate Change*. *Paris Agreement* does not intend to adopt an

表 5-1　碳市场体系层次结构

市场层级	交易对象	参与主体	主要功能
初始分配市场	配额初始分配	政府、控排企业（含新建项目）	创设碳配额
现货交易市场	配额现货交易	控排企业及其他合格投资者	基础价格发现、资源流转
期货与金融衍生品交易市场	碳期货、碳期权及其他碳金融衍生品等	控排企业、金融机构及其他合格投资者	价格发现、套期保值和规避风险

现阶段，中国的碳排放权初始分配市场一般由各省发展和改革委员会进行配额发放，采取无偿分配和有偿分配两种方式。其中，有偿分配遵循配额有偿、同权同价的原则，以封闭式竞价机制的方式进行。

而世界各国，确定"碳定价"或者"碳价格"的方法有两种：一是"碳税"，即对二氧化碳排放征税；二是要求企业有二氧化碳的排放许可证，并允许转让，即总量管制并允许排放权交易。

在初始分配市场，笔者认为，可以将财政学中的以下三类定价法用于碳排放权的配额分配。

第一，平均成本定价法。区域政府在保持各碳排放主体收支平衡的情况下，采取尽可能使经济福利最大化的定价方式。

第二，二部定价法。由两种要素构成定价体系，一是与碳排放量无关的按月或年支付的基本费，二是按碳排放量支付的从量费。

第三，负荷定价法。根据不同时间段或时期的需要，制订不同的价格，碳排放量最高峰时，收费最高；碳排放量最低时，收费最低。

这里，就有一个区域或一个国家的市场领域和空间的拓展、建设与完善的问题。碳市场的发展路径为：碳排放→碳排放权凭证发放→碳排放权凭证交易→碳商品→碳市场→碳市场体系层次的发展与完善。

《巴黎协定》是基于《联合国气候变化框架公约》和《联合国气候变化框架公约》京都议定书的一个更强有力、更新的协议。《巴黎协定》不是采取一种绝

absolute rule to promote the emission reduction of all countries, but a bottom-up approach that stimulates "independent contribution" to drive each country to make more efforts in reducing emission. The global climate change governance system is built on the *United Nations Framework Convention on Climate*, the *Kyoto Protocol to the United Nations Framework Convention on Climate Change*, and the *Paris Agreement*.

Let's take EU and China as examples to explain the methods for reducing carbon emissions.

The spot commodities in the EU carbon market include carbon emission quotas and certified emission reductions; and derivatives include the futures contract for certified emission reductions, the options contract for certified emission reductions, the futures contract for carbon emission quotas, and the options contract for carbon emission quotas.

The development of EU carbon market can be divided into the following four stages.

The first stage (2005—2007): The EU carbon emission trading system was officially put into operation, and it is the largest carbon emission trading market in the world.

The second stage (2008—2012): the EU carbon emission trading amount accounted for 99.3% of the global quota trading market, and held a dominant pricing power in the international carbon market.

The third stage (2013—2020): the scope of emission reduction was extended to petroleum and chemical industries.

The fourth stage (2021—2030): all quotas will be allocated through paid auctions by 2027.

EU is expected to achieve carbon neutrality by 2050.

China's carbon market system construction began with pilot projects in eight provinces and cities. In 2011, carbon emission trading pilot projects were launched in Beijing, Tianjin, Shanghai, Guangdong, Shenzhen, Hubei and Chongqing. In 2016, Fujian launched the carbon emission trading market, which was the eighth carbon emission trading pilot in China.

The development of China's carbon market can be divided into the following three stages.

2014—2016 was the preliminary preparation stage of the carbon emission permit trading market.

2016—2019 was the official launch stage of the carbon emission permit trading market.

The high-speed operation stage of promoting the development of the carbon emission permit trading market began in 2019.

In October 2020, the Ministry of Ecology and Environment, the National Development and Reform Commission, the People's Bank of China, the China Banking and Insurance Regulatory Commission, and the China Securities Regulatory Commission jointly issued the *Guiding Opinions on Promoting Investment and Financing in Response to Climate Change*. In December 2020, the Ministry of Ecology and Environment issued the *Measures for the*

对的准则来推动各国减排，而是更多地采取一种自下而上、"自主贡献"的激励方式，推动每个国家做出更多的减排努力。全球气候变化治理体系建立在《联合国气候变化框架公约》，以及《联合国气候变化框架公约》京都议定书和《巴黎协定》的基础上，它们共同成为全球气候变化治理体系中的一部分。

以欧盟与中国为例，介绍碳气体减排的方法。

欧盟碳市场的现货品种有碳排放配额和核证减排量；衍生品种有核证减排量期货合约、核证减排量期权合约、碳排放配额期货合约和碳排放配额期权合约。

欧盟的碳市场发展可以分为以下四个阶段。

第一阶段(2005—2007年)，欧盟碳交易体系正式运行，是世界上最大的碳交易市场。

第二阶段(2008—2012年)，欧盟碳交易金额占全球配额交易市场的99.3%，掌握着国际碳市场主要定价权。

第三阶段(2013—2020年)，减排范围扩大至石油、化工等行业。

第四阶段(2021—2030年)，2027年，将实现全部配额的有偿拍卖分配。

在未来，2050年，欧盟预期将实现碳中和。

中国的碳市场体系建设是从八个省市的试点开始的。2011年，确定在北京、天津、上海、广东、深圳、湖北、重庆开展碳交易试点；2016年，福建启动碳交易市场，作为国内第八个碳交易试点。

中国的碳市场发展可以分为以下三个阶段。

2014—2016年，为碳排放权交易市场的前期准备阶段。

2016—2019年，为碳排放权交易市场的正式启动阶段。

2019年后，为推动碳排放权交易市场发展的高速运转阶段。

2020年10月，生态环境部、国家发改委、中国人民银行、银保监会和证监会共同发布《关于促进应对气候变化投融资的指导意见》；2020年12月，生态

Management of Carbon Emissions trading (*for Trial Implementation*) and the *Implementation Plan for the Setting and Distribution of Total Amount of National Carbon Emission Permit Trading Quotas* (*Power Generation Industry*) *from 2019 to 2020*. In February 2021, Xi Jinping presided over the 18th meeting of the Commission for Further Reform Under the CPC Central Committee, and emphasized that we should establish and improve an economic system for green and low-carbon cycle development, and formulate a plan of action to reach the peak of carbon emissions by 2030. On October 12, 2021, Xi Jinping made a keynote speech at the leaders′ summit of CBD COP15 and pointed out that to achieve the goals of carbon peaking and carbon neutrality, China will successively release implementation plans and a series of supporting measures for carbon peaking in key areas and industries, and establish the "1+N" policy system for carbon peaking and carbon neutrality.

EU adopts a "up-bottom" and "synchronized futures and spot goods" path to construct a unified carbon market system across its member countries. China adopts a "bottom-up" path, or in other words, the path of "pilot before promotion, regional pilot before national pilot, and spot goods before futures".

China′s goal of carbon emission reduction, carbon emission trading and carbon neutrality are: carbon emission peaking by 2030; carbon neutrality by 2060.

In practice, we must address three issues: ①how to establish an "ecological compensation system"; ②how to improve the "ecological compensation mechanism"; ③how to promote "financial transactions in carbon market".

On the one hand, China is the second largest GHG emitter in the world and the most promising emission reduction market. On the other hand, China is still constructing its carbon emission permit trading, with its market operation being improved. In addition to carbon spot trading, markets such as carbon forward and carbon futures are still under exploration and product development.

First, due to the lack of a unified platform for carbon emission trading, obvious market segmentation and insufficient liquidity, the price discovery mechanism has not yet been formed. The competent authorities in some pilot areas blindly emphasize the allocation of quotas and achieving the goal of mandatory emission reduction through performance, while neglecting the development of spot trading market. Meanwhile, China′s carbon market is still short of carbon derivatives such as futures and options that provide risk hedging and price management for enterprises, which has prevented the normal functioning of the carbon market.

Second, financial institutions are not highly participating in the carbon market, and there is a lack of carbon financial professionals. At present, China is short of organizations and professionals related to carbon finance, as well as the investment in carbon financial tools, carbon product project development, and operating modes. We lack systematic and

环境部发布《碳排放权交易管理办法(试行)》和《2019—2020年全国碳排放权交易配额总量设定与分配实施方案(发电行业)》;2021年2月,习近平主持召开中央全面深化改革委员会第十八次会议,强调建立健全绿色低碳循环发展的经济体系,统筹制定2030年前碳排放达峰行动方案;2021年10月12日,习近平在《生物多样性公约》第十五次缔约方大会领导人峰会上的主旨讲话指出,为推动实现碳达峰、碳中和目标,中国将陆续发布重点领域和行业碳达峰实施方案和一系列支撑保障措施,构建起碳达峰、碳中和"1+N"政策体系。

相比较而言,欧盟采用的是"自上而下"和"期货、现货同步"的跨成员国统一碳市场体系建设路径;而当前中国在碳市场体系建设路径的选择上,采用的是"自下而上"的方式,即"先试点后推广、先区域后全国、先现货后期货"的方式。

中国的碳减排、碳交易与碳中和的目标为:2030年前二氧化碳排放力争达到峰值;2060年努力争取实现碳中和。

这就在现实中提出了三个问题:①如何确立"生态补偿体系";②如何健全"生态补偿机制";③如何推动"碳市场金融交易"。

一方面,中国属全球第二大温室气体排放国,是最具潜力的减排市场。另一方面,中国还处于碳排放权交易的建设阶段,市场运作正在逐步健全,除碳现货交易已经正式启动外,碳远期、碳期货等市场还处于探索和产品研发之中。

首先,由于缺乏碳交易统一平台,市场分割明显,流动性不足,价格发现机制尚未形成。个别试点地区的业务主管部门一味强调配额的分配以及通过履约达到强制减排的目的而忽视了现货交易市场的发展;同时,中国碳市场至今还缺乏为企业提供风险对冲和价格管理的期货、期权等碳衍生品种,这使碳市场功能未能得到正常发挥。

其次,由于金融机构参与度不高,碳金融专业人才缺乏。目前中国有关碳金融业务的组织机构和专业人才短缺,对碳金融工具、碳产品项目开发、操作模式等投入不足,缺乏系统、规范的碳金融政策文件作为指导,更缺乏碳基金、碳期

standardized carbon finance policy documents that can act as guidance, as well as various financial derivatives such as carbon funds, carbon futures, and carbon options, not to mention risk sharing and benefit compensation mechanisms.

Last, China's carbon emission trading is not highly global due to our low-profile voice in the global carbon trading market. The carbon emission trading systems in eight provinces and cities in China have no mechanisms to connect with external markets. The pricing power of the clean development mechanism market is controlled by overseas financial institutions. RMB has not become a main settlement currency. China is the largest seller in the clean development mechanism market, but sits at the lowest end of the industry chain in the clean development mechanism market.

The characteristics of carbon market itself and international experience indicate that the effective path to build a carbon market system is unified trading, to ensure synchronous docking of spot and futures markets. Therefore, the author believes that China ought to carry out innovation in concept, institution, organization and technology on the basis of the existing pilot projects of carbon spot market in various provinces and cities. First, China should speed up the establishment of a unified domestic carbon spot market in an all-round way. Second, China should simultaneously establish a carbon futures exchange. Third, China should establish a sound and diversified carbon financial organization and service system. The concept of a national unified carbon market system architecture is shown in Figure 5-2.

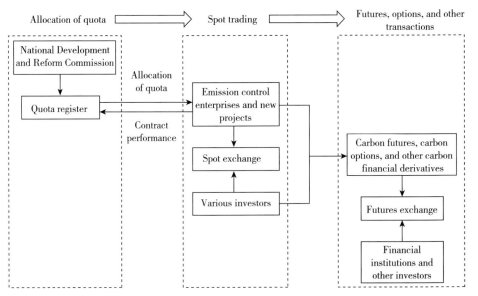

Figure 5-2　The Concept of a National Unified Carbon Market System Architecture

The author further believes that China should strengthen the top-level layout of carbon market construction: ①establish a sound carbon market system; ②create a carbon futures exchange; ③seize the discourse power in the Asian carbon futures market through standardization; ④strengthen the construction of rule of law, bundle carbon futures trading with RMB international settlement, and enhance the international status of RMB.

货、碳期权等各种金融衍生工具以及风险分担和利益补偿机制。

最后,由于在全球碳交易市场的话语权缺失,中国碳交易国际化程度不高。当前中国八省市的碳排放交易体系基本没有与外部市场连接的机制设置。清洁发展机制市场的定价权被国际金融机构掌握,人民币不是主要结算货币。中国是清洁发展机制市场的最大卖方,但处于清洁发展机制市场产业链的最低端。

碳市场本身的特性和国际经验均表明,碳市场体系建设的有效路径是统一交易,保证现货、期货市场同步对接。为此,笔者认为,中国应在现有各省市碳现货市场试点基础上,开展理念、制度、组织、技术的创新。第一,要全面提速建立统一的国内碳现货市场;第二,要同步创设碳期货交易所;第三,要建立健全多元化的碳金融组织服务体系。全国统一碳市场体系架构设想如图5-2所示。

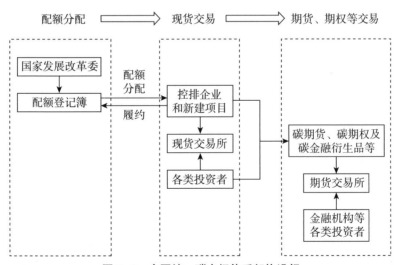

图5-2 全国统一碳市场体系架构设想

笔者进一步认为,中国应加强碳市场建设的顶层布局:①建立健全碳市场体系;②创建碳期货交易所;③以标准化建设为抓手,抢占亚洲碳期货市场话语权;④加强法治建设,捆绑碳期货交易与人民币国际结算,提升人民币的国际地位。

The internationalization of GBP went through several important milestones.

① Coal trading bundled with GBP payment and settlement.

② Government credit: issuance and management of treasury bond.

③ The establishment of the Bank of England.

④ The establishment of the GBP-gold standard.

⑤ The support of maritime power.

Coal trading bundled with GBP payment and settlement is a key element in this process. In the last 25 years of the 18th century, UK became the world's leader in trading power in the place of the Netherlands, and London became the most important financial center in the place of Amsterdam. Steam engine caused a series of technological revolutions and the leap from manual labor to power machine production. Coal became the main "food" for modern industry. The industrial revolution, the emergence and development of machine industry, and coal trading bundled with GBP payment and settlement made the GBP a key currency in international trade.

The internationalization of USD also went through several important milestones.

① The Bretton Woods Conference. After the Bretton Woods Conference, USD was linked to gold; the currencies of other countries were linked to USD; currencies of all countries were freely convertible; member states were not allowed to restrict the payment or settlement of current accounts of the balance of payments. As a result, USD was equivalent to gold in terms of position and became the main international reserve currency of various countries.

② The Marshall Plan. The Marshall Plan made USD fully involved in the international settlement process in Europe by establishing a multilateral payment system in Europe and combining remittance settlement with "conditional assistance".

③ Petroleum trading bundled with USD payment and settlement. During the fourth Middle East War, the United States allied with Saudi Arabia, the largest petroleum producer among the Arab countries, and signed an agreement with Saudi Arabia to make USD as the only pricing currency for petroleum, which was then agreed by other OPEC members. As a result, the United States gained a monopoly position in international petroleum trade pricing. On this basis, the United States also gained a monopoly position in the transactions of other commodities, thus further stabilizing the hegemony of USD.

Petroleum trading bundled with USD payment and settlement is a key element in this process. The reason why USD became the key currency in the place of GBP was the shift of core energy from coal to petroleum. In the 1970s, the United States reached an "unbreakable agreement" with Saudi Arabia, thereby making USD the sole currency for petroleum pricing. This provided the United States with international pricing power over petroleum commodities and USD standard in the global monetary structure.

纵观世界历史，英镑国际化的历程经过几个重要节点。
① 煤炭贸易绑定英镑支付结算；
② 政府信用——国债的发行与管理；
③ 英格兰银行成立；
④ 黄金－英镑本位制的确立；
⑤ 海域强权的支撑。

其中，煤炭贸易绑定英镑支付结算是个关键因素。18世纪的最后25年，英国取代荷兰成为世界领先的贸易强国，伦敦取代阿姆斯特丹成为最重要的金融中心。蒸汽机的问世引起一系列技术革命并实现从手工劳动向动力机器生产的飞跃转变，煤炭成为近代工业的主要"食粮"，工业革命及机器大工业的产生、发展，煤炭贸易绑定英镑支付结算使英镑成为国际贸易中的关键货币。

美元国际化的历程，也经历过几个重要节点。

① 布雷顿森林会议。布雷顿森林会议后，美元与黄金挂钩，其他国家货币与美元挂钩，各国货币自由兑换，会员国不得对国际收支经常项目的支付或清算加以限制。因此，美元处于等同于黄金的地位，成为各国外汇储备中最主要的国际储备货币。

② 马歇尔计划。马歇尔计划通过在欧洲建立多边支付体系，以及将汇兑结算与"有条件援助"相结合，使美元得以全面介入欧洲的国际结算环节。

③ 石油贸易绑定美元支付结算。第四次中东战争期间，美国选择阿拉伯国家中最大的石油产出国沙特阿拉伯作为盟友，与沙特阿拉伯签署协定，确定把美元作为石油的唯一计价货币，并得到了其他欧佩克成员国的同意。美国在国际石油贸易计价中获得了垄断地位。在此基础上，美国同样在其他大宗商品交易中获得了垄断地位，美元霸权进一步得到稳固。

其中，石油贸易绑定美元支付结算是个关键因素。美元取代英镑成为关键货币，受益于石油取代煤炭引起的核心能源的更迭。20世纪70年代，美国与沙特阿拉伯达成"不可动摇协议"，将美元确立为石油唯一计价货币。这确保了美国对石油大宗商品的国际定价权和国际货币格局中的美元本位制。

China is the second largest GHG emitter in the world and considered as the most promising emission reduction market by countries around the world. More and more enterprises will partake in carbon emission permit trading. According to the statistics released by the World Bank, the total volume of global carbon emission trading reached 1013 million tons in 2020, meaning that carbon became the world's largest trading market in the place of petroleum. We have sent away the coal-GBP international currency system and the petroleum-USD international currency system. China should seize the opportunity to establish a financial system for low-carbon economy development with Southeast Asia and other countries and regions by taking carbon emission trading—RMB as the carriers. In this way, China will be able to blaze a new trail of "corner overtaking" in which the internationalization of RMB rises in energy trade.

In order to seize this opportunity, China ought to strengthen its top-level layout, coordinate planning, and formulate relevant policies and measures, thereby expanding and constructing the transverse carbon market system as well as bettering the functions of the longitudinal carbon market system. The organic integration, coordination and unity of state and enterprise as well as government and market behavior are required. In particular, the following measures can be taken.

(1) Strengthen the cooperation with countries along the "Belt and Road" in terms of carbon market trading, bundle RMB with international settlement, build an international balance of payment structure for the current account and capital account deficits of countries along the "Belt and Road", and provide them with RMB liquidity.

(2) Develop the "Belt and Road" carbon market, increase the varieties of carbon emission trading, and enlarge the scale of RMB-bundled carbon emission trading.

(3) Urge Chinese-funded banks, fintech companies and Internet financial enterprises to speed up engaging in the "Belt and Road" countries, and raise the availability of RMB financial services.

(4) Deepen the "Belt and Road" regional carbon financial and monetary cooperation mechanism, extend the currency swap agreements with countries along the "Belt and Road", and provide them with liquidity from carbon emission permit trading bundled with RMB settlement through the swap mechanism.

(5) Speed up improving the carbon market system and standardizing the spot market;

create a carbon futures market; develop standards for carbon emissions, design standards for carbon emission trading, and build a carbon financial standard system that is consistent at home and abroad; improve the laws on protecting carbon asset property rights; develop national (international) regulatory guidelines for carbon finance markets; strive to achieve carbon peaking by 2030 and carbon neutrality by 2060.

中国是全球第二大温室气体排放国,也被世界各国认为是最具潜力的减排市场,有越来越多的企业参与碳排放权交易。根据世界银行测算,2020年全球碳交易总量达到10.13亿吨,超过石油成为世界第一大交易市场。在国际货币先后经历了煤炭－英镑、石油－美元这两个体系之后,若中国能抢占先机,以碳交易－人民币为载体,建立与东南亚等国家和地区的低碳经济发展的金融体系,那么将可以发展一条人民币国际化在能源贸易中崛起的"弯道超车"新路径。

为了抓住这一机遇,中国需要加强顶层布局,统筹谋划,制定相关政策和措施,既推动碳市场横向体系的拓展与建设,又推动碳市场纵向体系相关功能的健全与完善。它需要国家与企业、政府与市场行为的有机融合、协调统一。具体可以采取以下几个措施。

(1) 应加强与共建"一带一路"国家的碳市场交易合作,捆绑人民币国际结算,构建与共建"一带一路"国家经常项目和资本项目双逆差的国际收支结构,向共建"一带一路"国家提供人民币流动性。

(2) 应发展"一带一路"区域碳市场,丰富碳交易品种,扩大人民币捆绑碳交易的规模。

(3) 应促使中资银行、金融科技公司以及互联网金融企业加快进入"一带一路"国家,提高人民币金融服务的可获得性。

(4) 应深化"一带一路"区域碳金融和货币合作机制,扩大与"一带一路"国家的货币互换协议,通过互换机制为"一带一路"国家提供碳交易捆绑人民币结算的流动性。

(5) 加快完善碳市场体系,规范现货市场;创建碳期货市场;制定碳排放标准和设计碳交易标准,建设国内统一、国际接轨的碳金融标准体系;健全碳资产财产权保护法;制定碳金融市场国家(国际)监管准则;努力实现2030年前达到碳峰值,2060年前实现碳中和。

II. Modern Market Economy

In summary, we can see in the modern market economy that various fields of the transverse system are continuously extended and various functions of the longitudinal system are unceasingly bettered.

(I) Modern transverse market system

Like we see the quantity of factor of production increases from 2 to 6 (land, labor, capital, management, technology, and data) in industrial economy, the modern market system is also extended transversely from industrial economy to urban economy, and then to international economy (such as space economy, deep-sea economy, polar economy, and deep-exploration economy).

(II) Modern longitudinal market system

The modern longitudinal market system includes market factor system, market organization system, market law system, market supervision system, market environment system, and market infrastructure. It boasts the following characteristics.

(1) The formation of the longitudinal market system went through a progressive process.

(2) The six aspects of the longitudinal market system are unified.

(3) The six aspects of the longitudinal market system play their roles in an orderly way, which ensures the efficiency of the market system.

(4) The functions of the six aspects of the longitudinal market system are fragile.

(5) The six functions of the modern longitudinal market system are currently affecting or will soon affect the fields of the modern transverse market system.

Taking the United States as an example, we can see that the formation of the longitudinal market system is a progressive process. From 1776 to 1890, market liberalism got developed in the United States, which was mainly manifested in market factors and market organizations. In 1890, the first antitrust law in the United States was enacted, marking the beginning of establishing market legal system and market regulation. In the 1990s, with rapid development of the internet economy, the US market credit system and market infrastructure were further improved. It took more than 2 centuries for the United States to build and better a longitudinal market system.

二、现代市场经济

综上所述可见，现代市场经济存在横向体系中各个领域空间不断拓展、纵向体系中各项功能作用不断完善的问题。

（一）现代市场横向体系

正如产业经济中的生产要素从二要素到三要素、四要素，再到六要素(土地、劳动、资本、管理、技术、数据)一样，现代市场体系也在从产业经济向城市经济，再向国际经济(如太空经济、深海经济、极地经济、地球深探经济)等领域空间横向拓展。

（二）现代市场纵向体系

现代市场纵向体系包括市场要素体系、市场组织体系、市场法治体系、市场监管体系、市场环境体系和市场基础设施。其特点有以下几个。

(1) 现代市场纵向体系的形成，是个渐进的历史过程。

(2) 现代市场纵向体系的六个方面的内容是统一的。

(3) 现代市场纵向体系的六个方面的作用是有序的，有序的市场体系才是有效率的。

(4) 现代市场纵向体系的六个方面的功能又是脆弱的。

(5) 现代市场纵向体系的六个方面的功能，正在或即将作用于现代市场横向体系的各个领域。

以美国为例，我们可以看到现代市场纵向体系的形成是个渐进的历史过程。1776—1890年，美国早期市场自由主义经济发展，主要表现在市场要素与市场组织自身两大功能的活动上。1890年，美国第一部反垄断法颁布，开始逐步有了市场的法治与市场的监管。20世纪90年代，互联网经济快速发展，美国市场信用体系和市场基础设施才得到进一步的完善。可见，美国现代市场纵向体系的形成与完善也先后经历了二百多年的时间。

We also emphasize that the content, roles, and functions of the six aspects of the longitudinal market system are integral and impartible. First, the content is unified. The lack of content in a certain aspect will lead to defects of the market therein, which will further cause losses to the market and the country. Second, the roles are orderly. The price formation mechanisms of goods, factors, or projects are orderly; the formation mechanism of competition is orderly; and the formation mechanism of opening-up is orderly. Third, the functions are fragile. This is because of the lack of complete understanding among market entities, untimely policies, and the impact of economic globalization.

In fact, the functions of the six aspects of the modern longitudinal market system are currently acting on or will soon act on various fields of the modern transverse market system, thus forming three layers of the connotation of market economy operation: ①the reasonable core of market, namely market rules ②the spatial platform of market, namely market circulation; ③the operating conditions of market, namely market system.

The author believes that there are three market failures in the modern market system architecture: the "market mechanism defect", namely the defects in the functions of six aspects of the longitudinal market system; the "market mechanism gap", namely the absence of market mechanisms in the field of resource generation; the "market mechanism obstacle", which means that the interests of market entities deviate from market rules.

III. Mature Effective Government

The author believes that a mature effective government should achieve at least the following three points.

First, a mature effective government should grasp systematic concept and forward-looking thinking, or in other words, the government's foresighted leading. On the one hand, the government should respect market laws, maintain economic order, and effectively allocate resources; on the other hand, the government should participate in regional competition.

Second, a mature effective government should continue to build new development patterns. To plan, guide, support, coordinate, supervise, and manage the industrial economy; provide planning and layout, participate in construction, and achieve orderly management for the urban economy; achieve general underpinning, fairness, and practical improvement for the livelihood economy. Meanwhile, it is necessary to comprehensively grasp and coordinate the relationship between efficient market and effective government, the relationship between

我们同时强调，现代市场纵向体系六个方面的内容、作用和功能又是一个整体，是不能分割的。第一，内容是统一的。缺少哪个方面内容，就会带来市场哪一方面缺陷，造成市场与国家的损失。第二，作用是有序的。它表现在商品、要素或项目的价格形成机制是有序的；竞争形成机制是有序的；开放形成机制是有序的。第三，功能又是脆弱的。原因在于市场主体在认识上的不完整性、政策上的不及时性，以及经济全球化的冲击性。

现实中，现代市场纵向体系的六个方面的功能，正在作用或即将作用于现代市场横向体系的各个领域，形成市场经济运行的三个层次内涵：①市场的合理内核——市场规则；②市场的空间平台——市场流通；③市场的运作条件——市场体系。

笔者的研究结果是，在现代市场体系结构内，存在着三种市场失灵：一是"市场机制缺陷性"失灵，它表现在市场纵向体系六个方面功能存在缺陷；二是"市场机制空白性"失灵，它表现在资源生成领域市场机制缺位；三是"市场机制障碍性"失灵，它表现在市场主体利益与市场规则相背离。[①]

三、成熟有为政府

笔者认为，成熟有为政府至少应做到以下三个方面。

第一，要有系统性理念与前瞻性思考，即政府要超前引领。一方面，政府要尊重市场规律、维护经济秩序、有效调配资源；另一方面，政府要参与区域竞争。

第二，不断构建新发展格局。对产业经济，能够规划、引导、扶持、调节、监督、管理；对城市经济，能够规划布局、参与建设、有序管理；对民生经济，能够基本托底、公平公正、有效提升。同时需要统筹把握和协调发展有

---

① 陈云贤：《市场竞争双重主体论：兼谈中观经济学的创立与发展》，北京大学出版社，2020年，第217-221页。

the supply side and the demand side, and the relationship between domestic market and international market.

Third, a mature effective government should be able to promote the scientific and sustainable development of regional economy. For example, Foshan City, Guangdong Province seeks to use policies to promote industrial transformation and urban upgrading, and adopts the following five measures to boost sustainable development.

(1) Carry out "dual-transfer" and "cage swapping" to realize industrial transformation: close some projects, improve some projects, and cultivate some projects.

(2) Introduce large-scale projects to promote industrial upgrading.

(3) Boost technological progress and independent innovation.

(4) Utilize financial policies and measures to build industrial highlands.

(5) Promote the construction of "smart Foshan with integrated four modernizations", including the integration of informatization and industrialization; the integration of informatization and urbanization; the integration of informatization and internationalization.

The author believes that there are three government failures in fact. First, the government failure of "insufficient livelihood economy" or the "lack-of-cognition" failure, that is, the government regards the livelihood economy as a burden. Second, the government failure of "lacking industrial policy" or the "mistaken-cognition" failure, that is, the government does not intervene or intervenes improperly in the industrial economy. Third, the government failure of "urban construction gap" or the "cognitionless" failure, that is, the government does not play its allocating, participating, and marshoulding roles in the urban economy.

IV. Dual Entities of Market Competition

After analyzing carbon emissions and carbon market cases, we can see that a region or a country's transverse market system is constantly extending and longitudinal market system is continuously forming and improving, and that enterprises play a role in the micro field and regional governments play a role in the mezzo field. The author further concludes as follows.

效市场与有为政府的关系、供给侧与需求侧的关系、国内市场与国际市场的关系。

第三，能够推动区域经济科学可持续发展。广东省佛山市探索运用政策措施促进产业转型、城市升级，采用以下五大举措共同驱动可持续发展，就是一个很好的案例。

(1) 对产业转型采用"双转移"和"腾笼换鸟"：关转一批，提升一批，培植一批。

(2) 引进大项目，促进产业升级。

(3) 推动科技进步、自主创新。

(4) 运用金融政策和举措，建设产业高地。

(5) 推动"四化融合，智慧佛山"建设：促进信息化与工业化融合；促进信息化与城镇化融合；促进信息化与国际化融合。①

笔者经过研究认为，现实中存在三种政府失灵：一是"民生经济不足型"政府失灵，即政府"缺知型"的失灵，政府把民生经济当作一种负担；二是"产业政策缺失型"政府失灵，即政府"错知型"的失灵，政府对产业经济放任自流或干预失当；三是"城市建设空白型"政府失灵，即政府"无知型"的失灵，政府缺失对城市经济规划、参与、维序的作用。②

四、市场竞争双重主体

通过对碳排放与碳市场案例的分析，我们不仅看到了一个区域或一个国家的市场横向体系在不断拓展，市场纵向体系在不断形成与完善，还看到了企业在微观领域发挥着作用，区域政府在中观领域发挥着作用。为此，笔者进一步得出如下结论。

---

① 陈云贤：《市场竞争双重主体论：兼谈中观经济学的创立与发展》，第 222–226 页。
② 陈云贤：《市场竞争双重主体论：兼谈中观经济学的创立与发展》，第 227–229 页。

(I) There are two entities in market competition: regional government and enterprise

First, regional government and enterprise are the entities in resource allocation. Second, the competition mechanism always exists between regional government and enterprise, who are dual drives for regional economic development. Third, regional government and enterprise must take actions while respecting market rules. Fourth, both regional government and enterprise intend to maximize benefits in the first place.

(II) The dual entities of market competition are both separated and interdependent

First, enterprise competition is mainly manifested in the micro industrial economy field, while regional government competition is mainly manifested in the mezzo urban economy field, as shown in Figure 5-3. These two kinds of competition are seamlessly connected.

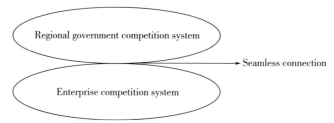

Figure 5-3 Relationship between the Dual Entities of Market Competition

Second, the core of enterprise competition falls on optimizing resource allocation in the case of resource scarcity, while the core of regional government competition optimizing resource allocation based on resource generation.

Third, the results of enterprise competition are similar to those of regional government competition as they both embody the phenomenon of 80/20 agglomeration.

V. Three Mezzoeconomic Laws

(1) The law of the phenomenon of 80/20 agglomeration. This law is featured in: co-growth of enterprise competition and regional government competition; different development trajectories of enterprise competition and regional government competition; and phenomenon

of 80/20 agglomeration always caused by enterprise competition and regional government competition. In the different economic development stages, driven by enterprise competition and regional government competition, the development of regional economies in various

(一)市场竞争存在区域政府和企业两大主体

第一,区域政府和企业都是资源调配的主体。第二,竞争机制在区域政府之间与企业之间始终存在,并成为区域经济发展的双重驱动力。第三,区域政府和企业的行为都必须在尊重市场规则的前提下展开。第四,区域政府和企业的最初目标都是利益最大化。

(二)市场竞争"双重主体"呈现相对独立又相互依存的关系

首先,企业竞争主要表现在微观产业经济领域,区域政府竞争主要表现在中观城市经济领域,两者无缝衔接,如图5-3所示。

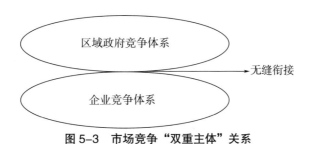

图5-3 市场竞争"双重主体"关系

其次,企业竞争的核心是在资源稀缺条件下的资源优化配置问题,区域政府竞争的核心是在资源生成基础上的资源优化配置问题。

最后,企业竞争的结果与区域政府竞争的结果相似,都有二八效应集聚律现象。

五、中观经济三大定律

(1)二八效应集聚律。此定律表现出三大特征:第一,企业竞争与区域政府竞争同生共长;第二,企业竞争与区域政府竞争的发展轨迹不同;第三,企业竞争与区域政府竞争最终都导致产生二八效应集聚律现象。随着不同经济发展阶段的历史进程,在企业竞争和区域政府竞争的双轮动力驱动下,世界各国区域经济

countries around the world is witnessing the agglomeration of industrial clusters, city clusters, and people's welfare in developed countries or developed regions.

(2) The law of gradient change equilibrium. This law operates in three stages. In the first stage, resource scarcity pairs with resource generation in the field of regional resource allocation. In the second stage, positive resources (primary and secondary resources) and negative resources (retrograde resources) are mutually constrained in the field of regional resource allocation. In the third stage, there is a shift from single regional economic growth goal to diversified regional economic growth goals. The law of gradient change equilibrium is reflected in both the balanced trend of industrial development, urban construction, and social progress in a certain region and that of industrial development, urban construction, and social progress among regions.

The participation of a regional government in competition leads to changes in the resource endowment of the region (especially the changes in advanced factors of production with economic development and resource input); changes in the industrial structure of the region (conventional industries, emerging industries, future low-carbon new technology industries); changes in industrial and supply chains of the region (digital industries, industrialization of digits, and comprehensive and full-chain transformation of existing industries); changes in industrial innovation capabilities of the region (new technologies, products, modes, business formats, and industries); changes in market environment, market field, and market space of the region. These changes push the economic competition among regions to do gradient transference.

(3) The law of coordination of competition and cooperation. This law is mainly reflected in the types of coordination in economic development among regions: coordinated policy; coordinated innovation; coordinated rules. In essence, this law refers to in different stages of regional economic development, various competition entities rely on various platforms such as industries, investment, and innovation to gather talents, capital, information, technology, and other factors for the development goals to achieve the coordination of competition policy, innovation-driven development, and competition rules, thereby breaching competition barriers and realizing effective cooperation and co-development.

Driven by the three laws of regional economic competition and development, the main behavioral orientations of a regional government in the four stages of economic development are shown in Table 5-2.

的发展，正逐渐出现先行发达国家或先行发展区域的产业集群、城市集群和民生福利越来越集中的现象。

(2) 梯度变格均衡律。此定律作用表现在三个阶段：第一阶段，区域的资源配置领域出现资源稀缺与资源生成相配对的阶段；第二阶段，区域的资源生成领域出现正向性资源(原生性资源和次生性资源)与负向性资源(逆生性资源)相掣肘的阶段；第三阶段，区域的经济增长目标由单一转向多元的阶段。梯度变格均衡律，既表现为某一区域产业发展、城市建设和社会民生进步的均衡性趋势，又表现为区域间产业发展、城市建设和社会民生进步的均衡性趋势。

区域政府参与竞争，使得区域的资源禀赋产生变化(特别是高级生产要素会随着经济发展和资源投入而发生变化)；使得区域的产业结构发生变化(传统产业、新兴产业、未来低碳绿色新技术产业)；使得区域的产业链、供应链产生变化(产业数字化、数字产业化，对现有产业的全方位、全角度、全链条改造)；使得区域的产业创新能力产生变化(新技术、新产品、新模式、新业态、新产业)；使得区域的市场环境、市场领域和市场空间等产生变化。它推动着区域之间的经济竞争梯度推移。

(3) 竞争合作协同律。此定律主要体现在区域间经济发展的三大协同上：第一，政策的协同性；第二，创新的协同性；第三，规则的协同性。竞争合作协同律，实质就是在区域经济发展的不同阶段，各竞争主体为了发展目标，依靠各种不同的产业、投资、创新等平台，汇聚人才、资本、信息、技术等要素，最终实现竞争政策的协同、创新驱动的协同和竞争规则的协同，从而突破竞争壁垒，有效合作，共同发展。

在区域经济竞争发展三大定律的驱动下，区域政府在经济发展四个阶段的主要行为取向如表5-2所示。

Table 5-2 Main Behavioral Orientations of a Regional Government in the
Four Stages of Economic Development

Stages of economic development	Main behavioral orientations of a regional government
The growth stage dominated by industrial economy	Industrial policy
The growth stage dominated by urban economy	Government participation
The growth stage dominated by innovative economy	Innovation approach
The growth stage dominated by shared economy	Shared Drive · Competition · Cooperation · Win-win Situation

China Development Research Foundation has released the *China City Cluster Integration Report*, which uses the ACEP index to measure regional integration. The ACEP index consists of four basic factors: economic agglomeration, regional connectivity, economic equalization, and policy coordination. This report also gives a range of empirical evidence based on the analysis of economic variables related to various city clusters in China.

VI. On Competitive Neutrality

Competitive neutrality emphasizes the equal market competition status between state-owned enterprises and private enterprises, and intends to eliminate the distorted state of resource allocation by state-owned enterprises through a fair market competition mechanism, thereby allowing the market to allocate resources and enhancing the competitiveness of all market participants. OECD launched a study on competitive neutrality in 2009, and pointed out that competitive neutrality is involved in eight criteria, namely, business form, cost recognition, commercial return rate, public service obligation, tax neutrality, regulatory neutrality, debt neutrality and subsidy constraint, and government procurement.

International institutions substantively advocate competitive neutrality through the business environment evaluation mechanism. For example, the World Bank's business environment evaluation index system also includes the essence of competitive neutrality, as shown in Table 5-3.

表 5-2 区域政府在经济发展四个阶段的主要行为取向

经济发展阶段	区域政府主要行为取向
产业经济驱动主导阶段	产业政策
城市经济驱动主导阶段	政府参与
创新经济驱动主导阶段	创新方式
共享经济驱动主导阶段	共享驱动·竞争·合作·共赢

中国发展研究基金会发布《中国城市群一体化报告》，运用 ACEP 指数测量区域一体化情况。ACEP 指数包括四个基本要素：经济集聚度、区域连接性、经济均等化和政策协同性。该报告从对中国各城市群相关经济变量的分析中也做出了系列实证。

六、关于竞争中性

竞争中性的原意是强调国有企业和民营企业间的平等市场竞争地位，通过公平的市场竞争机制消除国企在资源配置上的扭曲状态，实现市场配置资源，增强所有市场参与者的竞争力。经济合作与发展组织 (OECD) 在 2009 年也启动了对竞争中性的研究，指出竞争中性包括企业经营形式、成本确认、商业回报率、公共服务义务、税收中性、监管中性、债务中性与补贴约束、政府采购八方面标准。

国际机构通过营商环境评价机制在实质上推进这一准则。比如世界银行营商环境评价指标体系，也包含了竞争中性原则的要义，如表 5-3 所示。

Table 5-3 World Bank's Business Environment Evaluation Indicator System

Enterprise cycle	Tier-1 indicators	Tier-2 indicators
The stage of starting business	Establish an enterprise	Four indicators: processing procedures (item), processing time (day), expenses (as a percentage of per capita income), and the minimum registered capital required to establish a limited company (as a percentage of per capita income)
The stage of acquiring a premise	Apply for a construction permit	Four indicators: all procedures (item) before the commencement of housing construction, processing time (day), processing expense (as a percentage of per capita income), and the building quality control index
	Obtain the power utility	Four indicators: the procedures (item) required for connecting to the power grid, processing time (day), expense (as a percentage of per capita income), and the power supply stability and charging transparency index
	Register the property	Four indicators: the procedures (item) required for property transfer registration, processing time (day), expense (as a percentage of per capita income), and the quality of land use control system
The stage of obtaining funds	Obtain loans	Two indicators: chattel mortgage law index, credit information system index
	Protect minority investors	Six indicators: information disclosure index, director's responsibility index, shareholder litigation convenience index, shareholder's rights protection index, ownership and control protection index, and company transparency index
The stage of routine operation	Tax	Eight indicators: number of times the company pays taxes (times/year), time required for the company to pay taxes (hours/year), total tax rate (as a percentage of profits), post-tax practice process index, time of VAT refund declaration (hours), time of refund (weeks), time of audit and declaration of enterprise income tax (hours), completion time of enterprise income tax audit (weeks)
	Cross-border trade	Eight indicators: review time of export declaration (hours), time of export clearance (hours), review expense of export declaration (USD), expense of export clearance (USD), review time of import declaration (hours), time of import clearance (hours), review expense of import declaration (USD), and expense of import clearance (USD)
The stage of identifying default	Perform the contract	Three indicators: time to settle a commercial dispute (day), cost of settling a commercial dispute (as a percentage of claim amount), and the judicial process quality index
	Solve the bankruptcy	Two indicators: recovery rate, and bankruptcy law framework protection index

Enterprise and regional government are dual entities in the market. To focus on market entities, keep improving a market-oriented, legal, and international business environment, and better and enhance the principle of "competitive neutrality", we must apply this principle to the competition among enterprises and among governments. Therefore, from the perspective of improving and perfecting the six functions of the modern market system, the author put forwards that competition among governments should also follow the principle of "competitive neutrality", aiming to guide countries around the world to embark on a track of benign development of market economy, and a path to coordinated development of competition, cooperation, and win-win situation.

表 5-3 世界银行营商环境评价指标体系

企业周期	一级指标	二级指标
创业阶段	开办企业	四个：办理程序(项)、办理时间(天)、费用(占人均收入百分比)、开办有限公司所需最低注册资本金(占人均收入百分比)
获得场地阶段	办理施工许可	四个：房屋建筑开工前所有手续办理程序(项)、办理时间(天)、办理费用(占人均收入百分比)、建筑质量控制指数
获得场地阶段	获得电力	四个：办理接入电网手续所需程序(项)、办理时间(天)、费用(占人均收入百分比)、供电稳定性和收费透明度指数
获得场地阶段	登记财产	四个：办理产权转移登记所需程序(项)、办理时间(天)、费用(占人均收入百分比)、用地管控系统质量
获得融资阶段	获得信贷	两个：动产抵押法律指数、信用信息系统指数
获得融资阶段	保护少数投资者	六个：信息披露指数、董事责任指数、股东诉讼便利指数、股东权利保护指数、所有权和控制权保护指数、公司透明度指数
日常运营阶段	纳税	八个：公司纳税次数(次/年)、公司纳税所需时间(小时/年)、总税率(占利润百分比)、税后实务流程指数、增值税退税申报时间(小时)、退税到账时间(周)、企业所得税审计申报时间(小时)、企业所得税审计完成时间(周)
日常运营阶段	跨境贸易	八个：出口报关单审查时间(小时)、出口通关时间(小时)、出口报关单审查费用(美元)、出口通关费用(美元)、进口报关单审查时间(小时)、进口通关时间(小时)、进口报关单审查费用(美元)、进口通关费用(美元)
出现问题阶段	执行合同	三个：解决商业纠纷的时间(天)、解决商业纠纷的成本(占索赔金额百分比)、司法程序质量指数
出现问题阶段	解决破产	两个：回收率、破产法律框架保护指数

然而，市场主体不仅有企业，还包括地方区域政府。所以，要聚焦市场主体，持续打造市场化、法治化、国际化的营商环境，健全、完善与提升"竞争中性"原则，就不仅要将这一原则运用到企业之间的竞争过程，还应该运用到政府之间的竞争过程。因此，笔者从健全与完善现代市场体系六大功能的角度，提出政府之间的竞争也应该遵循"竞争中性"原则，从而引导世界各国在市场经济发展的进程中走上良性发展的轨道，走在竞争合作与合作共赢的协调发展的道路上。

First, the market factor system. All countries ought to establish and improve the principle of "competitive neutrality" in terms of factor acquisition, cost recognition, business operation, debt neutrality, and subsidy constraint.

Second, the market organization system. All countries ought to establish and improve the principle of "competitive neutrality" in terms of market access, business form, public service obligation, and fair competition among various business entities.

Third, the market law system. All countries ought to establish and improve the principle of "competitive neutrality" in terms of market value orientation, transaction behavior, contractual behavior, title behavior, and intellectual property right protection and tax neutrality.

Fourth, the market supervision system. All countries ought to establish and improve the principle of "competitive neutrality" in terms of project investment, bidding, government procurement, the review of institution, business, market and system, and regulatory neutrality.

Fifth, the market environment system. It involves three aspects: foundation of real economy, corporate governance structure, and the social credit system. Currently, all countries ought to establish and improve the principle of "competitive neutrality" in terms of the standards for legal system, trust relationship, credit tool, credit intermediary, and other relevant credit factors.

Sixth, the market infrastructure. It mainly includes market service network, supporting equipment and technology, various market payment and clearing systems, and technology information systems. All countries ought to establish and improve the principle of "competitive neutrality" in terms of the application of regional, national, and even international markets, as well as the formation of their relevant standards.

Hence, it can be concluded as follows.

(1) Taking global carbon emissions and carbon markets as an example, it is clear that: with the development of history and economic technologies, the transverse space in the market field is constantly extending, and the longitudinal functions of the market system are constantly improving, which require government and enterprise to provide dual support in the market economy.

(2) There are dual entities in modern market economy, and a mature effective government is able to achieve foresighted leading.

(3) Regional government competition presents three laws: the law of the phenomenon of 80/20 agglomeration, the law of gradient change equilibrium, and the law of coordination of competition and cooperation. They are objective laws shown in the four stages of economic development.

(4) The competition among governments around the world should also follow the principle of "competitive neutrality".

第一,市场要素体系。各国应在要素获取、成本确认、经营运行以及债务中性和补贴约束等方面健全和完善"竞争中性"原则。

第二,市场组织体系。各国应在准入许可、企业经营形式、公共服务义务和各类营商主体公平竞争等方面健全和完善"竞争中性"原则。

第三,市场法治体系。各国应在市场价值导向、交易行为、契约行为、产权行为,尤其是知识产权保护和税收中性等方面健全和完善"竞争中性"原则。

第四,市场监管体系。各国应在项目招商、招投标、政府采购和对机构、业务、市场、制度审查及监管中性等方面健全和完善"竞争中性"原则。

第五,市场环境体系。它主要包括实体经济基础、企业治理结构和社会信用体系三方面。目前,各国应在法律制度规范、信托关系规范、信用工具规范、信用中介规范以及其他相关信用要素规范上健全和完善"竞争中性"原则。

第六,市场基础设施。它主要包括市场服务网络、配套设备及技术、各类市场支付清算体系和科技信息系统等。各国在区域市场、国家市场乃至国际市场的运用及其相关标准的制定上,也应健全和完善"竞争中性"原则。

至此,本章得出如下结论。

(1) 以世界碳排放与碳市场为例,可以清晰地看到:随着历史进程和经济科技的发展,市场领域的横向空间在不断拓展,市场体系的纵向功能在不断完善,但它需要政府与企业在市场经济中的双重作用力支撑。

(2) 现代市场经济存在双重主体,成熟有为政府能够超前引领。

(3) 区域政府竞争呈现三大定律:二八效应集聚律,梯度变格均衡律和竞争合作协同律。这是在经济发展的四个阶段呈现出来的客观定律。

(4) 世界各国政府之间的竞争,也应该遵循"竞争中性"原则。

Chapter VI

A Mature Market Economy Is the Combination of Strong Effective Government and Strong Efficient Market

In this chapter, some of the key issues studied in this book will be discussed. What is modern market economy? Can our focus only fall on the two major roles: market factor and market institution's activity? When countries around the world pursue the goal of "fairness and efficiency", do they play the role in bettering legal system, supervision, social credit system construction, and market infrastructure? A government not only uses the troika (supply of factor, supply of environment, and supply of market) on the supply side of the mezzo economic field to boost economic growth, but also plays a role in the modern market economy system by using its effective hand. From this we derive the concept and scope of effective government and efficient market, as well as the concept and scope of mature market economy.

I. Classification of Efficient Market and Types of Effective Government

Modern market system consists of six parts, as shown in Figure 6-1.

By applying the concept of "efficient market" proposed by Fama in his analysis of the securities market in 1970 to the mezzo economics, the author divides the efficient market into three layers and defines the types of effective government.

第六章

成熟市场经济是强式有为政府与强式有效市场相融合的经济

本章将探讨此书研究的一些焦点问题：什么是现代市场经济？我们的着眼点还能够仅仅局限在市场要素与市场机构活动两大功能作用上吗？难道世界各国在追求"公平与效率"的目标时，没有法治监管、社会信用体系建设和市场基础设施完善等功能作用吗？政府不仅在中观经济领域的供给侧运用三驾马车（要素供给、环境供给、市场供给）助推经济增长，而且在现代市场经济体系中运用有为之手发挥着作用。由此就引申出有为政府与有效市场的概念与范畴，以及成熟市场经济的概念与范畴。

一、有效市场划分与有为政府类型

现代市场体系包括六大部分，如图6-1所示。

在此，笔者将法马在1970年分析证券市场时提出的"有效市场"概念应用到中观经济学科的理论中，将有效市场分为三个层次，同时也对有为政府类型做出界定。

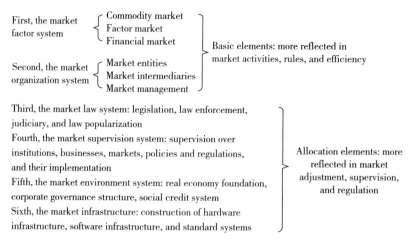

Figure 6-1 Modern Market System

(I) Classification of efficient market

A weak efficient market refers to the market where there are only market factor system and market organization system. The market development in the United States from 1776 to 1890 should be classified as a weak efficient market.

A semi-strong efficient market refers to the market where there are market factor system and market organization system and that has established a sound market law system and market supervision system. The market development in the United States from 1891 to 1990 should be classified as a semi-strong efficient market.

A strong efficient market refers to the market that has built sound market environment systems and market infrastructure on the basis of a semi-strong efficient market. The market development in the United States has been following this trend since the 1990s.

(II) Types of effective government

The core of an effective government's behaviors lies in the optimized allocation of the three types of resources in the region, namely non-operative resources, operative resources, and quasi-operative resources.

The author defines the following three types of effective government.

A weak effective government refers to the government that only focuses on the allocation of non-operative resources (the social public welfare resources related to people's livelihood) and their supporting policies.

A semi-strong effective government refers to the government that only focuses on the allocation of non-operative resources and operative resources and their supporting policies.

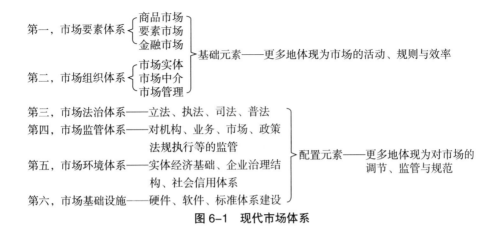

图 6-1　现代市场体系

（一）有效市场划分

弱式有效市场，即只存在市场要素体系和市场组织体系活动的市场。美国1776—1890年的市场发展状况属于弱式有效市场。

半强式有效市场，即在具备市场要素体系和市场组织体系的基础上，又逐步建立健全了市场法治体系和市场监管体系。美国1891—1990年的市场发展状况属于半强式有效市场。

强式有效市场，即在半强式有效市场的基础上，又建立并完善了市场环境体系和市场基础设施。美国20世纪90年代开始的市场发展状况，正是按照这一趋势前进的。

（二）有为政府类型

有为政府的行为核心在于对区域三类资源的优化配置，即对非经营性资源、可经营性资源、准经营性资源的优化配置。

为此，笔者把有为政府类型界定为以下三种。

弱式有为政府，即只关注非经营性资源（与社会民生相关的社会公益资源）的调配及相关政策配套的政府。

半强式有为政府，即只关注非经营性资源和可经营性资源的调配及相关政策配套的政府。

A strong effective government refers to the government that not only focuses on the support of non-operative resources and operative resources and their supporting policies, but also participates in and promotes the allocation of quasi-operative resources and their supporting policies.

The economic growth mode of "effective government + efficient market" is shown in Figure 6-2.

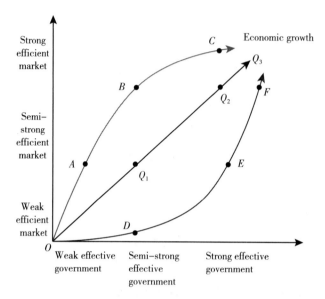

Figure 6–2　Economic Growth Mode of "Effective Government + Efficient Market"

In various countries around the world, effective government and efficient market merge in two ways: either the market takes the lead or the government. The economic growth path of a region or country is $Q_1 \to Q_2 \to Q_3$; the economic growth path that the market takes the lead and merges with the promising actions of the government is: $A \to Q_1 \to B \to Q_2 \to C \to Q_3$; the economic growth path that the government takes the lead and merges with the efficient market is: $D \to Q_1 \to E \to Q_2 \to F \to Q_3$; according to the results of empirical analysis, the former is similar to the mode taken by developed countries in Europe and America, while the latter is similar to the that taken by East Asian countries.

From the market perspective, countries around the world are different in four aspects.

(1) Different sources of market: spontaneous source of market and constructed source of market.

(2) Different scopes of market: the scope that focuses on operative resources and the scope that extends to quasi-operative resources.

(3) Different entities of market: single entity and dual entities.

(4) Different roles of market: one's emphasis is laid on the market's allocation of resources; and the other utilizes the supply-side troika.

From the government perspective, countries around the world are also different in the following four aspects.

强式有为政府，即不仅关注非经营性资源和可经营性资源的调配与政策配套，而且参与、推动准经营性资源的调配和政策配套的政府。

"有为政府＋有效市场"的经济增长路径模式如图 6-2 所示。

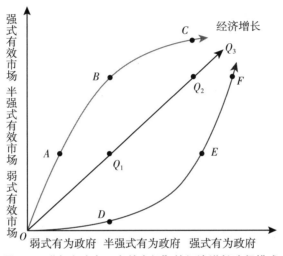

图 6-2 "有为政府＋有效市场"的经济增长路径模式

在世界各国，有为政府与有效市场相互融合呈现出两条路径：路径之一是市场先行；路径之二是政府先行。一个区域或一个国家的经济增长路线是：$Q_1 \to Q_2 \to Q_3$；市场先行与有为政府相互结合的经济增长路径是：$A \to Q_1 \to B \to Q_2 \to C \to Q_3$；政府先行与有效市场相结合的经济增长路径是：$D \to Q_1 \to E \to Q_2 \to F \to Q_3$。从实证分析的结果看，前者类似于欧美发达国家，后者类似于东亚国家。

从市场的视角看，世界各国有两条沿革路径，但存在着四点不同。

(1) 市场的来源不同：自发的与建设的。

(2) 市场的范围不同：集中在可经营性资源与扩展到准经营性资源。

(3) 市场的主体不同：单一的与双重的。

(4) 市场的作用不同：强调市场配置资源与同时发挥供给侧三驾马车作用。

从政府的视角看，世界各国也有两条沿革路径，同样存在着四点不同。

(1) Different behavioral nodes of government: pre-event guidance; and mid-event and post-event interventions.

(2) Different behavioral focuses of government: supply side or demand side.

(3) Different government policies: all-round development in the field of resource generation; or relying solely on fiscal policy.

(4) Different roles of government behaviors: a comprehensive and effective role throughout the entire process; only appropriate interventions as "backup".

Regardless of the path, the key to achieving optimal economic growth for a region or country lies in the integration of strong effective government and strong efficient market. This is the sustainable development goal that a region or a country should pursue.

II. Potential Economic Growth Rate and Real Economic Growth Rate

Potential economic growth rate refers to the highest growth rate of the total products and services produced by a region or country in the modern market system, or the highest economic growth rate that a region or country can achieve in the case of optimal allocation of various resources. This definition includes two connotations. First, the market is effective. The basic functions of the market (including market factor system and market organization system), the basic order of the market (including market law system and market supervision system), and the foundation of the market environment (including market environment system and market infrastructure) in the modern market system should be sound. Second, the government should be effective. The government of a region or a country should be able to effectively allocate operative resources, non-operative resources, and quasi-operative resources, and be able to formulate effective supporting policies and systems. Potential economic growth rate is the growth rate that can be achieved when the government of a region or a country maximizes the utilization of the three types of resources when the modern market system is sound, or that can be achieved under the mode of "strong effective government + strong efficient market".

Real economic growth rate, also known as actual economic growth rate, refers to the comparison between the final GDP of a region or a country and the base-period GDP. Nominal economic growth rate can be obtained by calculating the final GDP at current prices, while real economic growth rate can be obtained by calculating the final GDP at base-period prices (i.e. constant prices). Real economic growth rate is a dynamic indicator that reflects the degree of change in the economic development of a region or a country over a certain period of time.

(1) 政府的行为节点不同：事前引领与事中、事后干预。

(2) 政府的行为侧重点不同：供给侧与需求侧。

(3) 政府的政策手段不同：在资源生成领域全方位开拓与仅依靠财政政策。

(4) 政府的行为作用不同：全方位、全过程发挥有为作用与只作为"候补"的适机干预。

不管如何选择路径，一个区域或一个国家获得最优经济增长的关键，都在于强式有为政府与强式有效市场的融合作用。这是一个区域或一个国家需要追求的可持续发展目标。

二、潜在经济增长率与现实经济增长率

潜在经济增长率，是指在现代市场体系中，一个区域或一个国家所生产的总的产品和劳务的最高增长率，或者说在各种资源得到最优配置的条件下，一个区域或一个国家所能达到的最高经济增长率。该定义包括两方面内涵：一是市场有效，即现代市场体系中的市场基本功能(包括市场要素体系和市场组织体系)、市场基本秩序(包括市场法治体系和市场监管体系)与市场环境基础(包括市场环境体系和市场基础设施)是健全的；二是政府有为，即一个区域或一个国家的政府能够有效调配可经营性资源、非经营性资源和准经营性资源，并能够制定有效的配套政策和制度。潜在经济增长率是在现代市场体系健全的条件下，一个区域或一个国家的政府对三类资源最大限度地利用时所能实现的增长率，是在"强式有为政府＋强式有效市场"模式下实现的增长率。

现实经济增长率，也称实际经济增长率，是指一个区域或一个国家末期国内生产总值与基期国内生产总值的比较。以末期现行价格计算末期国内生产总值，属名义经济增长率，以基期价格(即不变价格)计算末期国内生产总值，属现实经济增长率。现实经济增长率是反映一个区域或一个国家一定时期内经济发展水平变化程度的动态指标。

The gap between potential economic growth rate and real economic growth rate represents the potential for economic growth of a region and country.

As for how to establish mathematical models or evaluation systems for the potential economic growth rate, how to apply them in the actual economic operations of various countries around the world, and whether or how to explore the mechanisms for realizing the value of ecological products and accounting for the gross domestic products of ecosystem, let's leave these topics for economists from various countries to discuss.

III. Washington Consensus and the Middle Income Trap

In the late 1980s, the world economy fell into recession; the economic growth rate of each country shrank; international trade and investment remained sluggish; insufficient driving force for economic growth; and economic market remained volatile. In view of this, the Institute for International Economics, the International Monetary Fund, the World Bank, and other institutions put forward the Washington Consensus in 1989.

(1) Fiscal policy discipline, with avoidance of large fiscal deficits, reduce the inflation rate, and stabilize the macroeconomic situation.

(2) Redirection of public spending from subsidies toward broad-based provision of key pro-growth, pro-poor services areas.

(3) Tax reform, broadening the tax base and adopting moderate marginal tax rates.

(4) Interest rates that are market determined and positive (but moderate) in real terms.

(5) Competitive exchange rates.

(6) Trade liberalization: liberalization of imports.

(7) Liberalization of inward foreign direct investment.

(8) Privatization of state enterprises.

(9) Loosen the grip of government.

(10) Legal security for property rights.

We can see that the core of the Washington Consensus is "advocating the minimization of the role of government, property privatization, and economic and financial freedom".

Therefore, in a specific stage, the ten measures of the Washington Consensus played a certain role in stimulating the economic development of various countries. Why is the effect of Washington Consensus hard to sustain? The author believes that the Washington Consensus ignored the importance of building and improving the six functions of the modern market

潜在经济增长率与现实经济增长率之间的差距,就是各区域、各国家经济增长的潜力所在。

至于如何设置潜在经济增长率的数理模型或评价体系,如何在世界各国实际经济运行中应用,是否或如何探索生态产品价值实现机制和生态系统生产总值核算机制,我们把这些课题留给各国的经济学同人来共同探讨。

三、华盛顿共识与中等收入陷阱

20世纪80年代末,世界经济陷入衰退,各国经济增长率萎缩,国际贸易和投资持续低迷,经济增长动力不足,经济全球化市场动荡。面对这一状况,美国国际经济研究所、国际货币基金组织、世界银行等,在1989年提出华盛顿共识。

(1) 加强财政纪律,压缩财政赤字,降低通货膨胀率,稳定宏观经济形势。

(2) 把政府开支的重点转向经济效益高的领域和有利于改善收入分配的领域。

(3) 开展税制改革,降低边际税率,扩大税基。

(4) 利率市场化。

(5) 采用一种具有竞争力的汇率制度。

(6) 贸易自由化,开放市场。

(7) 放松对外资的限制。

(8) 国有企业私有化。

(9) 放松政府的管制。

(10) 保护私人财产权。

可以看出,华盛顿共识的核心是"主张政府角色最小化,财产私有化和经济、金融自由化"。

应该说,在特定的阶段内,华盛顿共识的十条政策措施对刺激各国经济发展起到了一定的作用。但为什么华盛顿共识的作用力难以持久?笔者认为,因为它

system, as well as the important role of governments in allocating the three types of economic resources. As such, these propositions, policies, and growth modes are hard to sustain.

In 2006, the World Bank put forward the concept of "middle income trap". The emerging economies that have reached the middle income level will soon reach the "takeoff stage" of GDP between USD 1000 and USD 3000 after breaching the "poverty trap" of per capita GDP of USD 1000. When per capita GDP reached USD 3000, the contradictions accumulated in rapid development will erupt. As a result, these economies will see bottlenecks in their own institutional and system updates, making them difficult to overcome contradictions and fall into a period of decline or stagnation of economic growth. This is the middle income trap.

A country caught in the middle income trap will face two dilemmas. On one hand, the costs of resources, raw materials, labor, capital, and management remain high. On the other hand, they lack core and cutting-edge technologies, for which it is difficult for them to innovate, and lack competitiveness as they are positioned in the lower reaches of industrial chain. The resulting economic downturn or stagnation will further lead to difficulties in employment, shortage of social public services, fragile financial systems, polarization between the rich and the poor, frequent corruption, lack of faith, and social unrest. As a result, these countries hover in the middle-income stage and fail to enter the ranks of high-income countries.

Argentina is a typical case. Since the 1960s, Argentina has been deeply trapped in the middle income trap and its development has been sluggish. According to the data from the World Bank, Argentina's per capita GDP in 1977 was USD 7743. In 2018, its per capita GDP was USD 10040. Its compound growth rate over the past 41 years was only 0.63%.

Why has Argentina, which followed the Washington Consensus to promote economic reform, has become a typical case of middle income trap? The author believes that the reason is the Washington Consensus ignored the effective role of government in the market economy.

The author or this book claims that a mature market economy has to be the combination of strong effective government and strong efficient market.

既忽视了现代市场体系六大功能建设与完善的重要性,又忽视了各国政府调配三类经济资源的重要作用。因此,这种理论主张、政策措施或者增长模式,是没有持久生命力的。

2006年,世界银行提出"中等收入陷阱"的概念:那些中等收入的新兴市场国家,在突破人均国内生产总值1000美元的"贫困陷阱"后,会很快奔向1000美元至3000美元的"起飞阶段";但在人均国内生产总值达到3000美元左右时,快速发展中积聚的矛盾会集中爆发,这些经济体自身的体制与机制更新会陷入瓶颈,难以克服困难,落入经济增长的回落或停滞期,即中等收入陷阱阶段。

陷入中等收入陷阱的国家会面临两方面的困境:一方面,资源、原材料、劳动力、资金和管理等成本居高不下;另一方面,它们缺乏核心的尖端技术,难以创新,处于产业链条的中低端,缺乏竞争力。由此而来的经济增长的回落或停滞进一步导致就业困难、社会公共服务短缺、金融体系脆弱、贫富分化、腐败多发、信仰缺失、社会动荡等。于是这些国家长期在中等收入阶段徘徊,迟迟不能进入高收入国家行列。

阿根廷是一个典型的案例。从20世纪60年代开始,阿根廷一直深陷中等收入陷阱,发展长期迟滞不前。据世界银行数据,阿根廷1977年的人均国内生产总值为7743美元;2018年的人均国内生产总值为10040美元;41年间复合增速仅为0.63%。

为什么遵循华盛顿共识推进经济改革的阿根廷,成了陷入中等收入陷阱的典型代表?笔者认为,这是由于华盛顿共识倡导"头痛医头、脚痛医脚",忽视了政府在市场经济中的有为作用。

笔者或者说此书所倡导的是,成熟市场经济一定是强式有为政府与强式有效市场相融合的经济。

IV. The Mode of Integrating Effective Government With Efficient Market and the Evaluation of It

The combination of strong effective government and strong efficient market is shown in Figure 6-3.

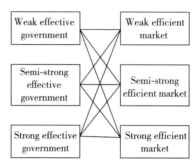

Figure 6-3　Nine Combinations

Mode 1: weak effective government + weak efficient market. The government rarely plays a regulatory role in the economy; the market development is not improved; the market competition mechanism is often blocked; the legal system is missing; and the order is chaotic. This mode is common in low-income and middle-income countries.

Mode 2: weak effective government + semi-strong efficient market. This mode is hard to exist in the real economy, as a semi-strong efficient market must be regulated under the market law system and the market supervision system and a weak effective government is unable to establish these systems.

Mode 3: weak effective government + strong efficient market. This mode is a theoretical assumption, but it has no actual case in the real world.

Mode 4: semi-strong effective government + weak efficient market. Under this mode, the government is able to better fulfill its responsibilities in allocating non-operative resources and provide basic public goods. The government is able to allocate and support operative resources, but fails to properly grasp market development trends and independently solve problems that arise in market operation. China's situation in 1978—1984 was similar to this mode, or the operation or regulation mode in the early stage of market economy.

四、有为政府与有效市场相融合的模式组合及评价

有为政府与有效市场相融合的模式组合如图6-3所示。

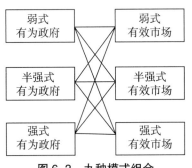

图6-3 九种模式组合

模式一是"弱式有为政府+弱式有效市场"。即政府基本没对经济发挥调控作用，市场发育也不完善，市场竞争机制常被阻断，法治欠缺，秩序混乱，这种模式常见于中低收入国家。

模式二是"弱式有为政府+半强式有效市场"。该模式在现实经济中难以存在，因为半强式有效市场必定存在市场法治体系和市场监管体系，而弱式有为政府不可能建立这些体系。

模式三是"弱式有为政府+强式有效市场"。这种模式是一种理论假定，现实世界中没有实际案例支撑。

模式四是"半强式有为政府+弱式有效市场"。该模式下，政府在非经营性资源调配上可以较好地履行职责，提供基本的公共物品。同时，政府也开始具备对可经营性资源的调配和扶持能力，但对市场发展趋势把握不好，不能自主解决市场运行中出现的问题。中国改革开放后的1978—1984年的情形类似这种模式，属于市场经济初期的运行或调控模式。

Mode 5: semi-strong effective government + semi-strong efficient market (semi-mature market economy mode). Under this mode, on one hand, the government is able to plan and guide industrial layout, as well as support and regulate production and operation; on the other hand, the government is able to continuously improve the market supervision mechanism, the legal protection mechanism, and the environmental support mechanism. This mode is common in countries in the mid stage of market economy development. China was very similar to this situation before joining WTO.

Mode 6: semi-strong effective government + strong efficient market. The United States is in line with this mode. In the economic development of the United States, the market plays a decisive role in allocating resources and the government plays an important role in allocating non-operative resources. Restricted by institution or concept, the United States is ambiguous and inconsistent in the allocation of operative resources, as well as in the definition and development of quasi-operative resources. It is difficult for the United States to make breakthroughs in these two aspects as its overall economic growth and urban improvement are not planned, systematic, and forward-looking.

Mode 7: strong effective government + weak efficient market. This mode is hard to exist in reality as the role of a strong effective government should be at least corresponding to that of a semi-strong efficient market. The country with a planned economy system does not fall under this mode.

Mode 8: strong effective government + semi-strong efficient market. At present, China is in line with this mode. China's economic mode is usually considered a market economy that gets mature under the leadership of the government. China has achieved remarkable economic achievements worldwide, but it also faces challenges in further improving market competition, market order, market credit, and market infrastructure.

Mode 9: strong effective government + strong efficient market. This is the best mode for the combination of government and market, the goal of practical exploration and theoretical breakthroughs in various countries around the world, and the only way for the market economy to truly mature.

The author believes that "a strong effective government and a strong efficient market contribute to a mature market economy", or that a truly mature market economy is the combination of strong effective government and strong efficient market.

模式五是"半强式有为政府 + 半强式有效市场",属于半成熟市场经济模式。该模式下,一方面,政府能够规划、引导产业布局,扶持、调节生产经营;另一方面,政府能够不断改善市场监管机制、法律保障机制、环境支撑机制。这种模式常见于处在市场经济中期发展阶段的国家。中国在加入世界贸易组织之前的情况与此非常类似。

模式六是"半强式有为政府 + 强式有效市场"。美国当前的状况很符合这种模式。在美国经济的发展中,市场在配置资源方面具有决定性作用,同时政府也在非经营性资源的调配中发挥着重要作用。但碍于制度或理念的限制,美国在可经营性资源的调配、准经营性资源的界定与开发上存在模糊或言行不一的问题。所以在这两方面美国难有突破,其整体经济增长和城市的提升缺少规划性、系统性和前瞻性。

模式七是"强式有为政府 + 弱式有效市场"。这种模式在现实中难以存在,因为强式有为政府的功能作用起码是与半强式有效市场相对应的。计划经济国家不属于此模式。

模式八是"强式有为政府 + 半强式有效市场"。现阶段的中国很符合这种模式。现阶段中国经济模式通常被认为是政府主导的逐渐成熟的市场经济,中国取得了世界瞩目的经济成就,但也面临着进一步完善市场竞争、市场秩序、市场信用及市场基础设施的挑战。

模式九是"强式有为政府 + 强式有效市场"。这是政府与市场组合的最佳模式,是世界各国实践探索和理论突破的目标,也是市场经济达到真正成熟的必由之路。

笔者认为,"强式有为政府 + 强式有效市场 = 成熟市场经济",或者进一步说,真正成熟的市场经济是强式有为政府与强式有效市场相融合的经济。

V. A Strong Effective Government and a Strong Efficient Market Contribute to a Mature Market Economy

Studies have shown that there are three criteria for a strong effective government: respecting market laws; maintaining economic order and stabilizing economic development; and effectively allocating resources and participating in regional competition and cooperation.

A strong efficient market should exhibit sufficient market competition, orderly legal supervision, and a sound social credit system.

A strong effective government should meet at three conditions: keep up with the times, carry out all-round competition and cooperation, and make government affairs public.

The economic performance indicators of a strong effective government can also be analyzed in three aspects.

The first aspect is the dual attributes of regional government: quasi-macro attribute and quasi-micro attribute.

The second aspect is the dual indicators for a government to be effective: the social role (public performance indicators), with social stability being the core (coordination); and the economic role (regional resource allocation efficiency index), with economic development being the core (profit seeking).

The third aspect is the measurement of economic performance indicators for an effective government. ①The government should be able to use the supply-side troika to promote economic growth. ②The government should be able to effectively regulate the efficiency of allocating the three types of resources in the region. ③The government should be able to leverage the effects of regional government in "9-in-3" Competition in competition and cooperation in the region. ④The government should be able to achieve positive combination with the competitiveness of micro enterprises at different stages of economic development.

The author believes that the combination of effective government and efficient market represents the path to sustainable economic development in a region or country. Here are three cases.

◎ **Case 6-1 The "Singapore Consensus" That Promoted Comprehensive Social Progress**

Singapore's per capita GDP was USD 427 in 1960, USD 4927 in 1980, and USD 56389 in 2013. During this period, Singapore managed to finish five economic transformations: the establishment of labor-intensive industries in the 1960s; the

五、强式有为政府+强式有效市场=成熟市场经济

研究表明，强式有为政府标准有三个：一是尊重市场规律；二是维护经济秩序，稳定经济发展；三是有效调配资源，参与区域竞争与合作。

强式有效市场标准有三个：一是市场充分竞争；二是法治监管有序；三是社会信用体系健全。

强式有为政府至少需要具备三个条件：一是与时俱进；二是全方位竞争与合作；三是政务公开。

强式有为政府经济绩效指标的衡量也可以从三个层面来分析。

第一，区域政府的双重属性，即准宏观属性与准微观属性。

第二，有为政府的双重指标。社会作用（公共绩效指标），以社会稳定性为核心（协调性）；经济作用（区域资源配置效率指标），以经济发展性为核心（逐利性）。

第三，有为政府经济绩效指标的衡量。①能够推动供给侧三驾马车促进经济增长的政府；②能够有效调节区域三类资源配置效率的政府；③能够发挥区域"三类九要素"竞争与合作作用力的政府；④能够在经济发展不同阶段与微观企业竞争力形成"正正叠加"效率的政府。

笔者认为，有为政府与有效市场相融合，是一个区域或者一个国家经济可持续发展的路径选择，下面三个案例可以很好地说明这一点。

◎ **案例6-1 推动社会全面进步的"新加坡共识"**

1960年，新加坡的人均国内生产总值为427美元，到1980年为4927美元，而到2013年为56389美元。在这期间，新加坡成功实现了五次经济转型：20世纪60年代建立劳动密集型产业，20世纪70年代打造资源密集型产业，20世纪

establishment of resource-intensive industries in the 1970s; the shift towards capital-intensive industries in the 1980s; the development of technology-intensive industries in the 1990s; the focus on knowledge-intensive industries in the 21st century. The government played a promoting role all along.

◎ **Case 6-2　The Rise of a World-class City Cluster in the Guangdong-Hong Kong-Macao Greater Bay Area**

In 2017, the Chinese government's work report stressed the construction of the Guangdong-Hong Kong-Macao Greater Bay Area and made it a globally first-class bay area and a world-class city cluster. The following measures have been taken. First, increase the connectivity of infrastructure, build world-class city clusters, speed up the coordinated development of ports, airports, and rapid transportation networks in there, and actively construct infrastructure for import-export ports. Second, accelerate the development of logistics and shipping industries, and set up world-class shipping clusters, including quickening the construction of free trade ports, vigorously developing intermodal logistics systems, enhancing the shipping service functions of the area, etc.Third, promote technological innovation and resource sharing, create international centers for technological innovation, strengthen the construction of technology infrastructure there, set up a mechanism for technology transfer and transformation, encourage the youth to innovate and start businesses, promote the development of fintech, vigorously develop technology service outsourcing, and carry out cooperation in intellectual property right protection. Fourth, promote the integrated development of manufacturing industries and build demonstration zones for "Made in China 2025"; promote the coordinated development of the manufacturing industry chain, strengthen the information-based development of industries, promote the cooperation in international productivity, and encourage the equipment manufacturing industry to go global. Fifth, enhance the innovative development of the financial industry and establish international finance, including cultivating and strengthening the shipping finance, actively innovating fintech, promoting the integration of industry and finance, accelerating the construction of financial platforms, and promoting the integration of offshore finance and onshore finance. Sixth, strengthen the integration level of the area, and create high-quality circles that are suitable for living, business, and tourism. The rise of the area has created a new development pattern and become a new engine of regional economy. All of these are attributable to the dual roles of effective government and efficient market. Only with such strategic planning and implementation can the area score substantial development results.

80年代转向资本密集型产业,20世纪90年代致力于科技密集型产业,21世纪主攻知识密集型产业,其主要背后推手一直是政府。

◎ 案例6-2 粤港澳大湾区世界级城市群的崛起

2017年,中国政府工作报告强调推进粤港澳大湾区建设,使其朝国际一流湾区和世界级城市群迈进。具体举措如下。第一,推进基础设施互联互通,建设世界级城市群。既加快湾区港口、机场、快速交通网络协同发展,又积极实施进出口岸基础设施建设。第二,加快物流航运发展,建立世界级航运群。这包括加快建设自由贸易港,大力发展联运物流体系,提升湾区航运服务功能,等等。第三,促进科技创新、资源共享,打造国际科技创新中心。除了加强湾区科技基础设施建设、建立科技转移转化机制、鼓励青年创新创业、推动科技金融发展,还要大力发展科技服务外包、开展知识产权保护协作。第四,推动制造业一体化发展,建设"中国制造2025"示范区。推动制造业产业链协同发展、加强工业信息化建设、促进国际产能合作、鼓励装备制造业走向国际市场。第五,提升金融业创新发展,建立国际金融枢纽。这包括培育壮大航运金融、积极创新科技金融、推动产融结合、加快金融平台建设、促进离岸金融与在岸金融对接。第六,强化湾区一体化水平,打造宜居、宜业、宜游的优质生活圈。粤港澳大湾区的成功崛起,打造出一种新的发展格局,成为区域经济新引擎。而这一切都归功于有为政府和有效市场的双重作用,有了这样的战略规划与实施推动,粤港澳大湾区才能取得实质性的发展成效。

At present, China accurately grasps the new development stage, deepens the implementation of new development concepts, speeds up the construction of new development patterns, and gives play to the dual driving forces of effective government and efficient market.

The new development stage is included in the primary stage of socialism, and marks a new starting point of the next stage. The new development stage represents a historic leap for the Chinese people to go from standing up, to becoming rich, and to growing strong. After years of unremitting efforts since the founding of the new China, especially since its reform and opening-up, China has built a solid material foundation to embark on a new journey and achieve new and higher goals. Therefore, China has put forward the goal of building a socialist modernized country, and the next three decades will be a new development stage for it to fulfill this historic aspiration.

As a systematic theoretical system, the new development concept offers answers to a range of theoretical and practical questions about the purpose, motivation, mode, and path of development, and clarifies major issues related to China's value orientation, development mode, and development path. It is necessary to grasp the new development concept from its fundamental purpose, issue orientation, and risk awareness.

The new development pattern focuses on accelerating the construction of the domestic circulation and promoting both domestic and international circulations. As a strategic task proposed in the "14th Five Year Plan" of China, it should be accurately grasped and actively promoted from the overall perspective. Only by relying on ourselves and unblocking the domestic circulation can we always survive and develop with vitality, regardless of international changes. We must enhance China's viability, competitiveness, development and sustainability in various predictable and unpredictable difficulties.

◎ **Case 6-3**

The third case is the economic behaviors of the US government to be studied. The five pillars of the U.S. financial system established by the first U.S. Treasury Secretary Hamilton, Roosevelt's New Deal, the layout of the Bretton Woods system, the Marshall Plan, and the large-scale infrastructure investment and construction of the Biden administration are all economic behaviors of the U.S. government. These behaviors not only interfere with the domestic economy of the U.S., but also affect international economy. However, economists in the United States have never revealed these behaviors.

In this chapter, the author proposes the following four questions for economists from all over the world to discuss and study.

当前，中国正在准确把握新发展阶段，深入贯彻新发展理念，加快构建新发展格局，发挥有为政府与有效市场相结合的双轮驱动力。

新发展阶段是社会主义初级阶段中的其中一个阶段，是经过几十年积累、站到了新起点上的一个阶段。新发展阶段是中国人民从站起来、富起来到强起来的实现历史性跨越的新阶段。经过中华人民共和国成立以来，特别是改革开放以来多年的不懈奋斗，中国已经拥有开启新征程、实现新的更高目标的雄厚物质基础。因此，中国提出全面建设社会主义现代化国家的目标，未来30年将是完成这个历史宏愿的新发展阶段。

新发展理念是一个系统的理论体系，回答了关于发展的目的、动力、方式、路径等一系列理论和实践问题，阐明了中国关于发展的价值导向、发展模式、发展道路等重大问题。必须完整、准确、全面贯彻新发展理念，从根本宗旨把握新发展理念，从问题导向把握新发展理念，从忧患意识把握新发展理念。

新发展格局以加快构建国内大循环为主体、促进国内、国际双循环。它是中国"十四五"规划提出的一项关系发展全局的重大战略任务，需要从全局高度准确把握和积极推进。只有立足自身，把国内大循环畅通起来，才能任由国际风云变幻，始终充满朝气地生存和发展下去。要在各种可以预见和难以预见的狂风暴雨、惊涛骇浪中，增强国家的生存力、竞争力、发展力、持续力。

◎ 案例6-3

第三个案例是有待破解的美国政府经济行为。从美国第一任财政部部长汉密尔顿建立美国财政金融体系的五大支柱，到罗斯福新政、布雷顿森林体系的布局、马歇尔计划等，再到现阶段拜登政府的大规模基础设施投资建设，都是美国政府的经济行为。此行为不仅干预着国内经济，还影响着国际经济，但美国的经济理论界却不去揭示。

在本章也就是本书的结束部分，笔者提出下面四个问题供世界各国经济学同人共同思考探研。

First, what is the difference between the effective government in industrial economy and the effective government in urban economy? As for the effective government in industrial economy, the point is whether industrial policies and subsidies are needed. In the development of urban economy, the focus of effective government falls on the planning, guidance, support, coordinating, supervision, and management of operative resources (industrial economy); providing general underpinning, fairness, and practical improvement for the non-operative resources (livelihood economy); and carrying out planning and layout, participating in construction, and achieving orderly management for quasi-operative resources (urban economy). These two effective governments contain different connotations.

Second, what are the connections and differences between the theory of comparative advantage and the theory of competitive advantage? The theory of comparative advantage is essentially the theory of comparative cost trade. A country or region should rely on its own resource advantages, and focus on producing and exporting the products in which it has comparative advantages and importing the products in which it has comparative disadvantages. A country or region moves on from a low-income agricultural economy to a high-income industrialized economy. Only through reasonable division of labor can resources be fully utilized, thereby helping the country or region achieve a balance in total import and export trade. However, countries around the world have discovered the "comparative advantage trap" when they develop their economy. This is a debated topic in economics. Regarding the theory of competitive advantage, Porter believes that the trade advantage of a country does not simply depends on its natural resources, labor, interest rates, and exchange rates, as claimed by traditional international trade theories, but largely depends on a country's capabilities of innovating and upgrading its industries. The author believes that the economic development of a country is driven by both enterprise competition and regional government competition; there is competition among regional governments in terms of the "9-in-3" Competition, which runs through the factor-driven stage, the investment-driven stage, the innovation-driven stage, and the sharing-driven stage of development; the fundamental path towards a mature market economy consists of government's foresighted leading and the combination of effective government and efficient market; the competition between dual economic entities in a country may overcome the "comparative advantage trap" and promote the economic and social transformation of a region or country.

Third, from the perspective of economic growth, how do we answer the three basic questions that exist in various countries in the real world: why are some countries rich and the other poor; what are the factors that affect a country's economic growth; how to understand the economic growth miracle in some countries or regions. We must not think about these questions solely from merely the perspective of natural endowment or market economy and deny the role of effective government.

需要延伸思考并清晰的问题之一是，产业经济中的有为政府与城市经济中的有为政府的区别是什么？产业经济中的有为政府的关注点主要集中在是否需要产业政策及产业补贴的问题上。而在城市经济发展中，有为政府的关注点涉及对可经营性资源（产业经济）的规划、引导、扶持、调节、监督、管理；对非经营性资源（民生经济）的基本托底、公平公正、有效提升；对准经营性资源（城市经济）的规划布局、参与建设、有序管理。在这二者中，有为政府的内涵不一样。

需要延伸思考并清晰的问题之二是，比较优势理论与竞争优势理论的联系与区别是什么？比较优势理论，实质是比较成本贸易理论。各国或各区域，依靠资源禀赋，集中生产并出口其具有比较优势的产品，进口其具有比较劣势的产品。各国或各区域是一条从低收入农业经济一直到高收入工业化经济的连续频谱，只有各国或各区域合理分工，资源才能得到充分利用，从而实现进出口贸易总额平衡。但现实中，世界各国经济发展时，却出现了"比较优势陷阱"。这是一个有争议的经济学话题。对于竞争优势理论，波特认为：一国的贸易优势并不像传统的国际贸易理论宣称的那样简单地取决于一国的自然资源、劳动力、利率、汇率，而是在很大程度上取决于一国的产业创新和升级的能力。而笔者认为：一国经济发展存在企业竞争和区域政府竞争的双重驱动力；区域政府存在"三类九要素"竞争，并且该竞争贯穿于要素驱动竞争导向、投资驱动竞争导向、创新驱动竞争导向和共享驱动竞争与合作导向发展的全过程；政府超前引领、有为政府与有效市场相融合，是走向成熟市场经济的根本路径；一国经济双重主体的竞争，能够克服"比较优势陷阱"，推动一个区域或者一个国家的经济转轨、社会转型。

需要延伸思考并清晰的问题之三是，从经济增长的角度，如何回答现实世界各国存在的三个基本问题，即为什么一些国家富有，一些国家贫穷；影响一国经济增长的因素是什么；怎样理解一些国家或地区的经济增长奇迹。回答这些问题都不能仅仅从自然禀赋或市场经济等单个角度去思考，而否定有为政府的作用。

Fourth, are we already in an era of competition in economic development modes? Economic development mode refers to the development strategies, economic growth mechanisms, and implementation modes for a country's national economy in a certain stage. It is determined by a range of optional elements and means such as economic development goals, development focuses, development steps, and implementation methods. The author believes that we will witness clear answers when economists around the world compare the mode of liberal economy with the mode that integrates effective government and efficient market, and analyze their pros and cons.

需要延伸思考并清晰的问题之四是,世界是否已经进入经济发展模式竞争的时代?经济发展模式,是指在一定阶段,一国国民经济发展战略、经济增长机制和运行实现方式的类型。它由经济发展目标、发展重心、发展步骤和实现方式等一系列可供选择的要素手段来确定。那么,当世界各国经济学同人实事求是地展开对自由主义经济模式和有为政府与有效市场相融合的经济模式的比较,并做出利弊分析时,必然会有着清晰的答案!

Conclusions

Consensus on Micro, Mezzo, and Macroeconomic Analysis and Government's Economic Behaviors

Let's compare microeconomic entity and macroeconomic entity and their behaviors with mezzoeconomic entity and its behaviors to reveal the consensus on government's economic behaviors, and then look into the prospects for addressing the relationship between government and market.

I. Analysis of Micro, Mezzo, and Macroeconomic Behaviors

(I) Analysis of microeconomic entity and its behaviors

Relevant microeconomic theories are shown in Figure A-1.

According to Figure A-1, the microeconomics mainly studies the economic behaviors of individual economic production units (enterprises) and their consequences. The object of study is the resource allocation issue in the case of resource scarcity. It focuses on the price determination mechanism in main economic variables. The content of study is shown by the theories in the figure. The purpose of study is to understand and grasp the laws of microeconomic operation, so as to effectively implement enterprise management, reform, and innovation.

Microeconomics assumes that resource utilization is a piece of cake when it aims to study resource allocation, meaning that microeconomics studies resource allocation under the condition of resource scarcity. The author believes that it contains three fatal flaws.

结 语

微观、中观、宏观经济行为分析与政府经济行为的几点共识

在结语中,我们先把微观、宏观经济主体及其行为与中观经济主体及其行为进行比较,从中揭示出政府经济行为的几点共识,进而展望"政府与市场"关系难题的破解前景。

一、微观、中观、宏观经济行为分析

(一)微观经济主体及其行为分析

微观经济学的相关理论可以用图 A-1 来表述。

从图 A-1 中我们可以看出,微观经济学的研究主体主要是单个经济生产单位(企业)的经济行为及其后果;研究对象是资源稀缺条件下的资源配置问题;研究焦点是其主要经济变量中的价格决定机制;研究内容及其展开就形成了如图所示的系列理论;研究目的是了解和把握微观经济运行规律,从而有效实施企业管理、改革和创新。

微观经济学在以研究资源配置为目标时假定资源利用不成问题,即微观经济学的研究对象是在资源稀缺条件下的资源配置问题。笔者认为,其存在着三个致命的基本缺陷。

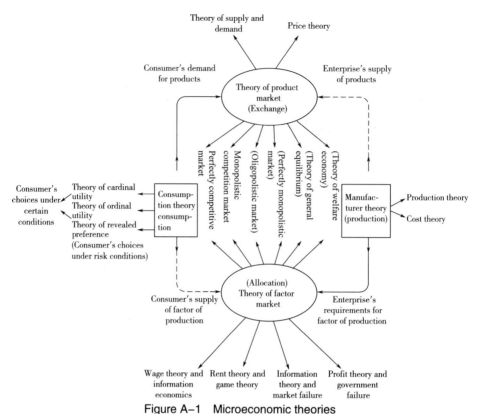

Figure A-1　Microeconomic theories

(1) Resource scarcity is assumed to be the only prerequisite in resource allocation.

(2) Industrial economy is regarded as the only form of market economy.

(3) The mechanism of market allocating resources is limited to enterprise's behavior.

Microeconomics has been through the following stages.

The period from the mid-17th century to the mid-19th century was the early stage of microeconomics, or the embryonic stage of microeconomics.

The period from the late 19th century to the early 20th century was the stage of neoclassical economics or the foundation stage of microeconomics.

The period from the 1930s to the 1960s was the establishment stage of microeconomics.

Since the 1960s, microeconomics has undergone further development, extension and evolution.

(II) Analysis of macroeconomic entity and its behaviors

Relevant macroeconomic theories are shown in Figure A-2.

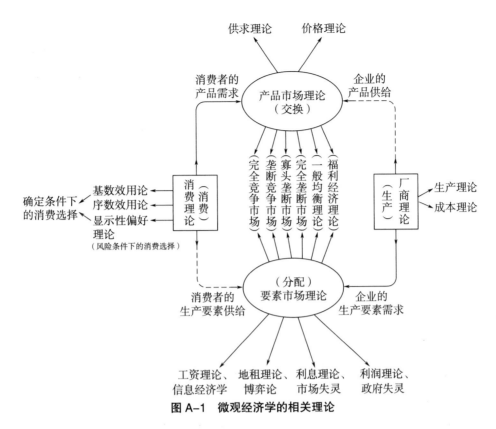

图 A-1 微观经济学的相关理论

(1) 把资源稀缺视为资源配置中唯一的前提假设。

(2) 把产业经济视为唯一的市场经济形态。

(3) 把市场配置资源的机制局限于企业行为。

微观经济学的发展大体经历了以下四个阶段。

第一阶段：17 世纪中期到 19 世纪中期，是早期微观经济学阶段，或者说微观经济学萌芽阶段。

第二阶段：19 世纪晚期到 20 世纪初期，是新古典经济学阶段，也是微观经济学奠定阶段。

第三阶段：20 世纪 30 年代到 60 年代，是微观经济学完成阶段。

第四阶段：20 世纪 60 年代至今，是微观经济学进一步发展、扩充和演变的阶段。

(二) 宏观经济主体及其行为分析

宏观经济学的相关理论可以用图 A-2 来表述。

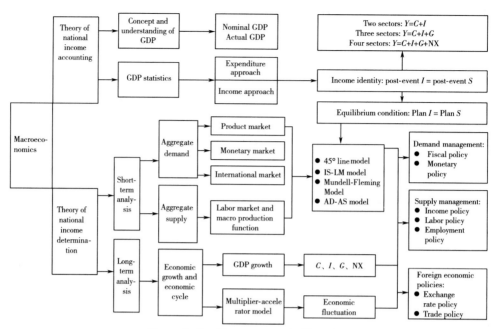

Figure A-2　Macroeconomic Theories

According to Figure A-2, the macroeconomics mainly studies the economic behaviors of activity units in the overall socioeconomic process (countries) and their consequences. The object of study is the resource utilization issue in optimizing a country's resource allocation. It focuses on the national income determining and operating mechanism in economic growth variables. The content of study is shown by the relevant core indicators and theoretical models in Figure A-2. The purpose of study is to understand and grasp the laws of macroeconomic operation, so as to carry out effective macro management, reform, and innovation.

Macroeconomics assumes that resource allocation is a piece of cake when studying resource utilization issues, meaning that macroeconomics studies resource utilization in optimized resource allocation. The author believes that macroeconomics contains three fatal fundamental flaws.

(1) The definitions of government and country are unclear.

(2) The definitions of government service behavior and government economic behavior are unclear.

(3) The definitions of pure public goods and quasi-public goods are unclear.

Macroeconomics has been through the following stages.

The period from the mid-17th century to the mid-19th century was the early stage of macroeconomics, or the stage of classical macroeconomics.

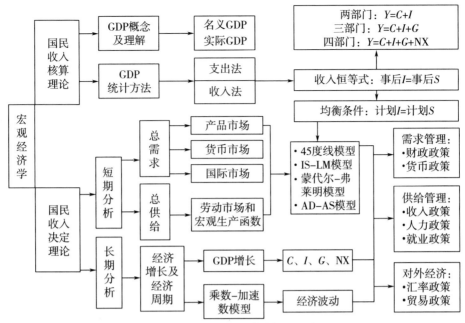

图 A-2 宏观经济学的相关理论

从图 A-2 中我们可以看出，宏观经济学的研究主体主要是社会经济总过程中活动单位(国家)的经济行为及其后果；研究对象是一国资源配置优化中的资源利用问题；研究焦点是其经济增长变量中的国民收入决定及其运行机制；研究内容就是图 A-2 中的相关核心指标和理论模型；研究目的是了解和把握宏观经济运行规律，从而有效进行宏观管理、改革和创新。

宏观经济学在以研究资源利用问题为目标时假定资源配置不成问题，即宏观经济学的研究对象是在资源配置优化中的资源利用问题。笔者认为，宏观经济学也存在三个致命的基本缺陷。

(1) 对政府与国家的界定模糊不清。

(2) 对政府服务行为与政府经济行为的界定模糊不清。

(3) 对纯公共产品与准公共产品的界定模糊不清。

宏观经济学的发展也大体经历了四个阶段。

第一阶段：17 世纪中期到 19 世纪中期，是早期宏观经济学阶段，或称古典宏观经济学阶段。

The period from the late 19th century to the 1930s was the foundation stage of modern macroeconomics.

The period from the 1930s to the 1960s was the establishment stage of macroeconomics.

Since the 1960s, macroeconomics has undergone further development and evolution.

By analyzing microeconomic and macroeconomic entities and their behaviors, we can conclude as follows.

Breakthroughs are needed in terms of the object of study, field of study, scope of study, system of study, method of study, market theory, and theoretical system of economics.

(III) Analysis of mezzoeconomic entity and its behaviors

Relevant mezzoeconomic theories are shown in Figure A-3.

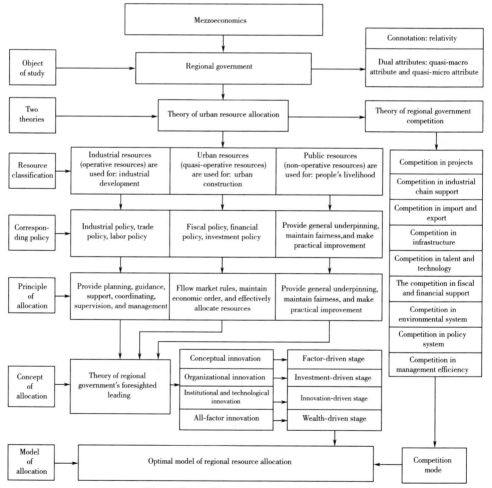

Figure A-3　Mezzoeconomic Theories

第二阶段：19世纪后期到20世纪30年代，是现代宏观经济学的奠基阶段。
第三阶段：20世纪30年代到60年代，是现代宏观经济学的建立阶段。
第四阶段：20世纪60年代以后，是宏观经济学进一步发展和演变的阶段。
通过对微观、宏观经济主体及其行为的分析，可以引申出以下三点思考。
第一，经济学的研究对象和研究领域需要突破。
第二，经济学的研究范畴、研究体系和研究方法需要突破。
第三，经济学的市场理论和经济学体系需要突破。

(三) 中观经济主体及其行为分析

中观经济学的相关理论可以用图A-3来表述。

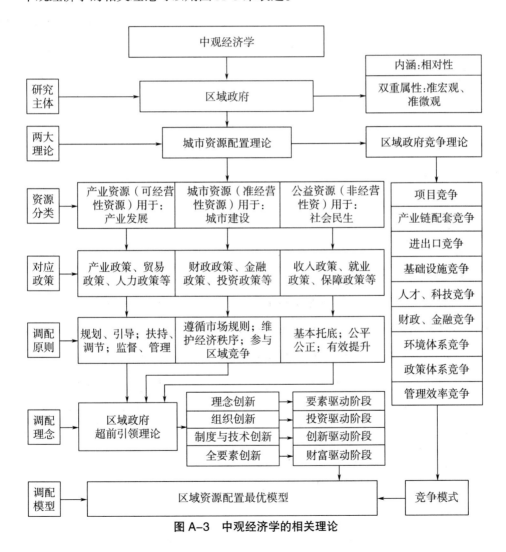

图A-3 中观经济学的相关理论

225

According to Figure A-3, the mezzoeconomics mainly studies the economic behaviors of regional economic development units (regional governments) and their consequences. The object of study is the resource allocation issue on the basis of resource generation. It focuses on the key economic variables that affect regional government competition, namely the fiscal revenue determination mechanism and the fiscal expenditure structure. Mezzoeconomic studies have delivered resource generation, government's dual attributes, regional government competition, four-stage resource allocation, government's foresighted leading, economic new engine, dual entities of market competition, "strong effective government and strong efficient market" in a mature market economy, and other theories. The purpose of study is to understand and grasp the operational laws of mezzoeconomy, establish scientific concepts of the government's management, formulate scientific guidelines for the government's management behaviors, select suitable policy tools, and promote sustainable economic development.

The concept of "mezzoeconomics" was first put forward by Dr. Peters, a professor of national economics in Germany in the mid-1970s. In the mid-1980s, Wang Shenzhi, a Chinese scholar, published the book *Mezzoeconomics*, which explained Peters' concept of "mezzoeconomics" and summarized the objects of study of mezzoeconomics as sector economy, regional economy and collective economy. However, these works did not substantively address the economic issues related to China or other countries around the world.

The author published a paper named *Controlling Investment Scale From a Mezzo Economic Perspective* in 1986; published a monograph titled *Foresighted Leading: Practice and Reflection on China's Regional Economic Development* in 2011; co-authored *Government Foresighted Leading: Theory and Practice of the World Regional Economic Development* with Qiu Jianwei in 2013; co-authored *Mezzoeconomics: Innovations and Developments in Theoretical Configuration of Economics* with Gu Wenjing in 2015; co-authored *On Regional Government Competition* with Gu Wenjing in 2017; published a monograph titled *New Economic Engine: Effective Government and Efficient Market* in 2019; published a monograph named *On the Dual-Entity of Market Competition: the Establishment and Development of Mezzoeconomics* in 2020. These works have systematically elaborated on the theory of regional government's foresighted leading, the dual roles of regional government, the dual entities of market competition, and the "strong effective government and strong efficient market" in a mature market economy, established the theoretical system of mezzoeconomics, and explained its development prospects.

从图 A-3 中我们可以看出，中观经济学的研究主体主要是区域经济发展单位(区域政府)的经济行为及其后果；研究对象是资源生成基础上的资源配置问题；研究焦点是影响区域政府竞争的主要经济变量，即区域财政收入决定与财政支出结构机制；研究内容及其展开将形成资源生成理论、政府双重属性理论、区域政府竞争理论、四阶段资源配置理论、政府超前引领理论、经济新引擎理论以及市场竞争双重主体理论和成熟市场经济"双强机制"理论等；研究目的是了解和把握中观经济运行规律，确立科学的政府管理理念，制定科学的政府管理行为准则，选择适合的政策工具，从而推动经济可持续发展。

"中观经济学"概念的提出源于 20 世纪 70 年代中叶德国的国民经济学教授彼得斯博士；20 世纪 80 年代中期，中国学者王慎之出版了《中观经济学》一书，阐述了彼得斯的中观经济理念，把中观经济的研究对象概括为部门经济、地区经济和集体经济。然而，这些著述没有实质性地解决与中国或世界各国相关的经济问题。

1986 年，笔者发表论文《从中观经济入手控制投资规模》；2011 年，出版了专著《超前引领：对中国区域经济发展的实践与思考》；2013 年，与邱建伟合著了《论政府超前引领：对世界区域经济发展的理论与探索》；2015 年，与顾文静合著了《中观经济学：对经济学理论体系的创新和发展》；2017 年，与顾文静合著了《区域政府竞争》；2019 年，出版了专著《经济新引擎：兼论有为政府与有效市场》；2020 年，出版了专著《市场竞争双重主体论：兼谈中观经济学的创立与发展》；等等。这些著作系统地阐述了区域政府超前引领理论、区域政府双重角色理论、市场竞争双重主体理论、成熟市场经济"双强机制"理论，确立了中观经济学的理论体系，阐述了它的发展前景。

(IV) Graphical analysis of micro, mezzo, and macroeconomic entities and their behaviors

The author summarizes the micro, mezzo, and macroeconomic entities and their behaviors within a country's modern market system and puts forward four core viewpoints as follows: ①we should grasp the full picture of the modern market system; ②we should fully grasp the dual competition entities of the modern market system; ③we should fully realize that a mature market economy is the fruit of strong effective government fusing with strong efficient market; ④we should strengthen the coordination of micro, mezzo, and macroeconomic activities.

The correlation effects in micro, mezzo, and macroeconomic operations mainly focus on a country's tax system, tax categories, tax rates, and total tax revenue. The relationship between total fiscal revenue (N) and total tax revenue (T) is shown in Figure A-4.

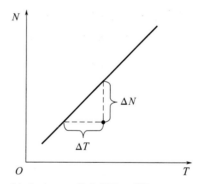

Figure A-4 Relationship between Total Fiscal Revenue and Total Tax Revenue

$$\delta = \frac{\Delta N}{\Delta T} \qquad \text{A-1}$$

$$N = \delta T \qquad \text{A-2}$$

Wherein, N represents the total fiscal revenue of a country; δ represents the tax sharing ratio between national and local governments; T represents the total tax revenue that all enterprises and individuals should pay.

From a macro perspective, a country's fiscal revenue depends not only on regional governments at the mezzo level, but also on enterprises and individuals at the micro level.

From a mezzo perspective, the regional government not only acts as the agent of the national government to regulate regional economy, but also seeks support from the national government on behalf of the economic interests of the region.

（四）微观、中观、宏观经济主体及其行为图析

笔者在书中把微观、中观、宏观经济主体及其行为取向概括在一国现代市场体系之内，提出并强化了四个核心观点：①应完整把握现代市场体系；②应完整把握现代市场体系双重竞争主体；③应完整把握成熟市场经济是强式有为政府与强式有效市场相融合的经济；④应强化微观、中观、宏观经济活动的协调性。

微观、中观、宏观经济运行中的关联效应主要聚焦在一国的税收体系及税种、税率、税收总额上。财政总收入(N)与上缴税收总额(T)的关系如图A-4所示。

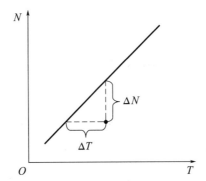

图A-4 财政总收入与上缴税收总额的关系

$$\delta = \frac{\Delta N}{\Delta T} \qquad \text{A-1}$$

$$N = \delta T \qquad \text{A-2}$$

其中，N表示国家政府的财政总收入；δ表示国家政府与地方政府的税收分成比例；T表示所有企业和个人需要上缴的税收总额。

从宏观层面看，国家的财政收入既依赖于中观层面的区域政府，也依赖于微观层面的企业及个人。

从中观层面看，区域政府既作为国家政府的代理，对区域经济进行调控，也代表本区域的经济利益，去争取国家的支持。

From a micro perspective, the taxes paid by enterprises and individuals constitute the source of fiscal revenue for both national and regional governments.

The correlations among macro, mezzo, and microeconomic entities and their behaviors are manifested as: country-national income—region-tax sharing—enterprise-total taxes (tax categories and tax rates). With this manifestation, the macro, mezzo, and microeconomic operations indicate the source and attribution of a country's national income. In other words, they elaborate on how does the country apply tax categories and tax rates; how does the central and local governments share tax revenue; how to use secondary distribution policies and policy tools; and how to achieve the three major economic goals of national and regional industrial development, urban construction, and people's livelihood after the primary distribution in the material production sector.

II. Code of Conduct of an Effective Government

The author believes that region is a relative concept. Each country is a region relative to the world. Each province or city is a region relative to the country. A regional government boasts "quasi-macro" attribute (coordinating) and "quasi-micro" attribute (seeking profit), both of which drive the regional government to take different actions in different stages of development. The line diagram of a regional government's economic behaviors is shown in Figure A-5, and the plane diagram of a regional government's economic behaviors is shown in Figure A-6.

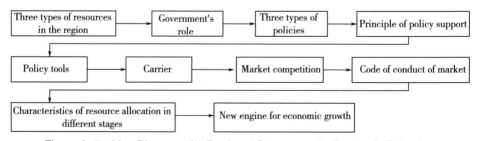

Figure A-5   Line Diagram of a Regional Government's Economic Behaviorsr

从微观层面看,企业及个人缴纳的税款既是国家政府的,也是区域政府的财政收入来源。

宏观、中观、微观经济主体及其行为之间关联效应的扭结点表现在:国家－国民收入—区域－税收分成—企业－税收总额(税种、税率)。宏观、中观、微观经济运行通过这一关联效应扭结点,叙述了一国国民收入的来源与归属,即在物质生产部门经过初次分配以后,国家如何运用税种、税率,如何进行中央与地方的税收分成,如何运用二次分配政策及其政策工具,如何实现国家和区域的产业发展、城市建设和社会民生三大经济目标。

二、有为政府行为准则

笔者认为,区域是个相对的概念。对全球而言,每个国家就是一个区域;对国家而言,每个省、市就是一个区域。区域政府具有"准宏观"和"准微观"双重属性,"准宏观"的协调性与"准微观"的逐利性驱动着区域政府在不同发展阶段中的行为选择。鸟瞰区域政府的经济行为,其一线图如图 A-5 所示,其平面图如图 A-6 所示。

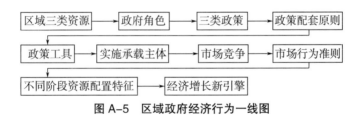

图 A-5 区域政府经济行为一线图

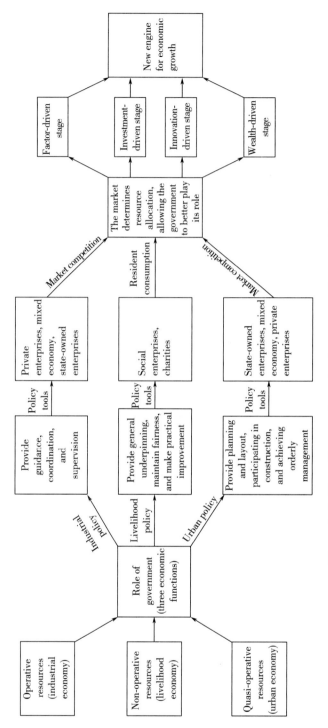

Figure A–6 Plane diagram of a regional government's economic behaviors

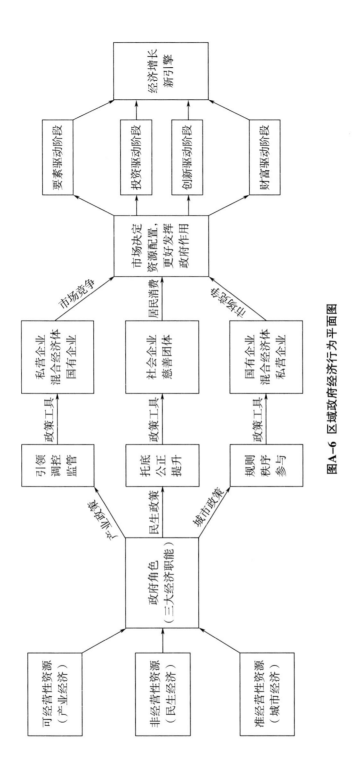

图A-6 区域政府经济行为平面图

The characteristics of a regional government's economic behaviors are divided into five layers. Layer 1: studying the three economic functions of the government, namely industrial development, urban construction, and safeguarding people's livelihood. Layer 2: studying the main economic variables of the government, namely fiscal revenue determination and fiscal expenditure structure. Layer 3: studying the main influencing factors of government revenue and expenditure, namely the effects and manifestations of "9-in-3" Competition among regional governments. Layer 4: studying the rationality and necessity of the government's economic policies, policy tools, policy coordination, and policy effectiveness in different stages. Layer 5: studying and discovering the laws of government economic activities or the operational laws of government economic activities, in order to reveal the theoretical foundation for the scientific governance of a region or a country's government.

From the perspective of regional economic operation or mezzoeconomic studies, several guidelines for an effective government's behaviors should be discussed or agreed upon.

First, in the field of resource generation, the government should utilize the supply-side troika to promote economic growth in the region or country, namely supply of factors (tangible and intangible factors), supply of environments (hard and soft environments), and supply of markets (transverse and longitudinal market systems), to boost economic growth.

Second, the government should play a coordinating role at the "quasi-macro" level and seek profits at the "quasi-micro" level. Its behaviors are determined by the goals in different stages of economic development.

Third, there is "9-in-3" Competition among governments, such as major projects, supply chain support, and import and export trade.

Fourth, comparative advantage and natural endowment are only the first steps in the economic development of a region or a country. To boost sustainable growth, it is necessary to follow a competitive economic growth trail that moves on from competition, to competition and cooperation, and finally to win-win cooperation.

Fifth, the government should carry out conceptual innovation, institutional innovation, organizational innovation, and technological innovation through foresighted leading.

Sixth, governments (in the mezzoeconomic field) should form dual drives for the development of market economy jointly with enterprises (in the microeconomic field).

Seventh, mature market economy is the combination of strong effective government and strong efficient market.

Eighth, governments around the world ought to create new investment engines, innovation engines, and rules engines, so as to achieve sustainable economic growth.

区域政府具备五个层次的经济行为特征。第一层次：研究政府的三大经济职能——产业发展、城市建设、社会民生；第二层次：研究政府的主要经济变量——财政收入决定与财政支出结构；第三层次：研究政府收支的主要影响因素——区域政府"三类九要素"竞争作用与表现；第四层次：研究政府经济政策、政策工具、政策协调及其政策效果在不同阶段的合理性与必要性；第五层次：研究、探索政府经济活动的行为规律，或政府经济活动的运行规律，从而揭示一个区域或一个国家政府的科学执政理论基石。

从区域经济运行或中观经济学研究的角度看，需要探索或达成共识的有为政府行为准则有以下几个。

第一，在资源生成领域，政府运用供给侧三驾马车推动一个区域或一个国家经济增长，即运用要素供给（有形要素与无形要素）、环境供给（硬环境与软环境）和市场供给（横向市场领域与纵向市场体系），推动经济增长。

第二，政府具有"准宏观"的协调性与"准微观"的逐利性，其行为选择由不同经济发展阶段的目标取向所决定。

第三，政府存在以重大项目、产业链配套、进出口贸易大小为标的的"三类九要素"竞争行为。

第四，比较优势、自然禀赋，只是一个区域或一个国家经济发展的第一步，要推动可持续增长，需要走以竞争为主、竞争与合作、合作共赢的竞争型经济增长路径。

第五，政府需要超前引领，在理念、制度、组织、技术四大方面创新发展。

第六，政府（在中观经济领域）与企业（在微观经济领域）共同形成市场经济发展的双轮驱动力。

第七，强式有为政府与强式有效市场相融合形成成熟市场经济。

第八，世界各国政府，需要开拓经济可持续增长的投资新引擎、创新新引擎和规则新引擎。

III. Mezzoeconomics and China

The author constructs mezzoeconomics by exploring and decoding the "relationship between government and market" in economic theories and practices around the world, aiming to breach the limitations of mainstream economic configuration in the western world and the theoretical framework of market economy, and discover the current and future market drivers and new economic engines in countries around the world by refining practical experience of China's reform and opening-up over the past years.

Experts at home and abroad have discussed the successful experience of China's economic system reform and opening-up from at least five perspectives.

(1) The explanations provided by neo-institutional economics: the property rights theory proposed by Coase; the transaction cost theory proposed by Williamson et al.; the institution change theory proposed by North et al.; the inter-county competition theory proposed by Zhang Wuchang et al.; the cultural factor theory advocated by Liu He et al.

(2) The explanations provided by development economics: the opening-up theory proposed by Chenery; the latecomer advantage theory proposed by Gerschenkron et al.; the "dualistic economy" development model proposed by Lewis; the three stages of economic development proposed by Porter and Schwab.

(3) The explanations provided by transition economics: development should move on from easy to difficult undertakings; resistance of reform should be solved via compensation; market relations should be reflected in the "dual price system"; the cost of reform should be transferred through decentralization of authority; local institutional innovation should drive overall institutional innovation.

(4) The explanations provided by neoclassical economics. According to Krugman and other neoclassical economists, the success of China's reform and opening-up mainly lies in the government's targeted choice of the "prescription" of neoclassical economics and its gradual implementation of neoclassical economics.

(5) The explanations provided by political economics: the neutral central government theory proposed by Yao Yang et al.; the decentralized authority theory proposed by Zhang Weiying et al.; the official selection system; etc.

三、中观经济学与中国

笔者从探索与破解世界各国经济学理论和实践中"政府与市场关系"的难题入手，构建中观经济学，力图突破西方主流经济学体系和市场经济理论框架的局限，在提炼中国改革开放成功实践经验的基础上，发掘世界各国现在与未来的市场驱动力和经济新引擎。

对中国经济体制改革开放成功经验的解释，国内外专家至少从以下五个角度进行了探讨。

(1) 新制度经济学的解释。一是科斯提出的产权理论；二是威廉姆森等提出的交易费用理论；三是诺思等提出的制度变迁理论；四是张五常等提出的县际竞争理论；五是刘鹤等主张的文化因素论。

(2) 发展经济学的解释。一是切纳里提出的对外开放理论；二是格申克龙等提出的后发优势论；三是刘易斯提出的"二元经济"发展模型；四是波特和施瓦布提出的经济发展三阶段论。

(3) 转轨/过渡经济学的解释。一是由易到难推进；二是通过利益补偿化解改革阻力；三是通过"价格双轨制"来演绎市场关系；四是通过分权来转移改革成本；五是由局部制度创新带动全局制度创新。

(4) 新古典经济学的解释。在克鲁格曼等新古典经济学家看来，中国改革开放的成功主要在于政府有针对性地选择了新古典经济学的"药方"，并采取了渐进的实施方式。

(5) 政治经济学的解释。一是姚洋等提出的中性中央政府论；二是张维迎等提出的分权理论；三是官员选拔体制；等等。

The author's studies of mezzoeconomics take roots in the great practice of China's reform and opening-up.

First, from the perspective of theoretical connotation, there are at least six aspects of mezzoeconomics that stem from the forefront of reform and opening-up. ①The theory of resource generation and the definition of the three types of regional resources are derived from the author's practical experience in Foshan City in 2004. ②The theory of government's foresighted leading is derived from the author's practical experience in Shunde District, Foshan City in 2005. ③The dual attributes theory of governments is derived from the author's practical experience in Shenzhen. ④The theory of "9-in-3" Competition among regional government is derived from the practical experience of various cities in the Pearl River Delta. ⑤The theory of dual entities of market competition and the "strong effective government and strong efficient market" mechanism of mature market economy stem from China's practical experience of reform and opening-up. ⑥The theory of new engine for economic growth stems from the development of China's economic practice.

Second, looking at the subject of study, competition among regional governments in China can be divided into at least at two layers: ①the "9-in-3" Competition among regional governments; ②state-owned enterprises established by the government participate in market competition.

Third, in terms of time span, China's reform and opening-up has achieved three leaps from the factor-driven stage to the investment-driven stage, and then to the innovation-driven stage.

Fourth, from the perspective of spatial range, China's reform and opening-up have moved from coastal areas to the mainland, and from special zones to the entire country. The "China Proposal" has been exposed to the world. China still faces three economic issues. How do government and market coexist in a country? How do private enterprise and state-owned enterprise coexist in a market? How do oligarchic private enterprises and SMEs coexist? The reasonable core of the theoretical system of mezzoeconomics addresses the relevant difficulties in China's economic development, and points out the path to and direction for building a new global economic governance system.

IV. Mezzoeconomics and the World

The author believes that mezzoeconomics is consistent with the development of economic practices in various countries around the world in at least the following seven aspects.

笔者的中观经济学研究源于中国改革开放的伟大实践。

第一,从理论的内涵来界定,中观经济学至少有六个方面源自改革开放最前沿:①资源生成理论和对区域三类资源界定源于笔者 2004 年在佛山市的实践经历;②政府超前引领理论源于笔者 2005 年在佛山市顺德区的实践经历;③政府双重属性理论源于笔者在深圳市的实践经历;④区域政府"三类九要素"竞争理论源于珠三角各城市的实践经验;⑤市场竞争双重主体论、成熟市场经济"双强机制"论源于中国改革开放的实践经验;⑥经济增长新引擎理论源于中国经济实践的发展。

第二,从研究主体来分析,中国区域政府的竞争至少存在于两个层面:①区域政府间的"三类九要素"竞争;②政府设立的国有企业参与市场竞争。

第三,从时间跨度来分析,中国改革开放已经实现了从要素驱动阶段到投资驱动阶段再到创新驱动阶段的三次飞跃。

第四,从空间范围来分析,中国的改革开放已经从沿海走向内地,从特区走向全国,"中国方案"已经摆在世人面前。但是中国仍需直面三大经济问题。其一,在国家中,政府与市场如何共处?其二,在市场中,私企与国企如何共处?其三,在私企中,寡头与小微如何共处?可以说,中观经济学理论体系中的合理内核,破解了中国经济发展中的相关难题,同时也为全球构建经济治理新体系探索了路径,指明了方向。

四、中观经济学与世界

笔者认为,中观经济学理论至少在以下七大方面与世界各国经济实践的发展相吻合。

First, the field of resource generation.

Second, the competition among governments around the world in the investment, development, and construction of domestic and international projects.

Third, competitive economic growth.

Fourth, the principle of competitive neutrality.

Fifth, new engine of economic growth.

Sixth, government's foresighted leading.

Seventh, a mature market economy is the combination of strong effective government with strong efficient market.

Traditional economics derives relevant theories based on the assumption of resource scarcity. Mezzoeconomics puts forwards that the government should use the troika on the supply side to boost the development of the market economy from the perspective of "resource generation". Traditional economics considers government economic behavior an exogenous variable and explains it at the market boundary or outside the market. Mezzoeconomics believes that government economic behavior acts as a market entity in the mezzo field (endogenous variable), and the government should achieve foresighted leading. Traditional economics believes that enterprise is the only market entity. Mezzoeconomics believes that there are enterprise and regional government acting as dual entities in the development of modern market economy and they both play a driving role. Traditional economics believes that a country's economic operation boasts a macro and micro dual structure. Mezzoeconomics believes that it is a ternary structure that includes macro, mezzo, and microeconomic operations, and they are correlated. Traditional economics believes that the single market plays a role. Mezzoeconomics believes that the government has dual attributes; there is competition among regional governments; a mature market economy the combination of strong effective government and strong efficient market. Traditional economics puts forwards the "trade engine" of economic growth on the demand side. Mezzoeconomics affirms the role of the "trade engine" and proposes new engines, namely "investment" "innovation" "rules", on the supply side, providing new paths for the sustainable development of economies around the world.

The theoretical and practical significance of mezzoeconomics are reflected in the following three aspects.

First, mezzoeconomics has breached the limitations of the mainstream economics systems and market theoretical framework in the western world.

(1) In the theory of market economy, it is proposed that a mature market economy is the combination of strong effective government and strong efficient market.

第一,资源生成领域。

第二,世界各国政府对国内与国际项目的投资、开发、建设的竞争。

第三,竞争型经济增长。

第四,竞争中性原则。

第五,经济增长新引擎。

第六,政府超前引领。

第七,成熟的市场经济,是强式有为政府与强式有效市场相融合的经济。

传统经济学从资源稀缺的假定前提出发,推导出相关理论,而中观经济学以"资源生成"作为研究起点,提出了政府在供给侧运用三驾马车助推市场经济发展的课题;传统经济学认为政府经济行为是个外生变量,把它放置在市场边界或市场之外来阐述,而中观经济学认为政府经济行为是作为中观领域的市场主体在发生作用(内生变量)的,政府应该超前引领;传统经济学认为只有企业是市场主体,而中观经济学认为现代市场经济发展存在微观企业与中观区域政府双重主体或双重驱动作用;传统经济学认为一国经济运行是宏观、微观二元结构论,而中观经济学认为它是包括宏观、中观、微观经济运行的三元结构论,三者之间存在关联效应;传统经济学认为单一市场功能在发挥作用,而中观经济学认为政府存在双重属性,区域政府之间存在竞争行为,成熟市场经济是强式有为政府与强式有效市场相融合的经济;传统经济学在需求侧提出经济增长的"贸易引擎",而中观经济学肯定了"贸易引擎"的作用,同时在供给侧提出了"投资""创新"与"规则"新引擎,为世界各国经济的可持续发展指引了新的增长路径。

中观经济学的理论和现实意义包括以下三个方面。

第一,中观经济学的设立,突破了西方主流经济学体系和市场理论框架的局限。

(1)在市场经济理论中提出了成熟市场经济是强式有为政府和强式有效市场相融合的经济。

(2) A framework of mezzoeconomics is created within the system of economics.

(3) The theory of new engine for economic growth is proposed in global economic development.

Second, mezzoeconomics accurately explains the successful experience of China's reform and opening-up over the past 40 years from an economic perspective.

Third, the establishment of mezzoeconomics and the creation of new economic system and modern market theory do not mention "China", but China has provided vast materials for the evolution of mezzoeconomics. The reasonable core of mezzoeconomics will effectively address the relationship between government and market in economic theories, and refine the successful practices and experience of China's reform and opening-up over the past 40 years. It will become a new engine for discovering the current and future market drives for the economic development of various countries around the world, effectively solve relevant problems in the economic development of various countries around the world, essentially boost their sustainable economic development, and seek to build new systems and paths for building global economic governance!

(2) 在经济学体系中创建了中观经济学架构。

(3) 在世界经济发展中提出了经济增长新引擎理论。

第二，中观经济学的设立，能够从经济学角度正确解释中国改革开放四十多年来的成功经验。

第三，中观经济学的设立，新经济学体系和现代市场理论的创建，都没有用到"中国"这个定语，但中国为这一理论发展提供了广阔素材。中观经济学的合理内核，将有效破解经济学理论中的"政府与市场"关系的难题，并将提炼中国改革开放四十多年来的成功实践与经验，成为发掘世界各国现在与未来的市场驱动力与经济新引擎，从而有效破解世界各国经济增长中的相关难题，实质推动世界各国经济的可持续发展，并探索构建全球经济治理的新体系、新路径！